FUZZY LOGIC-BASED MATERIAL SELECTION AND SYNTHESIS

FUZZY LOGIC-BASED MATERIAL SELECTION AND SYNTHESIS

Mustafa B Babanli

Azerbaijan State Oil and Industry University, Azerbaijan

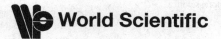

V JERSEY · LONDON · SINGAPORE · BEIJING · SHANGHAI · HONG KONG · TAIPEI · CHENNAI · TOKYO

Published by

World Scientific Publishing Co. Pte. Ltd.
5 Toh Tuck Link, Singapore 596224
USA office: 27 Warren Street, Suite 401-402, Hackensack, NJ 07601
UK office: 57 Shelton Street, Covent Garden, London WC2H 9HE

Library of Congress Cataloging-in-Publication Data
Names: Babanli, Mustafa B., author.
Title: Fuzzy logic-based material selection and synthesis / by Mustafa B Babanli
    (Azerbaijan State Oil and Industry University, Azerbaijan).
Description: New Jersey : World Scientific, [2018] | Includes bibliographical references and index.
Identifiers: LCCN 2018040646 | ISBN 9789813276567 (hc : alk. paper)
Subjects: LCSH: Fuzzy logic. | Materials--Mathematical models. | Artificial intelligence.
Classification: LCC QA9.64 .B22 2018 | DDC 511.3/13--dc23
LC record available at https://lccn.loc.gov/2018040646

British Library Cataloguing-in-Publication Data
A catalogue record for this book is available from the British Library.

For any available supplementary material, please visit
https://www.worldscientific.com/worldscibooks/10.1142/11164#t=suppl

Desk Editor: Herbert Moses

Typeset by Stallion Press
Email: enquiries@stallionpress.com

Printed in Singapore

To my parents Baba and Dunya Babanli

and my family

To the memory of the Father of Fuzzy Logic,
Prof. Lotfi Zadeh who supported idea
of publishing this book

Preface

Development of new materials is of theoretical and practical interest. In particular, it includes synthesis of new materials with predefined characteristics and selection of optimal materials for exploitation. Traditionally, these tasks are solved on the basis of intensive (and sometimes *ad-hoc*) experiments which are time and recourse consuming. This mandates the use of computer-guided methods of material synthesis and selection on the basis of a huge amount of obtained complex experimental data. In this regard, big data driven knowledge based models and other computational schemes allow to alternate hard experimental works. Such approaches provide ability of systematic and computationally effective analysis for prediction of composition, structure and properties of materials. Analyzing a wide diversity of approaches to material selection and synthesis, one can observe a tendency to shift research efforts from physical experiments to systematic analysis based on mathematical models and computational schemes. The latter, in turn, evolves from traditional analytical methods and computational schemes to modern approaches that are based on collaboration of fuzzy logic and soft computing, machine learning, big data and other new methods. The aim to apply fuzzy logic is to improve research using the advantage of dealing with: imprecision of experimental data; partial reliability of experimental data, prediction results and expert opinions; uncertainty of material properties stemming from complex relationship between material components; a necessity to analyze, summarize, and reason with large amount of information of various types (numeric data, linguistic information, graphical information, geometric information, etc). The use of fuzzy logic and computational intelligence approaches for material engineering is kernel of the proposed book.

The book is organized into five chapters and three appendices. In Chapter 1 we provide preliminary information on fuzzy sets theory, fuzzy logic, fuzzy modeling, fuzzy mathematics and Z-numbers, etc., which will be used in latter chapters for new materials selection and synthesis.

Chapter 2 is devoted to overview of the state-of-the-art of material selection and synthesis methods. It is considered different multicriteria decision making methods such as AHP, TOPSIS, VIKOR, etc., applied to material selection and synthesis problems. The chapter also includes modern computational approaches, mainly fuzzy logic and soft computing-based methods.

Fuzzy material selection methodology is considered in Chapter 3. The chapter embraces a spectrum of fuzzy data mining methods such as fuzzy K-means and fuzzy C-means clustering methods, ANFIS method, fuzzy reasoning-based approaches for selection of materials from big database. Different multiattribute decision making methods are applied to select different types of alloys. The chapter includes study on material selection by using expert systems, also new approach to material selection problems by using Z-valued If-Then rules. Comparative analysis of different material selection methodologies is given.

Fuzzy methods for synthesis of new materials with characteristics required are given in Chapter 4. Here emphasis is put on construction of materials database and modeling of fuzzy relationship between performance of new materials and affecting factors. The new approach for construction of knowledge-based model as Z-clustering approach is described. For the first time, fuzzy approach to estimation of phase diagram under fuzzy thermodynamic data is described. This chapter includes a large number of applications of fuzzy model-based synthesis of different alloys.

The case studies on material selection and synthesis by using fuzzy methods are given in Chapter 5. Validity of the suggested approaches is also considered in this chapter.

The book includes three appendices. The first two appendices are fragments of big data for candidate alloys and material synthesis. The third appendix is a description of software for operations over Z-numbers.

The book is intended for researchers and practitioners and will be useful for anyone who is interested in modern approaches to material selection and synthesis. The book is self-containing and includes details on application of a wide spectrum of fuzzy methods. At the same time, the book will be helpful for teachers and students of universities and colleges, for specialists in material science and engineering.

About the Author

Prof. Dr. M.B. Babanli received the PhD degree in 1992 and Doctor of Science degree in 2008. He served as a Researcher in Academy of Sciences of Ukraine, as an Associate Professor and Professor at Azerbaijan Technical University and as a Vice-President of Azerbaijan Technical University. His major field of research is analysis and synthesis of new smart materials, especially engineering of shape memory alloys, by using experimental and computer-aided approaches. His research breaks away traditional approaches to new material synthesis and selection. The research results of Prof. Babanli were published in more than 180 refereed publications including 6 books and 174 papers in journals and patents. Prof. Babanli was the head and the project member of more than 10 international research projects, such as ECONET-1 (2002–2005), STCU-5980 (2013–2015), etc.

Contents

Chapter 1

Preliminary Information on Fuzzy Logic

1.1. Fuzzy sets

Definition 1.1. *Classical set.* Let X be a classical set of elements which are denoted x and A be a subset of X. Membership of elements X in A is characterized by characteristic function μ_A from X to $\{0,1\}$.

$$\mu_A(x) = \begin{cases} 1 & \text{if} \quad x \in A \\ 0 & \text{if} \quad x \notin A \end{cases}$$

$\{0,1\}$ is called a valuation set.

In case when valuation set is real interval $[0,1]$ then $\mu_A(x)$ is grade of membership of x in A.

In this chapter, we provide preliminary material for fuzzy sets, fuzzy numbers, fuzzy relations, Z-numbers etc. which will be used in latter chapters for new materials selection and synthesis.

Definition 1.2. *Fuzzy set.* A fuzzy set A is a mapping

$$\mu_A : X \to [0,1],$$

where $\mu_A(X)$ is the grade of x to the fuzzy set [210]. Fuzzy set A is described as $A = \{(x, \mu_A(x)), x \in X\}$.

Example Fuzzy sets for mass fraction are shown in Fig. 1.1.

If X is finite set $X = \{x_1, x_2, ..., x_n\}$, discrete fuzzy subset of X can be represented as n dimensional vector $A = \{a_1, a_2, ..., a_n\}$ with $a_i = \mu_A(x_i)$.

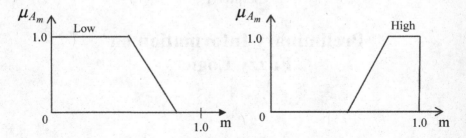

Fig. 1.1. Membership function of mass fraction.

Example Discrete fuzzy set for "Temperature" is shown in Fig. 1.2.

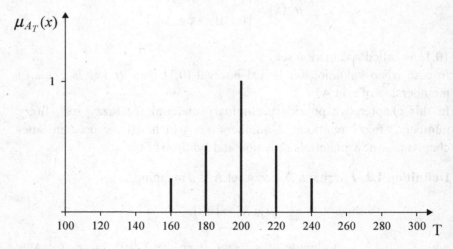

Fig. 1.2. Fuzzy set A in a discrete universe.

In real-world problems, the form of the MFs usually is chosen depending on how it is reflective to the problem at hand. Typical membership functions (MFs) are given below [12].

Bell-shaped MFs

Analytical representation of these MFs is described as follows:

$$\mu_A(x) = c \cdot \exp\left(-\frac{(x-a)^2}{b}\right)$$

Graphical representation of these MFs is shown in Fig. 1.3.

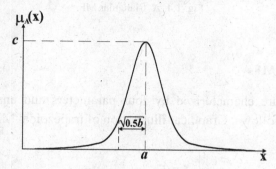

Fig. 1.3. Bell-shaped membership function.

Triangular MFs

Triangular MFs are the simplest model of the fuzzy sets and are characterized only by three parameters. Analytical representation of triangular MF is given as follows. Also see graphical representation in Fig. 1.4.

$$\mu_A(x) = \begin{cases} \dfrac{x - a_1}{a_2 - a_1} r & \text{if } a_1 \leq x \leq a_2 \\[2mm] \dfrac{a_3 - x}{a_3 - a_2} r & \text{if } a_2 \leq x \leq a_3 \\[2mm] 0 & \text{otherwise} \end{cases}$$

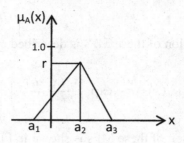

Fig. 1.4. A triangular MF.

Trapezoidal MFs

These MFs are characterized by four parameters and analytically are described as follows. Graphical illustration of trapezoidal MFs is given in Fig. 1.5.

$$\mu_A(x) = \begin{cases} \dfrac{x - a_1}{a_2 - a_1} r & \text{if } a_1 \leq x \leq a_2 \\[2mm] r & \text{if } a_2 \leq x \leq a_3 \\[2mm] \dfrac{a_4 - x}{a_4 - a_3} r & \text{if } a_3 \leq x \leq a_4 \\[2mm] 0 & \text{otherwise} \end{cases}$$

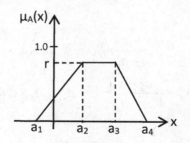

Fig. 1.5. A trapezoidal MF.

S-shaped MFs

Analytical representation of S-shaped MFs is of the following form

$$\mu_A(x) = \begin{cases} 0 & \text{if } x \le a_1 \\ 2\left(\dfrac{x-a_1}{a_3-a_1}\right)^2 & \text{if } a_1 < x < a_2 \\ 1-2\left(\dfrac{x-a_1}{a_3-a_1}\right)^2 & \text{if } a_2 \le x < a_3 \\ 1 & \text{if } a_3 \le x \end{cases}$$

Graphical representation of this type of MFs is illustrated in Fig. 1.6.

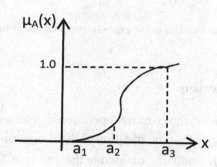

Fig. 1.6. S-shaped MF.

Exponential MFs

They have the following analytical form

$$\mu_{A(x)} = \frac{1}{1 + a_1(x - a_2)^2}, \quad k > 0$$

Graphical representation of this type of MFs is shown in Fig. 1.7.

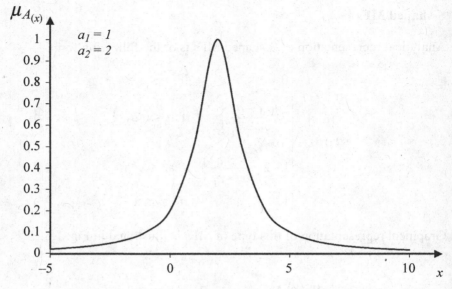

Fig. 1.7. An example of the exponential membership function.

Operations on fuzzy sets

At first let's consider three basic operations: intersection, union and complement of fuzzy sets. The mentioned three operations for fuzzy sets A and B with MFs μ_A and μ_B defined in the universe X are given below.

Standard intersection

The intersection of fuzzy sets A and B can be defined as

$$\forall x \in X \quad \mu_{A \cap B}(x) = \min(\mu_A(x), \mu_B(x))$$

Here $\mu_{A \cap B}(x)$ is MF of $A \cap B$.

Example

Let A and B be given [39]:

$$\mu_A(x) = \begin{cases} 1 & \text{if} \quad 60 \leq x < 70 \\ 1 - \dfrac{x-70}{10} & \text{if} \quad 70 \leq x < 80 \\ 0 & \text{if} \quad 80 \leq x \leq 100 \end{cases}$$

$$\mu_B(x) = \begin{cases} 0 & \text{if} \quad 60 \leq x < 70 \\ \dfrac{x-70}{10} & \text{if} \quad 70 \leq x < 80 \\ 1 - \dfrac{x-80}{10} & \text{if} \quad 80 \leq x < 90 \\ 0 & \text{if} \quad 90 \leq x \leq 100 \end{cases}$$

The intersection is as follows:

$$\mu_{A \cap B}(x) = \begin{cases} 1 & \text{if} \quad 60 \leq x < 70 \\ \dfrac{x-50}{10} & \text{if} \quad 70 \leq x < 75 \\ 1 - \dfrac{x-50}{10} & \text{if} \quad 75 \leq x \leq 80 \\ 0 & \text{if} \quad 80 < x \leq 100 \end{cases}$$

The graphs of A, B and $A \cap B$ are given in Fig. 1.8.

Standard union

Standard union of fuzzy sets A and B is determined as

$$\forall x \in X \quad \mu_{A \cup B}(x) = \max(\mu_A(x), \mu_B(x))$$

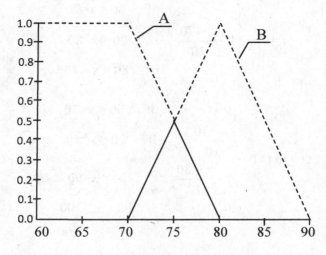

Fig. 1.8. Fuzzy intersection.

Example

For A and B given in previous example union is

$$\mu_{A \cup B}(x) = \begin{cases} 1 & \text{if} \quad 60 \le x < 70 \\ 1 - \dfrac{x-70}{10} & \text{if} \quad 70 \le x < 75 \\ \dfrac{x-70}{10} & \text{if} \quad 75 \le x \le 80 \\ 1 - \dfrac{x-80}{10} & \text{if} \quad 80 \le x \le 90 \\ 0 & \text{if} \quad 90 < x \le 100 \end{cases}$$

Graphical representation of union is shown in Fig. 1.9.

Complement of fuzzy set

The complement of fuzzy set A is the fuzzy set $\overline{A}$ defined as

$$\overline{A}(x) = 1 - A(x)$$

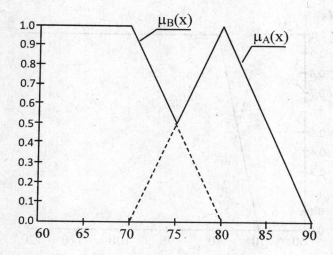

Fig. 1.9. Union of two fuzzy sets.

For fuzzy set A given in previous example $\overline{A}(x)$ is calculated as

$$\overline{A}(x) = \begin{cases} 0 & \text{if} \quad 60 \leq x < 70 \\ \dfrac{x-70}{10} & \text{if} \quad 70 \leq x < 80 \\ 1 & \text{if} \quad 80 \leq x \leq 100 \end{cases}$$

See also Fig. 1.10.

Associativity property is satisfied for fuzzy sets.

$$A \cap (B \cap C) = (A \cap B) \cap C$$

$$A \cup (B \cup C) = (A \cup B) \cup C$$

Also commutativity property for fuzzy sets holds true.

$$A \cap B = B \cap A$$

$$A \cup B = B \cup A$$

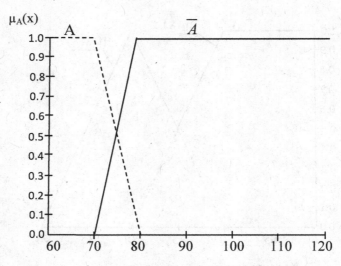

Fig. 1.10. The complement of a fuzzy set A.

Identity

$$A \cap X = A \qquad A \cup \varnothing = A$$

and absorption by $\varnothing$ and X

$$A \cap \varnothing = \varnothing \qquad A \cup X = X$$

properties are satisfied.

Idempotence

$$A \cap A = A \qquad A \cup A = A$$

and de Morgan Laws

$$\overline{A \cap B} = \overline{A} \cup \overline{B}$$

$$\overline{A \cup B} = \overline{A} \cap \overline{B}$$

properties hold true for fuzzy sets.

In general operators of intersection and union of fuzzy sets are triangular norms (t-norms) and co-norms (t-conorms). Main t-norms are [160]

1. Minimum: $at_m b = \min(a,b) = a \wedge b$
2. Product: $at_p b = ab$
3. Lukasiewicz: $at_L b = \max(a+b-1,0)$
4. Drastic product:
$$at_d b = \begin{cases} a & \text{if } b=1 \\ b & \text{if } a=1 \\ 0 & \text{otherwise} \end{cases}$$

Commonly used t-conorms are [160]

1. Maximum: $as_m b = \max(a,b) = a \vee b$
2. Probabilistic sum: $as_p b = a+b-ab$
3. Lukasiewicz: $as_L b = \min(a+b-1)$
4. Drastic sum: $at_d b = \{ b \quad \text{if } a=0$

Aggregation of fuzzy sets are often used in practice. T-norms and t-conorms provide a wide class of aggregation operators. Generalized mean-based commonly used aggregation operators are given below:

$$g(x_1, x_2, ..., x_n) = \frac{1}{n} \sum_{i=1}^{n} x_i$$ Arithmetic mean

$$g(x_1, x_2, ..., x_n) = \sqrt[n]{\prod_{i=1}^{n} x_i}$$ Geometric mean

$$g(x_1, x_2, ..., x_n) = \frac{n}{\sum_{i=1}^{n} 1/x_i}$$ Harmonic mean

$$g(x_1, x_2, ..., x_n) = \min(x_1, x_2, ..., x_n)$$ Minimum

$$g(x_1, x_2, ..., x_n) = \max(x_1, x_2, ..., x_n)$$ Maximum

Examples of arithmetic, geometric and harmonic means are illustrated in Fig. 1.11 (a,b,c), respectively [160].

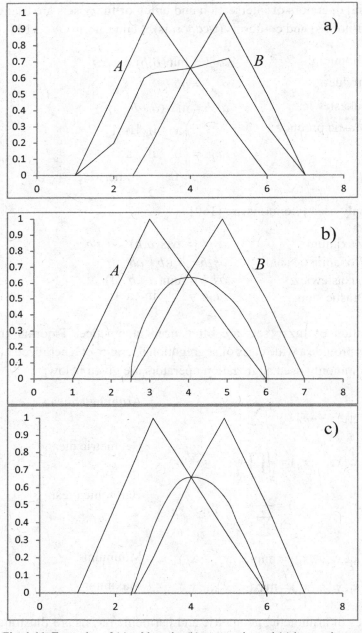

Fig. 1.11. Examples of (a) arithmetic; (b) geometric; and (c) harmonic mean.

Fuzzy measure considers another type of aggregation operators. Assume that X is finite universe and Ω family of subsets of X. Then fuzzy measure is

$$g:\Omega \to [0,1]$$

that satisfies

$g(\phi)=0 \quad g(X)=1$ Boundary conditions

If $A \subset B$, then $g(A) \le g(B)$ Monotonicity

If $h:X \to [0,1]$ is Ω measurable function, the fuzzy integral of h over A is described as

$$\int_A h(x) \circ g() = \sup_{\alpha \in [0,1]} \{\min[\alpha, g(A \cap H_\alpha)]\}$$

$$\int h(x) \circ g() = \max_{i=1,\dots,n} \{\min[h(x_i), g(A_i)]\}$$

is called Sugeno integral related to fuzzy measure.

$$\int f \circ g = \sum_{i=1}^{n} [h(x_i) - h(x_{i+1})]g(A_i), h(x_{n+1})$$

is called Choquet integral related to fuzzy measure.

Example

Assume that $\{h(x_i)\} = \{0.7, 0.4, 0.3, 0.1, 0.05\}$ and $\{g(A_i)\} = \{0.21, 0.412, 0.52, 0.833, 1\}$ are given. Then Choquet integral is calculated as [160]

$$\int f \circ g = (0.7 - 0.4)0.21 + (0.4 - 0.3)0.492 + (0.3 - 0.1)0.520$$
$$+ (0.1 - 0.005)0.833 + (0.05 - 0)1.0 = 0.3079$$

1.2. Fuzzy numbers

Definition 1.3. Fuzzy number is mapping from R (real numbers) to unit interval [0,1] that satisfies normality, boundness of support, continuity and unimodality.

Examples Triangular fuzzy number (TFN) A(2,3,4) is shown in Fig. 1.12.

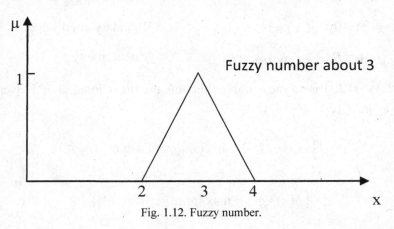

Fig. 1.12. Fuzzy number.

Trapezoidal fuzzy number (3,3.5,4.5,5) is shown in Fig. 1.13.

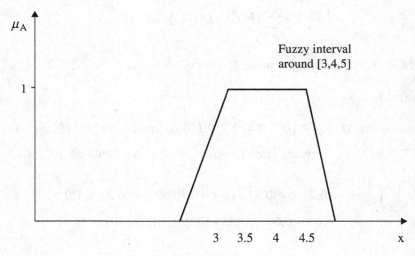

Fig. 1.13. Fuzzy interval.

Fuzzy numbers may be described in continuous (as in Fig. 1.13) and discrete forms.

Discrete fuzzy number "near 15" is described in Fig. 1.14.

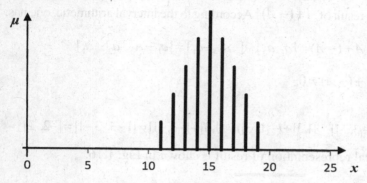

Fig. 1.14. Fuzzy integer number 15.

One of methods of fuzzy arithmetic exhibits its roots in the interval analysis. First, consider operations of interval arithmetic are given [9,149]. Assume that the following intervals $A = [a_1, a_2], B = [b_1, b_2] \subset \mathcal{R}$ are given.

Addition. If $x \in [a_1, a_2]$ and $y \in [b_1, b_2]$, then $x + y \in [a_1 + b_1, \ a_2 + b_2]$.

This can symbolically be expressed as

$$A + B = [a_1, \ a_2] + [b_1, \ b_2] = [a_1 + b_1, \ a_2 + b_2]$$

Example

$$[2,5] - [1,3] = [2-3, \ 5-1] = [-1, 4],$$

$$[0,1] - [-6,5] = [0-5, \ 1+6] = [-5, \ 7]$$

The graphical representation of result is shown in Fig. 1.15.

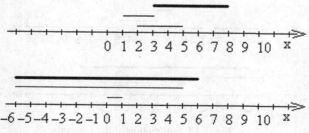

Fig. 1.15. Addition of the intervals.

The image of *A*. If $x \in [a_1, a_2]$ then $-x \in [-a_2, -a_1]$. In a symbolic form

$$-A = [-a_2, -a_1]$$

Consider the result of $A + (-A)$. According to the interval arithmetic, one has:

$$A + (-A) = [a_1, a_2] + [-a_2, -a_1] = [a_1 - a_2, \ a_2 - a_1]$$

Note that $A + (-A) \neq 0$.

Example

$$-[1,3] = [-3, -1] \quad [1,3] + (-[1, 3]) = [1,3] + [-3, -1] = [1-3, \ 3-1] = [-2, \ 2]$$

The graphical representation of result is shown in Fig. 1.16.

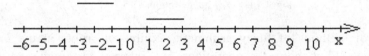

Fig. 1.16. Addition of *A* and –*A* intervals.

Subtraction. If $x \in [a_1, a_2]$ and $y \in [b_1, b_2]$, then

$$x - y \in [a_1 - b_2, a_2 - b_1]$$
$$A - B = [a_1, a_2] - [b_1, b_2] = [a_1 - b_2, a_2 - b_1]$$

Example

$$[2,5] - [1,3] = [2-3, \ 5-1] = [-1, 4]$$

$$[0,1] - [-6, 5] = [0-5, \ 1+6] = [-5, \ 7]$$

The graphical representation of result is shown in Fig. 1.17.

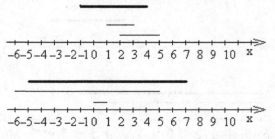

Fig. 1.17. Subtraction of the intervals.

Multiplication. The product of intervals $A, B \subset \mathcal{R}$ is defined as follows:

$$A \cdot B = [\min(a_1 \cdot b_1, a_1 \cdot b_2, a_2 \cdot b_1, a_2 \cdot b_2), \ \max(a_1 \cdot b_1, a_1 \cdot b_1, a_2 \cdot b_1, a_2 \cdot b_2)]$$

For the case $A, B \subset \mathcal{R}_+$ the result is obtained easily as

$$A \cdot B = [a_1, a_2] \cdot [b_1, b_2] = [a_1 \cdot b_1, a_2 \cdot b_2]$$

The scalar multiplication of A, $k \in \mathcal{R}$ is defined as follows:

$$\text{if } k > 0 \text{ then } k \cdot A = k \cdot [a_1, a_2] = [ka_1, ka_2]$$

$$\text{if } k < 0 \text{ then } k \cdot A = k \cdot [a_1, a_2] = [ka_2, ka_1]$$

Examples

$$[-1, 1] \cdot [-2, 0.5] = [\min(-1 \cdot (-2), -1 \cdot 0.5, \ 1 \cdot (-2), \ 1 \cdot 0.5),$$

$$\max(-1 \cdot (-2), -1 \cdot 0.5, \ 1 \cdot (-2), 1 \cdot 0.5)] =$$
$$= [\min(2, -0.5, -2, \ 0.5), \ \max(2, -0.5, -2, \ 0.5)] = [-2, \ 2]$$

The graphical representation of result is shown in Fig. 1.18.

Fig. 1.18. Multiplication of the intervals.

$$5 \cdot [3, 4] = [5 \cdot 3, 5 \cdot 4] = [15, 20]$$
$$-6 \cdot [2, 5] = [-6 \cdot 5, -6 \cdot 2] = [-30, -12]$$

Division. If $0 \notin B$ and $A, B \subset \mathcal{R}_+$ one has

$$A : B = [a_1, a_2] : [b_1, b_2] = [a_1 / b_2, a_2 / b_1] \qquad (1.1)$$

Based on (1.1), the inverse of A is defined as follows.
If $x \in [a_1, a_2]$ then

$$\frac{1}{x} \in \left[\frac{1}{a_2}, \frac{1}{a_1} \right]$$

and

$$A^{-1} = [a_1, a_2]^{-1} = [1/a_2, 1/a_1] \tag{1.2}$$

In general, the ratio of A and B is defined as

$$[a_1, a_2] : [b_1, b_2] = [a_1, a_2] \cdot [1/b_2, 1/b_1]$$

$$= [\min\{a_1/b_1, a_1/b_2, a_2/b_1, a_2/b_2\}, \max\{a_1/b_1, a_1/b_2, a_2/b_1, a_2/b_2\} \tag{1.3}$$

Note that,

$$A \cdot A^{-1} = [a_1/a_2, a_2/a_1] \neq 1$$

The division by a number $k > 0$ is equivalent to scalar multiplication by $1/k$.

Example

$$[-1, 1] / [-2, -0.5] = [-1, 1] \cdot [1/(-0.5), 1/(-2)]$$
$$= [\min(-1/(-2), -1/(-0.5), 1/(-2), 1/(-0.5)),$$
$$\max(-1/(-2), -1/(-0.5), 1/(-2), 1/(-0.5))] = \min(0.5, 2, -0.5, -2),$$
$$\max(0.5, 2, -0.5, -2)] = [-2, 2]$$

The graphical representation of result is shown in Fig. 1.19.

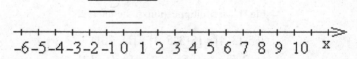

Fig.1.19. Division of the intervals.

In this arithmetic for interval numbers A, B, C following properties are satisfied:

1. Commutativity

$$A + B = B + A \qquad A \cdot B = B \cdot A$$

2. Associativity

$$A + (B + C) = (A + B) + C \qquad (A \cdot B) \cdot C = A \cdot (B \cdot C)$$

3. Identity
$$A+0=0+A=A \quad A\cdot 1=1\cdot A=A$$

4. Distributivity. This property is satisfied partially:

$$A\cdot(B+C)\subseteq A\cdot B+A\cdot C$$

There are different methods for arithmetic operations on fuzzy numbers. Here we present two commonly used methods.

Method based on the extension principle

Let f be function that maps a point in $X_1\times X_2\times...\times X_n$ to point in Y and $A_1\times A_2\times...\times A_n$ be fuzzy subsets of $X_1\times X_2\times...\times X_n$. According to the Zadeh's extension principle, the image of A under f is defined as [12,39,210].

$$\mu_B(y)=\max_{y=f(x_1,x_2,...,x_n)}\{\min[\mu_{A_1}(x_1),\mu_{A_2}(x_2),....,\mu_{A_n}(x_n)]\}$$

A fuzzy set $A*B$ in R can be defined as

$$\forall z\in R,\quad \mu_{(A*B)}(z)=\sup_{z=x*y}\min\{\mu_A(x),\mu_B(y)\}$$

or

$$A*B=\int_R \min(\mu_A(x),\mu_B(y))/(x*y)$$

* denotes one of arithmetic operations $\{+, -, . , :\}$. Then, the fuzzy set $A*B$ is defined as follows.

$$\mu_{(A+B)}(z)=\sup_{z=x+y}\min[\mu_A(x),\mu_B(y)] \text{ or }$$

$$A+B=\int_R \min(\mu_A(x),\mu_B(y))/(x+y)$$

$$\mu_{(A-B)}(z)=\sup_{z=x-y}\min[\mu_A(x),\mu_B(y)] \text{ or }$$

$$A - B = \int_R \min(\mu_A(x), \mu_B(y)) / (x - y)$$

$$\mu_{(A \cdot B)}(z) = \sup_{z = x \cdot y} \min[\mu_A(x), \mu_B(y)] \text{ or}$$

$$A \times B = \int_R \min(\mu_A(x), \mu_B(y)) / (x \times y)$$

$$\mu_{(A:B)}(z) = \sup_{z = x:y} \min[\mu_A(x), \mu_B(y)] \text{ or}$$

$$A : B = \int_R \min(\mu_A(x), \mu_B(y)) / (x : y)$$

Example

$$A = \frac{0.2}{1} + \frac{1}{2} + \frac{0.7}{3} , \; B = \frac{0.5}{1} + \frac{1}{2}$$

$$A \times B = \left(\frac{0.2}{1} + \frac{1}{2} + \frac{0.7}{3} \right) \times \left(\frac{0.5}{1} + \frac{1}{2} \right) = \left\{ \frac{\min(0.2, 0.5)}{1} \right.$$

$$+ \frac{\max[\min(0.2, 1), \min(0.5, 1)]}{2} + \frac{\max[\min(0.7, 0.5), \min(1, 1)]}{4}$$

$$+ \left. \frac{\min(0.7, 1)}{8} \right\} = \left\{ \frac{0.2}{1} + \frac{0.5}{2} + \frac{1}{4} + \frac{0.7}{8} \right\}$$

Method based on interval arithmetic and α-cuts

Let A and B be fuzzy numbers. For four arithmetic operations $* \in (+, -, \times, :)$ the α-cut of $A * B$ is described as

$$(A * B)^\alpha = A^\alpha * B^\alpha$$

The resulting fuzzy number is calculate of as

$$(A * B)^\alpha = \bigcup_{\alpha \in [0,1]} (A * B)^\alpha \qquad (1.4)$$

Using (1.4) we can calculate addition, subtraction, product and division of given fuzzy numbers [12].

Addition

Let A and B be two fuzzy numbers and A^α and B^α be their α-cuts

$$A^\alpha = [a_1^\alpha, a_2^\alpha] \; ; \; B^\alpha = [b_1^\alpha, b_2^\alpha]$$

Then we can write

$$A^\alpha + B^\alpha = [a_1^\alpha, a_2^\alpha] + [b_1^\alpha, b_2^\alpha] = [a_1^\alpha + b_1^\alpha, a_2^\alpha + b_2^\alpha]$$

here

$$A^\alpha = \{x / \mu_A(x) \geq \alpha\} \; ; \quad B^\alpha = \{x / \mu_B(x) \geq \alpha\}$$

Example

Consider fuzzy numbers A and B (Fig. 1.20).

$$\mu_A(x) = \begin{cases} 0 & \text{for } x < -1 \text{ and } x > 4 \\ (x+1)/2 & \text{for } -1 \leq x \leq 1 \\ (4-x)/3 & \text{for } \; 1 \leq x \leq 4 \end{cases}$$

$$\mu_B(x) = \begin{cases} 0 & \text{for } x < 2 \text{ and } x > 6 \\ (x-2)/2 & \text{for } \; 2 \leq x \leq 4 \\ (6-x)/2 & \text{for } \; 4 \leq x \leq 6 \end{cases}$$

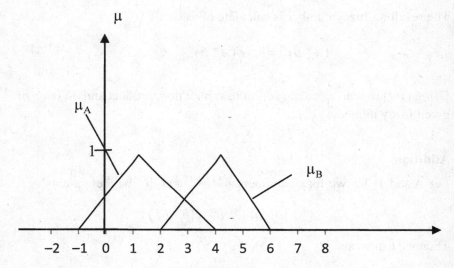

Fig. 1.20. Fuzzy numbers A and B.

Then

$$A(a_1^\alpha) = (a_1^\alpha + 1)/2 = \alpha$$
$$A(a_2^\alpha) = (4 - a_2^\alpha)/3 = \alpha$$

From these we obtain

$$a_1^\alpha = 2\alpha - 1 \quad a_2^\alpha = 4 - 3\alpha$$

Hence,

$$A^\alpha = [2\alpha - 1, \ 4 - 3\alpha]$$

Similarly,

$$B(b_1^{'\alpha}) = (b_1^\alpha - 2)/2 = \alpha$$

$$B(b_2^\alpha) = (6 - b_2^\alpha)/2 = \alpha$$

From these we obtain

$$b_1^\alpha = 2\alpha + 2 \quad b_2^\alpha = 6 - 2\alpha$$

that is

$$B^\alpha = [2\alpha + 2, \ 6 - 2\alpha].$$

Then

$(A+B)^{\alpha}=[2\alpha-1,\ 4-3\alpha]+[2\alpha+2,\ 6-2\alpha]=[4\alpha+1,\ 10-5\alpha]$.

Since $\alpha\in(0,1]$, the ranges of interval left and right endpoints are $(1,5]$ and $[5,10]$. This means that

$$4\alpha+1=x\quad\text{when } x\in(1,5]$$

and

$$10-5\alpha=x\quad\text{when } x\in[5,10)$$

Solving these equations for α, we obtain

$$\alpha=(x-1)/4=(A+B)(x)\quad\text{when } x\in(1,5]$$
$$\alpha=(10-x)/5=(A+B)(x)\quad\text{when } x\in[5,10)$$

That is, the MF of $A+B$ is expressed by the formula (see Fig. 1.21)

$$\mu_{A+B}(x)=\begin{cases}0 & \text{for } x<1 \text{ and } x>10\\ (x-1)/4 & \text{for } 1\le x\le 5\\ (10-x)/5 & \text{for } 5\le x\le 10\end{cases}$$

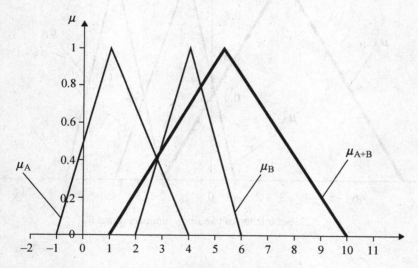

Fig. 1.21. Addition of two triangular fuzzy numbers A and B.

Subtraction

Subtraction of A and B can be defined as

$$(A - B)^\alpha = A^\alpha - B^\alpha = [a_1^\alpha - b_2^\alpha, a_2^\alpha - b_1^\alpha], \forall \alpha \in [0,1]$$

We can determine by addition of the image B^- to A

$$\forall \alpha \in [0,1], \qquad B^{\alpha^-} = [-b_2^\alpha, -b_1^\alpha]$$

Example

For the fuzzy numbers considered above, $A - B$ is calculated as

$$(A - B)^\alpha = [2\alpha - 1, \ 4 - 3\alpha] - [2\alpha + 2, \ 6 - 2\alpha]$$
$$= [2\alpha - 1, \ 4 - 3\alpha] + [2\alpha - 6, \ -2\alpha - 2] = [4\alpha - 7, \ 2 - 5\alpha]$$

and the corresponding MF is (see Fig. 1.22)

$$\mu_{A-B}(x) = \begin{cases} 0 & \text{for } x < -7 \text{ and } x > 2 \\ (x + 7)/4 & \text{for } -7 \le x \le -3 \\ (2 - x)/5 & \text{for } -3 \le x \le 2 \end{cases}$$

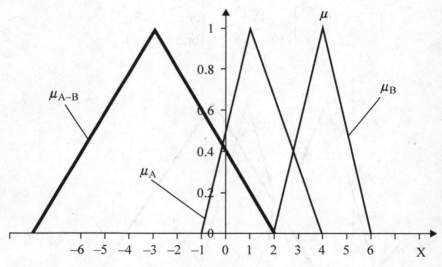

Fig. 1.22. Subtraction of two fuzzy numbers A and B.

Multiplication

Multiplication $A \cdot B$ fuzzy numbers A and B is defined as

$$(A \cdot B)^\alpha = A^\alpha \cdot B^\alpha = [a_1^\alpha, a_2^\alpha] \cdot [b_1^\alpha, b_2^\alpha] \qquad \forall \alpha \in [0,1]$$

Example

Let us compute multiplication of fuzzy numbers considered above. We have in terms of α-cuts:

$$(A \cdot B)^\alpha = [2\alpha - 1,\ 4 - 3\alpha] \cdot [2\alpha + 2,\ 6 - 2\alpha]$$

According to the principle of multiplication of intervals, we have obtained:

$$(A \cdot B)^\alpha = \begin{cases} [-4\alpha^2 + 14\alpha - 6,\ 6\alpha^2 - 26\alpha + 24] & \text{for } \alpha \in (0,\ 0.5] \\ [4\alpha^2 + 2\alpha - 2,\ 6\alpha^2 - 26\alpha + 24] & \text{for } \alpha \in (0.5,\ 1] \end{cases}$$

Therefore, the MF of $A \cdot B$ is as follows (see also Fig. 1.23)

$$\mu_{A \cdot B}(x) = \begin{cases} 0 & \text{for } x < -6 \text{ and } x > 24 \\ \dfrac{7 - \sqrt{25 - 4x}}{4} & \text{for } -6 \le x < 0 \\ \dfrac{-1 + \sqrt{9 + 4x}}{4} & \text{for } 0 \le x < 4 \\ \dfrac{13 - \sqrt{25 + 6x}}{6} & \text{for } 4 \le x \le 24 \end{cases}$$

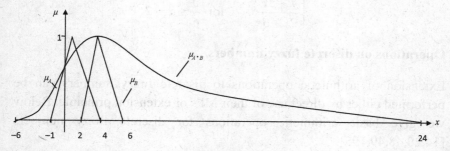

Fig. 1.23. Multiplication of two fuzzy numbers.

Division

Division of A by B is defined as (provided that $0 \notin \text{supp} B$)

$$(A / B)^\alpha = A^\alpha / B^\alpha = [a_1^\alpha, a_2^\alpha] / [b_1^\alpha, b_2^\alpha] \qquad \forall \alpha \in [0,1]$$

Example

Let us compute division of the fuzzy numbers considered above. α-cut of A / B is as follows:

$$\left(\frac{A}{B}\right)^{\alpha} = \begin{cases} \left[\dfrac{2\alpha-1}{2\alpha+2}, \dfrac{4-3\alpha}{2\alpha+2}\right] & \text{for } \alpha \in (0,\ 0.5] \\[4mm] \left[\dfrac{2\alpha-1}{6-2\alpha}, \dfrac{3-2\alpha}{2\alpha+2}\right] & \text{for } \alpha \in (0.5,\ 1] \end{cases}$$

and the MF

$$\mu_{\frac{A}{B}}(x) = \begin{cases} 0 & \text{for } x < -1 \text{ and } x > 2 \\[2mm] \dfrac{2x+1}{2-2x} & \text{for } -1 \leq x \leq 0 \\[2mm] \dfrac{6x+1}{2x+2} & \text{for } 0 \leq x \leq \dfrac{1}{4} \\[2mm] \dfrac{4-2x}{4x+3} & \text{for } \dfrac{1}{4} \leq x \leq \dfrac{5}{6} \\[2mm] \dfrac{4-2x}{2x+3} & \text{for } \dfrac{5}{6} \leq x \leq 2 \end{cases}$$

Operations on discrete fuzzy numbers.

Extension of arithmetic operations to discrete fuzzy numbers can be performed either by direct use of their MFs or extension principle. Below we give basic arithmetic operations for discrete fuzzy numbers [14,20,48,49,195].

Definition 1.4. Addition of discrete fuzzy numbers.

Addition of discrete fuzzy numbers A_1, A_2, $A_{12} = A_1 + A_2$ is the discrete fuzzy number whose α-cut is defined as

$$A_{12}^{\alpha} = \{x \in \{\text{supp}(A_1) + \text{supp}(A_2)\} \mid \min\{A_1^{\alpha} + A_2^{\alpha}\} \leq x \leq \max\{A_1^{\alpha} + A_2^{\alpha}\}\},$$

where

$$\text{supp}(A_1) + \text{supp}(A_2) = \{x_1 + x_2 \mid x_j \in \text{supp}(A_j), j = 1, 2\}$$

$$\min\{A_1^\alpha + A_2^\alpha\} = \min\{x_1 + x_2 \mid x_j \in A_j^\alpha), j = 1, 2\}$$

$$\max\{A_1^\alpha + A_2^\alpha\} = \max\{x_1 + x_2 \mid x_j \in A_j^\alpha, j = 1, 2\}$$

The MF is defined as

$$\mu_{A_1 + A_2}(x) = \sup\{\alpha \in [0,1] \mid x \in \{A_1^\alpha + A_2^\alpha\}\}$$

Consider discrete fuzzy numbers A_1 and A_2:

$$A_1 = 0/1 + 0.3/2 + 0.5/3 + 0.6/4 + 0.7/5 + 0.8/6 + 0.9/7 + 1/8$$
$$+ 0.8/9 + 0.6/10 + 0/11$$

$$A_2 = 0/1 + 0.5/2 + 0.8/3 + 1/4 + 0.8/5 + 0.7/6 + 0.6/7 + 0.4/8$$
$$+ 0.2/9 + 0.1/10 + 0/11$$

The approximated resulting $A_{12} = A_1 + A_2$ is as follows:

$$A_{12} = 0/1 + 0/2 + 0.19/3 + 0.36/4 + 0.5/5 + 0.58/6 + 0.65/7 + 0.73/8$$
$$+ 0.8/9 + 0.87/10 + 0.93/11 + 1/12 + 0.9/13 + 0.8/14 + 0.73/15 + 0.7/16$$
$$+ 0.6/17 + 0.45/18 + 0.3/19 + 0.17/20 + 0.086/21.$$

Definition 1.5. Standard subtraction of discrete fuzzy numbers.

For discrete fuzzy numbers A_1, A_2 their standard subtraction $A_{12} = A_1 - A_2$ is the discrete fuzzy number whose α-cut is defined as

$$A_j^\alpha = \{x \in \{\text{supp}(A_1) - \text{supp}(A_2)\} \mid \min\{A_1^\alpha - A_2^\alpha\} \leq x \leq \max\{A_1^\alpha - A_2^\alpha\}\}$$

where

$$\text{supp}(A_1) - \text{supp}(A_2) = \{x_1 - x_2 \mid x_j \in \text{supp}(A_j), j = 1, 2\}$$

$$\min\{A_1^\alpha - A_2^\alpha\} = \min\{x_1 - x_2 \mid x_j \in A_j^\alpha, j = 1, 2\}$$

$$\max\{A_1^\alpha - A_2^\alpha\} = \max\{x_1 - x_2 \mid x_j \in A_j^\alpha, j = 1, 2\}$$

and the MF is defined as

$$\mu_{A_1 - A_2}(x) = \sup\{\alpha \in [0,1] \mid x \in \{A_1^\alpha - A_2^\alpha\}\}$$

Definition 1.6. Standard multiplication of discrete fuzzy numbers.

For discrete fuzzy numbers A_1, A_2 their multiplication $A_{12} = A_1 \cdot A_2$ is the discrete fuzzy number whose α -cut is defined as

$$A_j^\alpha = \{x \in \{\text{supp}(A_1) \cdot \text{supp}(A_2)\} \mid \min\{A_1^\alpha \cdot A_2^\alpha\} \le x \le \max\{A_1^\alpha \cdot A_2^\alpha\}\}$$

where

$$\text{supp}(A_1) \cdot \text{supp}(A_2) = \{x_1 \cdot x_2 \mid x_j \in \text{supp}(A_j), j = 1, 2\}$$

$$\min\{A_1^\alpha \cdot A_2^\alpha\} = \min\{x_1 \cdot x_2 \mid x_j \in A_j^\alpha, j = 1, 2\}$$

$$\max\{A_1^\alpha \cdot A_2^\alpha\} = \max\{x_1 \cdot x_2 \mid x_j \in A_j^\alpha, j = 1, 2\}$$

and the MF is defined as

$$\mu_{A_1 \cdot A_2}(x) = \sup\{\alpha \in [0,1] \mid x \in \{A_1^\alpha \cdot A_2^\alpha\}\}$$

Definition 1.7. Standard division discrete fuzzy numbers.

For discrete fuzzy numbers A_1, A_2 given that $0 \notin \text{supp}(A_2)$ their standard division $A_{12} = {}^{A_1}\!/\!_{A_2}$ is the discrete fuzzy number whose α-cut is defined as

$$A_{12}^\alpha = \{x \in \{\text{supp}(A_1)/\text{supp}(A_2)\} \mid \min\{A_1^\alpha / A_2^\alpha\} \le x \le \max\{A_1^\alpha / A_2^\alpha\}\}$$

where

$$\text{supp}(A_1)/\text{supp}(A_2) = \{x_1/x_2 \mid x_j \in \text{supp}(A_j), j = 1,2\}$$

$$\min\{A_1^\alpha / A_2^\alpha\} = \min\{x_1/x_2 \mid x_j \in A_j^\alpha, j = 1,2\}$$

$$\max\{A_1^\alpha / A_2^\alpha\} = \max\{x_1/x_2 \mid x_j \in \text{supp}(A_j), j = 1,2\}$$

and the MF is defined as

$$\mu_{A_1/A_2}(x) = \sup\{\alpha \in [0,1] \mid x \in \{A_1^\alpha / A_2^\alpha\}\}$$

Linguistic variables [211]

Linguistic variable is variable whose values are fuzzy sets. These variables have values consisting of word or sentences described in natural language. Formally, a linguistic variable is expressed as $< u, T, X, G, M >$ where u is name of the variable whose values range over a universe X, $T(X)$ is a term set of X, G is a grammar for generation of linguistic terms, M is semantic rule that assigns to each linguistic term its meaning, which is a fuzzy set on X.

For example, consider a class of men aged near 30. In this case (Fig. 1.24) we may define a linguistic variable $Y_1, i = \overline{1,4}$ "Young men", consisting of four linguistic terms {very young, young, yet young, young for somebody}. The correspondent fuzzy sets may be defined intuitively as (see Fig. 1.24),

$$A_1 = \{1.0/15 + 0.7/18 + 0.3/21 + 0.1/24 + 0.0/27 + 0.0/30 + \cdots + 0.0/45\}$$
$$A_2 = \{0.1/15 + 0.3/18 + 0.7/21 + 1.0/24 + 0.7/27 + 0.3/30 + \cdots + 0.0/45\}$$
$$A_3 = \{0.0/15 + \cdots + 0.0/21 + 0.1/24 + 0.3/27 + 0.7/30 + 1.0/33 + 0.7/36$$
$$+ 0.3/39 + 0.1/42 + 0.0/45\}$$
$$A_4 = \{0.0/15 + \cdots + 0/33 + 0.1/36 + 0.3/39 + 0.7/42 + 1.0/45\}$$

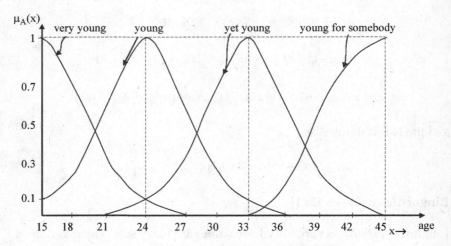

Fig. 1.24. Graphical representation of membership functions.

Fuzzy relations

Fuzzy relation R is fuzzy subset of the Cartesian product of universes X and Y that has partial association between elements of universes. Formally, R is

$$R: X \times Y \rightarrow [0,1]$$

For example, for temperature control system we have knowledge described through if-then rule given below

If the error e is negative large (NL) THEN the control action u is negative large (NL)

or through MF

$$\mu_{E1}(e) = 1.00/-10 + 0.73/-7 + 0.34/-3 + 0.20/0 + 0.13/3 + 0.08/7 + 0.06/10$$

$$\mu_{U1}(u) = 1.00/-1 + 0.92/-0.7 + 0.67/-0.3 + 0.50/0 + 0.37/0.3 + 0.26/0.7 + 0.20/1$$

then fuzzy relation matrix R with the MF $\mu_R(u,e) = \min(\mu_{E1}(e), \mu_{U1}(u))$ will be

	1.00	0.92	0.67	0.50	0.37	0.26	0.20
1.00	1.00	0.92	0.67	0.50	0.37	0.26	0.20
0.73	0.73	0.73	0.67	0.50	0.37	0.26	0.20
0.34	0.34	0.34	0.34	0.34	0.34	0.26	0.20
0.20	0.20	0.20	0.20	020	0.20	0.20	0.20
0.13	0.13	0.13	0.13	0.13	0.13	0.13	0.13
0.08	0.08	0.08	0.08	0.08	0.08	0.08	0.08
0.06	0.06	0.06	0.06	0.06	0.06	0.06	0.06

Now let's consider operations on fuzzy relations

Union
The union R of fuzzy relations P and Q defined in $X \times Y, R = P \cup Q$, is expressed as follows. Here s is a t-conorm.

$$R(x,y) = P(x,y)\, s\, Q(x,y) \quad \forall (x,y) \in X \times Y$$

Intersection
The intersection R of fuzzy relations P and Q defined in $X \times Y, R = P \cap Q$, is expressed as follows where t is a t-norm.

$$R(x,y) = P(x,y)\, t\, Q(x,y) \quad \forall (x,y) \in X \times Y$$

Complement
The complement R of the fuzzy relation R is defined as

$$\overline{R}(x,y) = 1 - R(x,y) \quad \forall (x,y) \in X \times Y$$

Example
Assume that mentioned above temperature control system has 7 rules as

1. If e is negative large THEN u is negative large
2. If e is negative average THEN u is negative average
3. If e is negative small THEN u is negative small
4. If e is zero THEN u is zero
5. If e is positive small THEN u is positive small
6. If e is positive average THEN u is positive average
7. If e is positive large THEN u is positive large

Through MFs they are expressed as

Rule 1

$$\mu_{E1}(e) = 1.00/-10 + 0.73/-7 + 0.34/-3 + 0.20/0 + 0.13/3 + 0.08/7 + 0.06/10$$

$$\mu_{U1}(u) = 1.00/-1 + 0.92/-0.7 + 0.67/-0.3 + 0.50/0 + 0.37/0.3 + 0.26/0.7 + 0.20/1$$

Rule 2

$$\mu_{E2}(e) = 0.73/-10 + 1/-7 + 0.61/-3 + 0.34/0 + 0.20/3 + 0.11/7 + 0.08/10$$

$$\mu_{U2}(u) = 0.91/-1 + 1.00/-0.7 + 0.86/-0.3 + 0.67/0 + 0.50/0.3 + 0.34/0.7 + 0.26/1$$

Rule 3

$$\mu_{E3}(e) = 0.34/-10 + 0.61/-7 + 1.00/-3 + 0.73/0 + 0.41/3 + 0.20/7 + 0.13/10$$

$$\mu_{U3}(u) = 0.61/-1 + 0.86/-0.7 + 1.00/-0.3 + 0.92/0 + 0.74/0.3 + 0.50/0.7 + 0.37/1$$

Rule 4

$$\mu_{E4}(e) = 0.20/-10 + 0.34/-7 + 0.73/-3 + 1.00/0 + 0.73/3 + 0.34/7 + 0.20/10$$

$$\mu_{U4}(u) = 0.50/-1 + 0.67/-0.7 + 0.92/-0.3 + 1.00/0 + 0.92/0.3 + 0.67/0.7 + 0.50/1$$

Rule 5

$$\mu_{E5}(e) = 0.13/-10 + 0.20/-7 + 0.41/-3 + 0.73/0 + 1.00/3 + 0.61/7 + 0.34/10$$

$$\mu_{U5}(u) = 0.37/-1 + 0.50/-0.7 + 0.74/-0.3 + 0.92/0 + 1.00/0.3 + 0.86/0.7 + 0.67/1$$

Rule 6

$$\mu_{E6}(e) = 0.08/-10 + 0.11/-7 + 0.20/-3 + 0.34/0 + 0.61/3 + 1.00/7 + 0.73/10$$

$$\mu_{U6}(u) = 0.26/-1 + 0.34/-0.7 + 0.50/-0.3 + 0.67/0 + 0.86/0.3 + 1.00/0.7 + 0.91/1$$

Rule 7

$$\mu_{E7}(e) = 0.06/-10 + 0.08/-7 + 0.13/-3 + 0.20/0 + 0.34/3 + 0.73/7 + 1.00/10$$

$$\mu_{U7}(u) = 0.20/-1 + 0.26/-0.7 + 0.37/-0.3 + 0.50/0 + 0.67/0.3 + 0.92/0.7 + 1.00/1$$

Relation matrices are given as follows:

Fuzzy relation matrix R_1

	1.00	0.92	0.67	0.50	0.37	0.26	0.20
1.00	1.00	0.92	0.67	0.50	0.37	0.26	0.20
0.73	0.73	0.73	0.67	0.50	0.37	0.26	0.20
0.34	0.34	0.34	0.34	0.34	0.34	0.26	0.20
0.20	0.20	0.20	0.20	0.20	0.20	0.20	0.20
0.13	0.13	0.13	0.13	0.13	0.13	0.13	0.13
0.08	0.08	0.08	0.08	0.08	0.08	0.08	0.08
0.06	0.06	0.06	0.06	0.06	0.06	0.06	0.06

Fuzzy relation matrix R_2

	0.91	1.00	0.86	0.67	0.50	0.34	0.26
0.73	0.73	0.73	0.73	0.67	0.50	0.34	0.26
1.00	0.91	1.00	0.86	0.67	0.50	0.34	0.26
0.61	0.61	0.61	0.61	0.61	0.50	0.34	0.26
0.34	0.34	0.34	0.34	0.34	0.34	0.34	0.26
0.20	0.20	0.20	0.20	0.20	0.20	0.20	0.20
0.11	0.11	0.11	0.11	0.11	0.11	0.11	0.11
0.08	0.08	0.08	0.08	0.08	0.08	0.08	0.08

Fuzzy relation matrix R_3

	0.61	0.86	1.00	0.92	0.74	0.50	0.37
0.34	0.34	0.34	0.34	0.34	0.34	0.34	0.34
0.31	0.61	0.61	0.61	0.61	0.61	0.50	0.37
1.00	0.61	0.86	1.00	0.92	0.74	0.50	0.37
0.73	0.61	0.73	0.73	0.73	0.73	0.50	0.37
0.41	0.41	0.41	0.41	0.41	0.41	0.41	0.37
0.20	0.20	0.20	0.20	0.20	0.20	0.20	0.20
0.13	0.13	0.13	0.13	0.13	0.13	0.13	0.13

Fuzzy relation matrix R_4

	0.50	0.67	0.92	1.00	0.92	0.67	0.50
0.20	0.20	0.20	0.20	0.20	0.20	0.20	0.20
0.34	0.34	0.34	0.34	0.34	0.34	0.34	0.34
0.73	0.50	0.67	0.73	0.73	0.73	0.67	0.50
1.00	0.50	0.67	0.92	1.00	0.92	0.67	0.50
0.73	0.50	0.67	0.73	0.73	0.73	0.67	0.50
0.34	0.34	0.34	0.34	0.34	0.34	0.34	0.34
0.20	0.20	0.20	0.20	0.20	0.20	0.20	0.20

Fuzzy relation matrix R_5

	0.37	0.50	0.74	0.92	1.00	0.86	0.67
0.13	0.13	0.13	0.13	0.13	0.13	0.13	0.13
0.20	0.20	0.20	0.20	0.20	0.20	0.20	0.20
0.41	0.37	0.41	0.41	0.41	0.41	0.41	0.41
0.73	0.37	0.50	0.73	0.73	0.73	0.73	0.67
1.00	0.37	0.50	0.74	0.92	1.00	0.86	0.67
0.61	0.37	0.50	0.61	0.61	0.61	0.61	0.61
0.34	0.34	0.34	0.34	0.34	0.34	0.34	0.34

Fuzzy relation matrix R_6

	0.26	0.34	0.50	0.67	0.86	1.00	0.91
0.08	0.08	0.08	0.08	0.08	0.08	0.08	0.08
0.11	0.11	0.11	0.11	0.11	0.11	0.11	0.11
0.20	0.20	0.20	0.20	0.20	0.20	0.20	0.20
0.34	0.26	0.34	0.34	0.34	0.34	0.34	0.34
0.61	0.26	0.34	0.50	0.61	0.61	0.61	0.61
1.00	0.26	0.34	0.50	0.67	0.86	1.00	0.91
0.73	0.26	0.34	0.50	0.67	0.73	0.73	0.73

Fuzzy relation matrix R_7

	0.20	0.26	0.37	0.50	0.67	0.92	1.00
0.06	0.06	0.06	0.06	0.06	0.06	0.06	0.06
0.08	0.08	0.08	0.08	0.08	0.08	0.08	0.08
0.13	0.13	0.13	0.13	0.13	0.13	0.13	0.13
0.20	0.20	0.20	0.20	0.20	0.20	0.20	0.20
0.34	0.20	0.26	0.34	0.34	0.34	0.34	0.34
0.73	0.20	0.26	0.37	0.50	0.67	0.73	0.73
1.00	0.20	0.26	0.37	0.50	0.67	0.92	1.00

Composed fuzzy relation R is defined as

$$R = R_1 \cup R_2 \cup ... \cup R_5 \cup ... \cup R_7$$

with the MF, $\mu_R(u,e) = \max[\mu_1(u,e),...,\mu_2(u,e),...,\mu_7(u,e)]$

Composition operators

Different types of composition operators are in existence based on the specific t-norms and t-conorms. Let X and Y be classical sets and $F(X \times Y)$ family of all fuzzy relations on $X \times Y$. For given fuzzy relations $R \in F(X \times Y)$ and $Q \in F(Y \times Z)$.

$$R \circ Q(X,Z) = \bigvee_{y \in Y} R(X,Y) \wedge Q(Y,Z) \qquad (1.5)$$

is called the max-min composition of R and Q. If X, Y and Z are finite sets and R and Q are discrete fuzzy relations then composition $T = R \circ Q \in F(X,Z)$ is defined as [160]

$$t_{ik} = \bigvee_{j=1}^{m} r_{ij} \wedge g_{jk}, \quad i = \overline{1,n}, \; j = \overline{1,m}, \; k = \overline{1,p} \qquad (1.6)$$

Example

If

$$R = \begin{pmatrix} 0.3 & 0.7 & 0.2 \\ 1 & 0 & 0.9 \end{pmatrix} \quad \text{and} \quad Q = \begin{pmatrix} 0.8 & 0.3 \\ 0.1 & 0 \\ 0.5 & 0.6 \end{pmatrix}, \quad \text{then } R \circ Q = \begin{pmatrix} 0.3 & 0.3 \\ 0.8 & 0.6 \end{pmatrix}$$

1.3. Fuzzy inference rules and reasoning

Definition 1.8. Fuzzy implication.

A fuzzy implication is a function $f_i : [0,1]^2 \rightarrow [0,1]$ with the following properties:

1. $B(y_1) \le B(y_2) \Rightarrow f_i(A(x), B(y_1)) \le f_i(A(x), B(y_2))$ Monotonicity

2. $f_i(0, B(y)) = 1$ Dominance of falsity

3. $f_i(1, B(y)) = B(y)$ Neutrality of truth

In addition to the list shown above, two properties are usually added:

4. $A(x_1) \le A(x_2) \Rightarrow f_i(A(x_1), B(y)) \ge f_i(A(x_2), B(y))$ Monotonicity

5. $f_i(A(x_1), f_i(A(x_2), B(y))) = f_i(A(x_2), f_i(A(x_1), B(y)))$ Exchange

There are a number of implication operators. The commonly used realizations of fuzzy implications are shown below [12].

    1) min-logic

$$a \underset{\min}{\rightarrow} b = \begin{cases} a & \text{if } a \le b \\ b & \text{otherwise} \end{cases}$$

    2) $S^{\#}$-logic

$$a \underset{S^{\#}}{\rightarrow} b = \begin{cases} 1 & \text{if } a \ne 1 \text{ or } b = 1 \\ 0 & \text{otherwise} \end{cases}$$

    3) S-logic ("Standard sequence")

$$a \underset{S}{\rightarrow} b = \begin{cases} 1 & \text{if } a \le b \\ 0 & \text{otherwise} \end{cases}$$

4) G-logic ("Gödelian sequence")

$$a \underset{G}{\to} b = \begin{cases} 1 & \text{if } a \le b \\ b & \text{otherwise} \end{cases}$$

5) G43-logic

$$a \underset{G43}{\to} b = \begin{cases} 1 & \text{if } a = 0 \\ \min(1, b/a) & \text{otherwise} \end{cases}$$

6) L-logic (Lukasiewicz's logic)

$$a \underset{L}{\to} b = \min(1, 1 - a + b).$$

7) KD-logic

$$a \underset{KD}{\to} b = ((1-a) \vee b) = \max(1-a, b).$$

8) ALI1-logic

$$a \underset{ALI1}{\to} b = \begin{cases} 1-a & \text{if } a < b \\ 1 & \text{if } a = b \\ b & \text{if } a > b \end{cases}$$

By using shown above implications on base of Fuzzy Conditional Inference Rules we can make logical inference when rules preconditions and conclusions are described by fuzzy concepts. In practice usually following types of propositions are used.

(i)=IF x is A THEN y is B
(ii)=IF x is A THEN y is B
OTHERWISE C
(iii)=IF x_1 is A_1 AND x_2 is A_2 AND ... x_n is A_n
THEN y is B.

Here A, B and C are fuzzy concepts.
For case (i) fuzzy conditional inference is expressed as

Proposition 1: IF x is A THEN y is B
Proposition 2: x is A′
_____

Conclusion: y is B′,

(1.7)

Here A and A′ are fuzzy sets in the universe U, B and B′ are fuzzy sets in the universe V. To perform logical conclusion the Proposition 1 and Proposition 2 must be transformed to the fuzzy binary relation $R(A(x), B(y))$ and fuzzy unary relation $R(A_1(x))$. Then

$$R(A_1(x))=A'$$

For example $R(A_1(x), A_2(y))$ may be defined as follows [38].

The maximin conditional inference:
$$R_m(A_1(x), A_2(y))=(A \times B) \cup (\neg A \times V)$$

The arithmetic conditional inference rule

$$R_a(A_1(x), A_2(y))=(\neg A \times V) \oplus (U \times B)$$

The mini-functional conditional inference rule

$$R_c(A_1(x), A_2(y))= A \times B$$

Then logical consequence $R(A_2(y))$ (B′ in (1.7)) can be defined as

$$R(A_2(y))=A' \subset [(A \times B)] \cup [\neg A \times U)]$$
$$R(A_2(y))=A' \subset [(\neg A \times V)] \oplus [U \times B)]$$

or

$$R(A_2(y))=A' \subset (A \times B)$$

where $\subset$ is the F-set maximin composition operator.
For the type of Proposition 2 as it is given in [12] logical consequence is obtained as

$$R(A_1(x), A_2(y)) = \left[\bigcap_{i=1,n} (\neg A_i \times V) \right] \oplus [(U \times B)]$$

$$R(A_1(x), A_2(y)) = \left[\bigcap_{i=1,n} (\neg A_i \times V) \right] \cup [(U \times B)]$$

$$R(A_1(x), A_2(y)) = \left[\bigcap_{i=1,n} A_i \right] \times B$$

Example

Assume that A from U and B from V are given. For ALI 1-logic fuzzy relation $R(A_1(x), A_2(y))$ is defined as

$$R_1(A_1(x), A_2(y)) = A \times V \underset{ALI1}{\rightarrow} U \times B = \int_{U \times V} \mu_A(u)/(u, v) \underset{ALI1}{\rightarrow}$$

$$\underset{ALI1}{\rightarrow} \int_{U \times V} \mu_B(v)/(u, v) = \int_{U \times V} (\mu_A(u) \underset{ALI1}{\rightarrow} \mu_B(v))/(u, v)$$

where

$$\mu_A(u) \underset{ALI1}{\rightarrow} \mu_B(v) = \begin{cases} 1 - \mu_A(u), & \mu_A(u) < \mu_B(v), \\ 1, & \mu_A(u) = \mu_B(v), \\ \mu_B(v), & \mu_A(u) > \mu_B(v) \end{cases}$$

Let U=V=0+1+2+3+4+5+6+7+8+9+10, A=*small*=1/0+0.8/1+0.6/2+0.4/3+0.2/4, B=*medium*=0.2/2+0.4/3+0.8/4+1/5+0.8/6+0.4/7+0.2/8.

Then the F-conditional proposition
IF x is small THEN y is medium
boils down to a binary relation of the following type
$R(A_1(x), A_2(y)) = [small]_{\times V} \underset{ALI1}{\rightarrow} U \times [medium]$

	0	1	2	3	4	5	6	7	8	9	10
0	0	0	0,2	0,4	0,8	1	0,8	0,4	0,2	0	0
1	0	0	0,2	0,4	1	0,2	1	0,4	0,2	0	0
2	0	0	0,2	0,4	0,4	0,4	0,4	0,4	0,2	0	0
3	0	0	0,2	1	0,6	0,6	0,6	1	0,2	0	0
4	0	0	1	0,8	0,8	0,8	0,8	0,8	1	0	0
= 5	1	1	1	1	1	1	1	1	1	1	1
6	1	1	1	1	1	1	1	1	1	1	1
7	1	1	1	1	1	1	1	1	1	1	1
8	1	1	1	1	1	1	1	1	1	1	1
9	1	1	1	1	1	1	1	1	1	1	1
10	1	1	1	1	1	1	1	1	1	1	1

Let $R(A_1(x))$=*small*, then $R(A_2(y)) = [small] ^c R_1(A_1(x)), (A_2(y))$

$=0.2/2+0.4/3+0.8/4+1/5+0.8/6+0.4/7+0.2/8=$ *medium*

When $R_1(A_1(x))=$*very small*, we get

$R(A_2(y))=[$*very small*$] ^c R_1(A_1(x)), (A_2(y))$

$=[$*small*$]^{2c} R_1(A_1(x),A_2(y))$

$=0.04/2+0.16/3+0.64/4+1/5+0.64/6+0,16/7+0,04/8$

$= [$*medium*$]^2=$ *very medium*

1.4. Fuzzy Modeling

Fuzzy modeling means description system characteristic and relationship between their input and output variables. Widely used classes of fuzzy models are [12]

    (i)   Linguistic models
    (ii)   Fuzzy relational models
    (iii)   TSK models

Linguistic fuzzy models

This type of models for objects with multi-input (n) and multi-output (m) objects (MIMO models) is expressed by means of fuzzy rules as:

Rule k:
$$IF \ x_1 \ is \ A_{i1} \ AND \ x_2 \ is \ A_{i2} \ AND \ ... \ x_n \ is \ A_{in} \ \ \ THEN$$
$$y_1 \ is \ B_{i1} \ AND \ y_2 \ is \ B_{i2} \ AND \ ... \ y_m \ is \ B_{im}$$

where $x_i (i = \overline{1,n})$, $y_j (j = \overline{1,m})$ are linguistic variables of inputs and outputs, A_{ij}, B_{ij} are fuzzy sets, (k=1,N).

For single input and single output models (SISO-models) one has:

$$IF \ x \ is \ A_k \ THEN \ y \ is \ B_k \ (k=1,...,K)$$

Example

Consider a fragment of a collection of fuzzy IF-THEN rules describing relationship between a composition of Ti-Ni alloy and its required characteristics. The use of fuzzy rules is motivated by the fact that information on this relationship is complex and uncertain. The inputs of the rules are portions of Ti, x_1, and Ni, x_2, and test temperature (experiment condition), x_3, the outputs are alloy characteristics as conventional ultimate strength (MPa), y_1, conventional yield strength (MPa), y_2, and unit elongation (%), y_3. The fuzzy rules are as follows [30]:

IF x_1 is High and x_2 is Low and x_3 is Very low

THEN y_1 is Very high and y_2 is Average high 2 and y_3 is Low,

IF x_1 is Very high and x_2 is Very low and x_3 is Very high

THEN y_1 is Very low and y_2 is Average high 1 and y_3 is Average

The linguistic terms used in the If-Then rules are described by trapezoidal fuzzy numbers as follows: for x_1, High=(49.16, 49.46, 49.65, 49.96), Very High=(49.27, 49.58, 49.78, 50.08); for x_2, Very Low=(49.92, 50.22, 50.42, 50.73), Low=(50.04, 50.35, 50.54, 50.84); x_3: Very Low=(−307.3, −222.3, −168, −83.02), Very High=(23.84, 166.8, 202.6, 345.5); for y_1: Very Low=(817.2, 868, 947.5, 998.6), Very High=(1128, 1223, 1284, 1380); for y_2: Average=(295.7, 371, 419, 494.3); for y_3: Low=(16.8, 30.8, 39.7, 53.7), Average=(37.69, 44.04, 48.1, 54.45).

Example

In this example a fragment of a collection of fuzzy rules that express relation between geological parameters as carbonate %, y_1, sand %, y_2, silt %, y_3, shale%, y_4, porosity %, y_5, changing with respect to the depth. The use fuzzy rules is conditioned by the complexity, nonlinearity and uncertainty of the considered behavior. The antecedents of the rules are the parameters values for the current depth, $y_{i,t}$ and the previous depth, $y_{i,t-1}$. The outputs are values of these parameters at the following depth, $y_{i,t+1}$, $i=1,...,5$. The rules are given below:

IF y_{1t-1} is *Low average and* y_{2t-1} is *Average and* y_{3t-1} is *Low average and*
 y_{4t-1} is *Low average and* y_{5t-1} is *Average and* y_{1t} is *Low average and*
 y_{2t} is *Average and* y_{3t} is *Low average and* y_{4t} is *Low average and*
       y_{5t} is *Average*
        THEN
y_{1t+1} is *Low average and* y_{2t+1} is *Low average and* y_{3t+1} is *Low average*
   y_{4t+1} is *Average and* y_{5t+1} is *Average*

  IF y_{1t-1} is *Average and* y_{2t-1} is *Low and* y_{3t-1} is *Average and*
 y_{4t-1} is *Average and* y_{5t-1} is *Average and* y_{1t} is *Low average and*
y_{2t} is *High Average and* y_{3t} is *Low average and* y_{4t} is *Low and* y_{5t} is *High*
        THEN
y_{1t+1} is *Low and* y_{2t+1} is *High average and* y_{3t+1} is *Low and*
  y_{4t+1} is *Average and* y_{5t+1} is *High*

Fuzzy relational model

Construction of fuzzy relational model means solving a following equation.

$$B = A \circ R$$

where A and B are fuzzy sets and R is fuzzy relation between input and output variables of a considered system.

Example

Assume that the following fuzzy set A and fuzzy relation R are given:

$$A = 0.2 / 1 + 0.4 / 2 + 1.0 / 3,$$

$$R = 1.0 / (1,5) + 1.0 / (1,6) + 1.0 / (1,7) + 1.0 / (2,5) + 1.0 / (2,6) +$$
$$+ 1.0 / (2,7) + 0.6 / (3,5) + 0.8 / (3,6) + 1.0 / (3,7)$$

or in the vector form

$$A = \begin{bmatrix} 0.2 & 0.4 & 1.0 \end{bmatrix}$$

$$R = \begin{bmatrix} 1.0 & 1.0 & 1.0 \\ 1.0 & 1.0 & 1.0 \\ 0.6 & 0.8 & 1.0 \end{bmatrix}.$$

Let us construct fuzzy set B by using the sup-min (max-min) composition:

$$B = A \circ R,$$

where

$$\mu_B(y) = \sup_{x \in A} \min(\mu_A(x), \mu_R(x, y)).$$

Computation is as follows.

$$\mu_B(y) = \sup_{x \in A} \min(\mu_A(x), \mu_R(x, y))$$

$$= \sup_{x \in A} \min\left\{ \begin{bmatrix} 0.2 & 0.4 & 1.0 \end{bmatrix}, \begin{bmatrix} 1.0 & 1.0 & 1.0 \\ 1.0 & 1.0 & 1.0 \\ 0.6 & 0.8 & 1.0 \end{bmatrix} \right\}$$

$$= \begin{bmatrix} \sup\{\min(0.2, 1.0), \min(0.4, 1.0), \min(1.0, 0.6)\} \\ \sup\{\min(0.2, 1.0), \min(0.4, 1.0), \min(1.0, 0.8)\} \\ \sup\{\min(0.2, 1.0), \min(0.4, 1.0), \min(1.0, 1.0)\} \end{bmatrix}$$

$$= \begin{bmatrix} \sup(0.2, 0.4, 0.6), \sup(0.2, 0.4, 0.8), \sup(0.2, 0.4, 1.0) \end{bmatrix} = \begin{bmatrix} 0.6, 0.8, 1.0 \end{bmatrix}.$$

Thus, $B = 0.6/5 + 0.8/6 + 1.0/3$.

TSK-model

Takagi-Sugeno-Kang (TSK) model for multi-input (n) and single output can be expressed as follows.

$$R^i : IF \ x_1 \ is \ A_1^i \ AND \ x_2 \ is \ A_2^i \ ... \ AND \ x_n \ is \ A_n^i$$
$$THEN \ y^i = f^i(x_1, x_2, ..., x_n)$$

where $R^i (i = 1, ..., m)$ — the ith rule, $x_1, x_2, ..., x_n$ are crisp input variables, A_j^i — the fuzzy values of $x_j (j = 1, ..., n)$, y^i — the output of the ith rule expressed as a linear or nonlinear function of the inputs.

Given values $(x_1^o, x_2^o, ..., x_n^o)$ of $x_1, x_2, ..., x_n$, the output of the fuzzy model is computed as:

$$y = \frac{\sum_{i=1}^{m} w_i y^i}{\sum_{i=1}^{m} w_i}.$$

w_i is the activation degree of the ith rule:

$$w_i = \bigwedge_{j=1}^{n} \mu_{A_j^i}(x_j^o).$$

Example

Consider TSK model of pressure in a fermenter. This model describes dependence of value of pressure the k+1 time step, y(k+1) on the previous value of pressure, y(k) and valve position x(k) (the k-th time step). The fuzzy rules are given below [12].

> IF y(k) is low AND x(k) is open
> THEN y(k+1)=0.67 y(k) + 0.0007 x(k) + 0.35
> IF y(k) is average AND x(k) is half-closed
> THEN y(k+1) = 0.80 y(k) + 0.0028 x(k) + 0.07
> IF y(k) is high AND x(k) is closed
> THEN y(k+1) = 0.90 y(k) + 0.0071 x(k) − 0.39

1.5. Z-numbers [16,20,201]

The Z-number concept is proposed to describe partial reliability of information. A Z-number is an ordered couple of fuzzy numbers, Z=(A,B), where A is a restriction on the values of random variable X and B is a value of probability measure of A. B is used to describe a level of reliability of information. A and B usually are described verbally. (X,A,B) is referred to as a Z-valuation. A collection of Z-valuations is termed as Z-information.

Examples of Z-valuations

Below several examples of Z-valuations are given for the real-world cases when the relevant information is actually imprecise and partially reliable. The examples relate to everyday activity situations and global phenomena:
Age estimation:

(Age (Tom), very young, likely)

Weather description:

(Wind, strong, usually).

Gold price forecasting:

(gold price, about 1.300 dollars, likely)

Travel time estimation:

(traveling from Paris to Berlin takes about 11 hrs, usually)

Weather forecasting:

(medium temperature in the middle of April, very likely)

World oil production prediction:

(Oil production will be about 93 mln. bbl/day next year, likely).

Now we give brief information on operations of discrete Z-numbers.

A discrete Z-number [9,16]

A discrete Z-number is denoted $Z=(A,B)$, where A and B are discrete fuzzy numbers playing the same roles as those for a continuous Z-number. Namely, B is a fuzzy value of $P(A)$:

$$P(A) = \sum_{i=1}^{n} \mu_A(x_i) p(x_i), \quad P(A) \in \text{supp}(B).$$

General framework for arithmetic operations is given in [38]. Let us describe this framework for computation of $Z_{12} = Z_1 * Z_2$, $Z_1 = (A_1, B_1)$, $Z_2 = (A_2, B_2)$, $* \in \{+, -, \cdot, /\}$. $A_{12} = A_1 * A_2, * \in \{+, -, \cdot, /\}$, is defined by using one of Definitions 1.4-1.7. The information on actual probability distributions p_{R_1} and p_{R_2} in $Z_1 = (A_1, B_1)$ and $Z_2 = (A_2, B_2)$ is uncertain and is described as fuzzy constraints:

$$\sum_{k=1}^{n} \mu_{A_1}(x_{1k}) p_{R_1}(x_{1k}) \text{ is } B_1, \quad \sum_{k=1}^{n} \mu_{A_2}(x_{2k}) p_{R_2}(x_{2k}) \text{ is } B_2$$

Using MFs these constraints may be expressed as

$$\mu_{B_1}\left(\sum_{k=1}^{n} \mu_{A_1}(x_{1k}) p_{R_1}(x_{1k})\right), \mu_{B_2}\left(\sum_{k=1}^{n} \mu_{A_2}(x_{2k}) p_{R_2}(x_{2k})\right)$$

Probability distributions p_{R_1} and p_{R_2} are defined as

$$\mu_{p_{R_1}}\left(p_{R_1}\right) = \mu_{B_1}\left(\sum_{k=1}^{n} \mu_{A_1}(x_{1k}) p_{R_1}(x_{1k})\right) \qquad (1.8)$$

$$\mu_{p_{R_2}}\left(p_{R_2}\right) = \mu_{B_2}\left(\sum_{k=1}^{n} \mu_{A_2}(x_{2k}) p_{R_2}(x_{2k})\right) \qquad (1.9)$$

$p_1 = p_{R_1}$ and $p_1 = p_{R_2}$ are found by solving goal linear programming problems:

$$\sum_{k=1}^{n} \mu_{A_j}(x_k) p_j(x_k) \rightarrow b_{jl}, \qquad (1.10)$$

subject to

$$\left. \begin{array}{c} \sum_{k=1}^{n_j} p_j(x_{jk}) = 1 \\ p_j(x_{jk}) \geq 0 \end{array} \right\} \qquad (1.11)$$

Now we calculate a degree

$$\mu_{P_j}(p_j) = \mu_{B_j}\left(\sum_{k=1}^{n} \mu_{A_j}(u_k) p_j(u_k)\right), j = 1, 2. \qquad (1.12)$$

The fuzzy constraint on convolutions $p_{12s}, s = 1, ..., l^2$ of p_{1l} and p_{2l} is defined as

$$\mu_{P_{12}}(p_{12}) = \max_{p_{12} = p_1 \circ p_2} \left[\min\left(\mu_{P_1}(p_1), \mu_{P_2}(p_2) \right) \right] \qquad (1.13)$$

Probability measure of A_{12} is calculated as

$$P(A_{12}) = \sum_{w} p_{12}(w) \mu_{A_{12}}(w)$$

Finally, the MF of B_{12} is computed:

$$\mu_{B_{12}}(b_{12s}) = \sup\left(\mu_{P_{12s}}(p_{12s}) \right) \qquad (1.14)$$

subject to

$$b_{12s} = \sum_{k} p_{12s}(x_k) \mu_{A_{12}}(x_k) \qquad (1.15)$$

Thus, $Z_{12} = Z_1 * Z_2, * \in \{+, -, \cdot, /\}$ is computed as $Z_{12} = (A_{12}, B_{12})$.

Let us outline four arithmetic operations on discrete Z-numbers [9]

Addition of discrete Z-numbers. $A_1 * A_2$ is a sum $A_1 + A_2$ computed by using Definition 1.4. Implementing step-by-step computations MFs (1.12) by solving (1.10)-(1.11), computations of a fuzzy restriction over convolutions $p_{12s}, s = 1, ..., l^2$, based on (1.13), and the MF $\mu_{B_{12}}$ of B_{12} based on (1.14)-(1.15), we obtain Z-number:

$$Z_{12} = (A_1 + A_2, B_{12})$$

An example. Let $Z_1 = (A_1, B_1)$ and $Z_2 = (A_2, B_2)$ be given:

$$A_1 = 0/1 + 0.3/2 + 0.5/3 + 0.6/4 + 0.7/5 + 0.8/6 + 0.9/7 + 1/8$$
$$+ 0.8/9 + 0.6/10 + 0/11$$
$$B_1 = 0/0 + 0.5/0.1 + 0.8/0.2 + 1/0.3 + 0.8/0.4 + 0.7/0.5 + 0.6/0.6$$
$$+ 0.4/0.7 + 0.2/0.8 + 0.1/0.6 + 0/1$$
$$A_2 = 0/1 + 0.5/2 + 0.8/3 + 1/4 + 0.8/5 + 0.7/6 + 0.6/7 + 0.4/8$$
$$+ 0.2/9 + 0.1/10 + 0/11$$
$$B_2 = 0/0 + 0.3/0.1 + 0.5/0.2 + 0.6/0.3 + 0.7/0.4 + 0.8/0.5$$
$$+ 0.9/0.6 + 1/0.7 + 0.9/0.8 + 0.8/0.6 + 0/1.$$

Compute addition $Z_{12} = Z_1 + Z_2$. First, we compute $A_{12} = A_1 + A_2$ (Definition 1.4):

$$A_{12} = \bigcup_{\alpha \in [0,1]} \alpha A_{12}^{\alpha}$$

The computed A_{12} is

$$A_{12} = 0/1 + 0/2 + 0.19/3 + 0.36/4 + 0.5/5 + 0.58/6 + 0.65/7 + 0.73/8$$
$$+ 0.8/9 + 0.87/10 + 0.93/11 + 1/12 + 0.9/13 + 0.8/14 + 0.73/15$$
$$+ 0.7/16 + 0.6/17 + 0.45/18 + 0.3/19 + 0.17/20 + 0.086/21.$$

Second, we proceed with computation of B_{12}. As information on we actual probability distributions p_1 and p_2 is uncertain, we constructed MFs μ_{p_j}, $j=1,2$, on the basis of the solutions of (1.10)-(1.11). For example, we found a probability distribution p_1 that induce $b_1 = 0.4$:

$$\sum_{k=1}^{n_1} \mu_{A_1}(x_{1k})p_1(x_{1k}) = 0 \cdot 0.27 + 0.3 \cdot 0 + 0.5 \cdot 0 + 0.6 \cdot 0.003$$
$$+0.7 \cdot 0.04 + 0.8 \cdot 0.075 + 0.9 \cdot 0.11 + 1 \cdot 0.15 + 0.8 \cdot 0.075$$
$$+0.6 \cdot 0.002 + 0 \cdot 0.27 = 0.4$$

Then $\mu_{p_1}(p_1) = \mu_{B_1}(0.4) = 0.8$. Analogously, we found that $\mu_{p_2}(p_2) = 1$ for p_2 described below:

$$p_2 = 0.09 \backslash 1 + 0 \backslash 2 + 0.18 \backslash 3 + 0.32 \backslash 4 + 0.18 \backslash 5 + 0.1 \backslash 6 + 0.036 \backslash 7 + 0 \backslash 8 + 0 \backslash 9 + 0 \backslash 10 + 0.09 \backslash 11.$$

Thus, we computed the membership degrees for all the considered p_1 and p_2.

Third, given μ_{p_1} and μ_{p_2} we need to construct $\mu_{p_{12}}$ over $p_{12} = p_1 \circ p_2$ convolutions according to (1.13). For example, for the convolution p_{12} obtained above:

$$\mu_{p_{12}}(p_{12}) = \mu_{p_1}(p_1) \wedge \mu_{p_2}(p_2) = 0.8 \wedge 1 = 0.8.$$

Fourth, we compute B_{12} as a fuzzy restriction on $P(A_{12})$ by using (1.14)-(1.15). The values of $P(A_{12})$ are found by using the convolutions p_{12}. For example, $P(A_{12})$ found by using the convolution p_{12} of p_1 and p_2 considered above is

$$P(A_{12}) = 0 \cdot 0 + 0 \cdot 0.243 + 0.19 \cdot 0 + 0.36 \cdot 0.0486 + 0.087 \cdot 0.5 + \cdots$$
$$+0.086 \cdot 0.243 = 0.63.$$

Thus, one of the basic values of B_{12} is found as $b_{12} = P(A_{12}) = 0.63$. As $\mu_{B_{12}}\left(b_{12} = \sum_k \mu_{A_{12}}(x_{12k})p_{12}(x_{12k})\right) = \mu_{p_{12}}(p_{12})$ and $\mu_{p_{12}}(p_{12}) = 0.8$, we obtain $\mu_{B_{12}}(b_{12} = 0.63) = 0.8$ for $b_{12} = \sum_k \mu_{A_{12}}(x_{12k})p_{12}(x_{12k})$. By using this procedure, we computed B_{12} :

$$B_{12} = 0/0.56 + 0.5/0.60 + 0.8/0.63 + 1/0.66 + 0.8/0.69 + 0.7/0.72$$
$$+ 0.6/0.75 + 0.4/0.78 + 0.2/0.81 + 0.1/0.84 + 0/0.86 + 0/1.$$

Thus, the resulting $Z_{12} = (A_{12}, B_{12})$ is shown in Fig. 1.25.

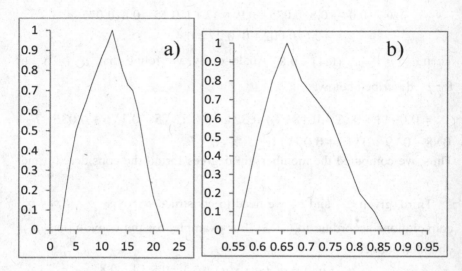

Fig. 1.25. The results of addition of the discrete Z-numbers: (a) A_{12}, (b) B_{12}.

Subtraction of discrete Z-numbers. $A_{12} = A_1 - A_2$ is defined using Definition 1.5. On the basis of the procedure described by (1.10)-(1.15) one finds the resulting Z-number as

$$Z_{12} = (A_1 - A_2, B_{12})$$

Example Consider computation of standard subtraction of $Z_1 = (A_1, B_1)$ and $Z_2 = (A_2, B_2)$ given in the example above.

First, $A_{12} = A_1 - A_2$ is we computed using Definition 1.5:

$A_{12} = 0/-10 + 0.075/-9 + 0.15/-8 + 0.24/-7 + 0.35/-6 + 0.45/-5$
$+ 0.53/-4 + 0.6/-3 + 0.65/-2 + 0.7/-1 + 0/0.75 + 0.8/1 + 0.87/2$
$+ 0.93/3 + 1/4 + 0.9/5 + 0.8/6 + 0.68/7 + 0.53/8 + 0.27/9 + 0/10.$

Second, MFs μ_{p_1} and μ_{p_2} should be derived. These MFs were constructed in the example above.

Third, we construct the MF $\mu_{p_{12}}$. Note that membership degrees $\mu_{p_{12}}(p_{12})$ are derived based only on the degrees $\mu_{p_1}(p_1)$ and $\mu_{p_2}(p_2)$ of p_1 and p_2 from which p_{12} is obtained. The membership degree of p_{12} obtained above is $\mu_{p_{12}}(p_{12}) = 0.8$.

Fourth, we construct B_{12} as a fuzzy constraint on values of $P(A_{12})$. For example, $P(A_{12})$ computed based on the convolution p_{12} of p_1 and p_2 considered above is

$$P(A_{12}) = 0 \cdot 0 + 0 \cdot 0.243 + 0.19 \cdot 0 + 0.36 \cdot 0.0486 + 0.087 \cdot 0.5$$
$$+ \cdots + 0.086 \cdot 0.243 = 0.71.$$

Thus, a basic value $b_{12} = 0.71$ of B_{12} is found, $\mu_{B_{12}}(b_{12} = 0.71) = 0.8$. The constructed B_{12} is given below:

$$B_{12} = 0/0.59 + 0.5/0.62 + 0.8/0.65 + 1/0.68 + 0.8/0.71 + 0.7/0.74$$
$$+ 0.6/0.77 + 0.4/0.8 + 0.2/0.83 + 0.1/0.86 + 0/0.88.$$

The resulting $Z_{12} = (A_{12}, B_{12})$ is shown in Fig. 1.26.

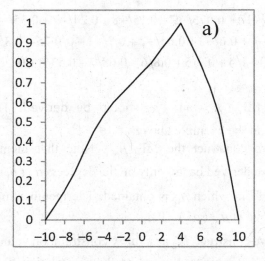

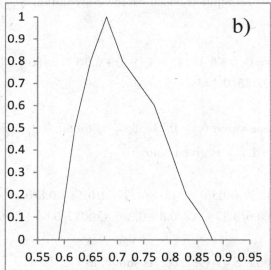

Fig. 1.26. The result of standard subtraction of the discrete Z-numbers:(a) A_{12}, (b) B_{12}.

Multiplication of discrete Z-numbers.

$A_{12} = A_1 \cdot A_2$ is defined by using Definition 1.6. On the basis of the procedure described by (1.10)-(1.15) one finds the resulting Z-number as

$$Z_{12} = (A_1 \cdot A_2, B_{12})$$

Example $A_{12} = A_1 \cdot A_2$ computed by using Definition 1.6 is shown below:

$$A_{12} = 0/1 + 0.16/2 + \ldots + 1/32 + \ldots + 0.17/100 + 0/121.$$

Second, we compute membership degrees $\mu_{p_1}(p_1)$ and $\mu_{p_2}(p_2)$ by using (12). Third, the membership degrees of the convolutions p_{12} are obtained on the basis of (13). Fourth, we compute B_{12}. For example, $P(A_{12})$ computed for the convolution p_{12} of the distributions p_1 and p_2 considered above is

$$P(A_{12}) = b_{12} = 0.67.$$

Thus, $\mu_{B_{12}}(b_{12} = 0.67) = 0.8$. The constructed B_{12} is given below:

$$B_{12} = 0/0.54 + 0.5/0.57 + 0.8/0.61 + 1/0.63 + 0.8/0.67 + 0.7/0.7 + 0.6/0.73$$
$$+ 0.4/0.76 + 0.2/0.79 + 0.1/0.819 + 0/0.82.$$

The resulting $Z_{12} = (A_{12}, B_{12})$ is shown in Fig. 1.27.

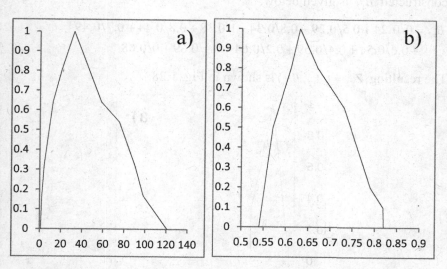

Fig. 1.27. The results of multiplication of the discrete Z-numbers: (a) A_{12}, (b) B_{12}.

Standard division of discrete Z-numbers

$A_{12} = A_1 / A_2$ is defined by using Definition 1.7. On the basis of the procedure described by (1.10)-(1.15) one finds the resulting Z-number as

$$Z_{12} = (A_1 / A_2, B_{12})$$

Example Let us compute standard division of the Z-numbers considered above. $A_{12} = \frac{A_1}{A_2}$ is computed on the basis of Definition 1.7:

$$A_{12} = 0.07/0.36 + 0.1/0.375 + \cdots + 1/1.6 + \cdots + 0.17/100 + 0/121$$

Second we compute membership degrees $\mu_{p_1}(p_1)$ and $\mu_{p_2}(p_2)$.

Third, we compute membership degrees $\mu_{p_{12}}(p_{12})$ of the convolutions p_{12}

Fourth, we construct B_{12}. Given the membership degrees $\mu_{p_{12}}(p_{12})$ of the convolutions p_{12}, we compute values of $P(A_{12})$. For example, $P(A_{12})$ computed on the base of the convolution p_{12} of the distributions p_1 and p_2 considered above is $P(A_{12}) = b_{12} = 0.44$. Thus, $\mu_{B_{12}}(0.44) = 0.8$. The constructed B_{12} is given below:

$$B_{12} = 0/0.24 + 0.5/0.29 + 0.8/0.34 + 1/0.38 + 0.8/0.44 + 0.7/0.49$$
$$+ 0.6/0.54 + 0.4/0.59 + 0.2/0.64 + 0.1/0.69 + 0/0.68.$$

The resulting $Z_{12} = (A_{12}, B_{12})$ is shown in Fig. 1.28.

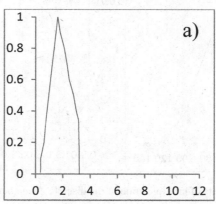

Fig. 1.28. The results of division of the discrete Z-numbers: (a) A_{12}, (b) B_{12}.

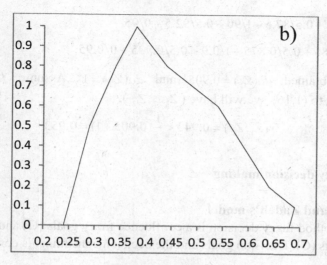

Fig. 1.28. (*Continued*)

Ranking of Z-numbers [8]

Fuzzy-optimality principle and pessimism degree-based approach to human-like comparison of Z-numbers is proposed in [8]. First, optimality degrees for two Z-numbers Z_j and Z_i are computed: $do(Z_j)$, $do(Z_i)$.

Given the optimality degrees, we define

$$r(Z_i, Z_j) = \beta do(Z_j) + (1 - \beta) do(Z_i)$$

$$Z_i > Z_j \text{ iff } r(Z_i, Z_j) > \frac{1}{2}(do(Z_i) + do(Z_j)) \quad (1.16)$$

$$Z_i < Z_j \text{ iff } r(Z_i, Z_j) < \frac{1}{2}(do(Z_i) + do(Z_j))$$

$$Z_i = Z_j \text{ otherwise}$$

Here β is a degree of pessimism.

Example. Consider comparison of Z-numbers $Z_1 = (A_1, B_1)$ and $Z_2 = (A_2, B_2)$:

$A_1 = 0/95 + 0.5/97.5 + 1/100 + 0.5/102.5 + 0/105$,

$B_1 = 0/0.75 + 0.5/0.775 + 1/0.8 + 0.5/0.825 + 0/0.85$;

$A_2 = 0/85 + 0.5/87.5 + 1/90 + 0.5/92.5 + 0/95,$

$B_2 = 0/0.85 + 0.5/0.875 + 1/0.9 + 0.5/0.925 + 0/0.95.$

We obtained $do(Z_1) = 0.905$ and $do(Z_2) = 1$. Assume $\beta = 0.6$. according to (1.16): we will have ($Z_1 > Z_2$).

$$r(Z_1, Z_2) = 0.943 < \frac{1}{2}(0.905 + 1) = 0.953.$$

1.6. Fuzzy decision making

Bellman and Zadeh's model
In this method fuzzy decision is a confluence fuzzy goals (G) and (fuzzy) constraints (C). Decision goals and the decision constraints is combined as

$$D = G \cap C \Leftrightarrow \mu_D(a) = \mu_G(a) \wedge \mu_C(a), a \in A$$

Optimal decision a* is defined as

$$a^* = \arg \max_{a \in A}(\mu_G(a) \wedge \mu_C(a))$$

Example
Assume that there are n fuzzy goals F_j, j=1,2,...,n and m fuzzy constraints G_i, i=1,2,...,m. MFs are $F_j(x), G_i(x): X \to [0,1]$. In accordance with Bellman and Zadeh model (Fig. 1.29), fuzzy decision will be

$$D(x) = F_1(x) \circ ... \circ F_n(x) \circ G_1(x) \circ ... \circ G_m(x)$$

Optimal decision is defined as

$$x^* = \arg \max_{x \in X} D(x)$$

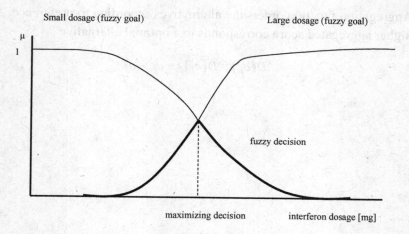

Fig. 1.29. Fuzzy decision by Bellman and Zadeh's model.

Now we consider multi-attribute decision making. Let $A = \{a_1,...,a_n\}$ be alternatives set and $C = \{c_1,...,c_m\}$ be set of criteria. μ_{ij} is evaluation of each alternative for each criterion. We have to create evaluation matrix D.

$$
D = \begin{array}{c|ccc}
 & a_1 & \cdots & a_n \\
\hline
c_1 & \mu_{11} & \cdots & \mu_{1n} \\
\cdot & \cdot & \cdot & \cdot \\
\cdot & \cdot & \cdot & \cdot \\
\cdot & \cdot & \cdot & \cdot \\
c_m & \mu_{m1} & \cdots & \mu_{mn}
\end{array}
$$

Now we assign importance weight factors to all criteria. Then an aggregation function combines weight factors and μ_{ij} for the criteria:

$$D^w\left(\mu_{1j},...,\mu_{mj}\right), \ j \in \{1,...,n\}$$

Aggregation function orders the alternatives according to preference. A higher aggregated score corresponds to a optimal alternative

$$D(a_k) > D(a_l) \Leftrightarrow a_k \succ a_l$$

Chapter 2

State-of-the-Art of Material Selection and Synthesis

2.1. Literature review on material selection

Material selection is an important problem attracting theoretical and practical interest [29,31,32]. Nowadays, a lot of materials and alloys are designed [33-35]. In most alloys some properties are good and in compliance with the requirements, but some of them are not acceptable [36,37]. Generally, for material selection methods a synergy of theoretical knowledge and practical experiences data is needed. Scientists used and developed some selection methods due to all of these.

Material selection includes three stages: initial screening, development and comparison of alternatives, and final one is determination of best solution [25, 92].

In [25] a systematic study of material selection in the mechanic field is provided. The author describe the main categories of materials, their properties, and in general, evolution of material selection study. The considered approaches mainly fall within the classical (analytical equations based) optimization techniques, such that property limits, geometric restrictions, material indexes (e.g. structural index), cost (cost and performance relation) and other criteria are considered. The book includes a series of important case studies.

A systematic study on quantitative approaches to material selection, including analytical and some computer-aided approaches is also provided in [92].

In [25,92,52] it is mentioned that two main kinds of information are relevant for selection:
a) Screening and ranking information
b) Supporting information.

Screening and ranking information is commonly related to shifting through the database due to the technical and economical requirements of design. Supporting information is based on knowledge about microstructure, performance in specific environment and other issues [215].

Let us consider the main categories of material selection methods.

2.1.1. *Multi-criteria decision-making methods (MCDM) and the related techniques*

We could say that using multi-criteria decision-making (MCDM) for selection of materials is considered for new materials with complex application, and when each material has a competitive advantage in performance criteria [114]. MCDM methods include multiobjective optimization and multiattribute decision making (MADM). MODM strategies can be fitted to material plan and improvement. MADM methods are used to compare materials by using set of characteristics.

A wrong selection of material(s) can unfavorably influence the efficiency and benefit and consequently reputation of organization. Therefore, importance of problem makes multicriteria analysis as an effective way in material selection.

One of the approaches for initial screening is the Ashby method [25]. This method is based on material selection charts where the axes for density and strength are used. Various lines describing fixed ratios of these properties are drawn. Materials placed on the line exhibit approximately the same ratio, those which are upper a line perform better, and those that are below — perform worse. An application of the Ashby method to initial screening in the framework of multiobjective optimisation is considered in [215].

Review of methods of material screening and choosing is provided in [151]. Authors discuss the existing literature in the field, including potential application and various approaches. Also, advantages and drawbacks of screening and choosing methods in material selection is discussed in the paper.

In [92] the simplest method for comparing candidate materials referred to as weighted properties method is described. According to this method, each material characteristic is assigned a weight measuring the importance for an alloy in a considered applied field. Values of attributes are multiplied by corresponding weights and then summed to produce the overall performance of alloy. Finally, an alloy with the highest overall performance is chosen as the best option. In realm of MADM such approach is referred to as simple additive weighting (SAW). This method is simple, but includes several well known disadvantages (mainly, difficulty of assigning weights and additive aggregation). In order to solve the problem of adequate determination of weights, a digital logic method (DLM) is used [92]. Weights are determined by using pairwise comparison of material properties. Only two properties are considered at a time and provided that all possible pairs are analyzed, the correct weight is found by using relative scaling.

As it is written in [51] many methods suffer from a lack of the support to the selection of proper engineering criteria or parameters which are desired especially for the new designers and those who have little knowledge about the operations in the selection process.

As it is mentioned in [116], one of the shortcomings of the existing tools is that there is a need for defining a weighting method which is both user-friendly and can clearly represent the project's requirements. In this article, it is underlined importance of ranking and selection of the optimal material during engineering design process. The authors indicate tending to focus on cost and benefit criteria as minuses for proposed methods of ranking in materials selection. According to the authors, due to these financial aspects, some technical or biological properties are missing. In response to this perceived gap, Technique for Order Preference by Similarity to Ideal Solution (TOPSIS) method and objective weighting were used in this paper. Accordingly, in this work the TOPSIS method was modified and updated. Further, the system for objective weighting was developed for cases with target values of attributes, and its drawbacks are addressed. Also it has been shown that the offered normalization technique is not only able to account for the impact of criteria, but also for the criteria goal values. TOPSIS method in this work was applied for several cases for validation of the proposed model results.

One of the most famous MADM methods is AHP method [214]. In this approach a decision problem is considered within three-level hierarchy: the aim of choice, criteria, and alternatives. Criteria evaluations and weights are determined by using pairwise comparison matrices. This comparison increases reliability of computation results but complicates the decision procedures. AHP method is widely applied for material selection purposes. In [214] they apply this method for analysis of Al/SiC composite material properties and making decisions. Paper [178] is devoted to application of AHP for semiconductor switching devices. In [129] an aluminum alloy was chosen by using AHP with the aim to minimize environmental impact in screw manufacturing. The paper [27] suggests that the designers can be able to work without preparing material selection decision matrices and can mainly stress on finding the most important criterion controlling the entire selection process. In the article, five material selection problems are examined from different point of views. VIKOR, TOPSIS and PROMETHEE methods are used. The comprehension of the matter hints at the impact of the criteria having maximum priority weight on the working efficiency of VIKOR, TOPSIS and PROMETHEE techniques. Amongst the five material selection were:

1) cryogenic storage tank material
2) High speed naval craft material
3) Light load wagon wall material
4) Material for a high temperature conditions
5) flywheel material

[120] is devoted to material selection for flywheel (Table 2.1). A flywheel is a device developed to store kinetic energy efficiently [181]. The application of a flywheel can be hindered by sudden failure. In order to ensure continuous work of a flywheel it is needed to delay the time to failure which is due to fatigue and/or brittle structure. Performance index in this particular case will be the ratio of fatigue limit over the material density [120].

If the failure occurs due to the brittle structure of the material then the fracture toughness (Kic) of the material will be the most important parameter to consider. The fragmentability (F) is also very important parameter while considering time to failure because if it is possible to break the flywheel into small parts such that the risk of the hazards can be minimized [166]. It is demonstrated that both methods VIKOR and ELECTRE II have determined the same optimal material for the flywheel design [120]. These methods have a great potential to solve such kind of material selection problems.

Table 2.1. Quantitative data of material selection for flywheel [120].

Sl. №	σ_{limit}/ρ	K_{IC}/ρ	C/m	F
300M (A_1)	100	8.6125	4200	3
2024-T3 (A_2)	49.6454	13.4752	2100	3
7050-T73651(A_3)	78.0142	12.5532	2100	3
Ti-6Al-4V (A_4)	108.8795	26.0042	10500	3
E glass-epoxy FRP (A_5)	70	10	2735	9
S glass-epoxy FRP (A_6)	165	25	4095	9
Carbon-epoxy FRP (A_7)	440.2516	22.0126	35470	7
Kevlar 29-epoxy FRP (A_8)	242.8571	28.5714	11000	7
Kevlar 49-epoxy FRP (A_9)	616.4384	34.2466	25000	7

In [57] 10 MCDM methods are compared in solving material selection problems for 3 various purposes. Among the considered methods, PROMETHEE II (EXPROM2), complex proportional assessment with gray relations (COPRAS-G), ORESTE (Organization, Rangement Et Synthese De DonnesRelationnelles), VIKOR (VlseKriterijumska Optimizacija I Kompromisno Resenje in Serbian, means Multicriteria Optimization and Compromise Solution) and operational competitiveness rating analysis (OCRA) are used. All these methods indicate selected materials which are best and worst. It is shown that for selection of any type of material with various criteria and number of alternatives the named methods can be efficiently used. The VIKOR method is proven to be the best method amongst these methods because of relatively better performance.

However, in [113] it is argued that though VIKOR method is quite a comprehensive tool for solving the problems of material selection it still does not account for constraints and goals of design with continuous variables.

[78] is devoted to comparison of VIKOR and ELECTRE methods in selection of materials for engineering purpose. VIKOR is a compromise ranking method and ELECTRE is an outranking method. At the same

time both of them are used to compare materials with under considered requirements.

One of the novel methods of material selection, referred to as Z-transformation method is applied in [89]. In the process of designing of every product the selection of materials is considered very important. Different researchers have offered and applied approaches in selection of various materials with the quantitative and qualitative properties. But some of these methods are complex. That is why modified digital logic (MDL) method is suggested to normalize the criteria. Three cases in mechanical design and lightweight naval structures have been carried out to compare capabilities of this new technique with MDL. Advantages of Z-transformation methods are illustrated to be compared with MDL method where it is difficult to identify any superiority of material properties when their selecting. Designers evaluated this advantage of the Z-transformation method because trades try to make use of the lower ranked materials.

Despite a wide range of studies on materials selection using different MCDM methods exist, Indian scientists suggested a new approach of MCDM [58]. As it is mentioned in this paper, applicability and capability of new methods (for a given engineering application): (a) evaluation of mixed data (EVAMIX), and (b) complex proportional assessment (COPRAS) methods. Also, statistic information for two illustrative examples given this work could be used which proves that these two methods can be successfully applied to solve practical problems in material selection. The main advantage of EVAMIX is that it different mathematical models are used to deal with the ordinal and cardinal decision. On the other hand, COPRAS method can be easily applied to evaluate the alternatives and select the optimal material, even if the physical meaning of the decision making process is not known. Two illustrative examples and comparison of MCDM methods provided in the work to test the capability, accuracy and applicability of EVAMIX and COPRAS for complex material selection problems with ordinal and cardinal criteria.

The authors of the article [146] use EXPROM2, COPRAS-G, ORESTE, OCRA methods in gear material selection. They have considered 9 different materials as the candidates for the gear design and amongst them were 5 selection criteria: core hardness, surface hardness, surface fatigue limit, bending fatigue limit and ultimate tensile strength. Quantitative data for this problem is given in the Table 2.2 below.

Table 2.2. Quantitative data for gear material selection problem [146].

Material	Surface hardness (SH)	Core hardness (CH)	Surface fatigue limit (SFL)	Bending fatigue limit (BFL)	Ultimate tensile strength (UTS)
Cast iron (1)	200	200	330	100	380
Ductile iron(2)	220	220	460	360	880
S.G.iron(3)	240	240	550	340	845
Cast alloy steel(4)	270	270	630	435	590
Through hardened alloy steel(5)	270	270	670	540	1190
Surface hardened alloy steel(6)	585	240	1160	680	1580
Carburised steels(7)	700	315	1500	920	2300
Nitrided steels(8)	750	315	1250	760	1250
Through hardened carbon steel(9)	185	185	500	430	635

It was observed that the results obtained with COPRAS-G and EXPROM 2 are very similar to that obtained by the two most popular MCDM methods VIKOR and PROMETHEE II [57].

2.1.2. *Fuzzy logic and soft computing based methods*

The methods based on fuzzy logic and soft computing have a capability to deal with complexity and uncertainty of real-world problems in material selection.

In the present study, we will consider some of these works to reflect the findings in the field.

In the research [96] they used fuzzy VIKOR as a tool to select alternative material for instrument panel of electric car. The fuzzy VIKOR is used to deal with linguistic evaluations provided by a decision maker.

In [5] they applied fuzzy logic and genetic algorithm to develop shape memory alloy (SMA) actuators with the ability to take the required shape while heating and having a lot of application fields. Playing the main role in the system design actuators are based on hydraulic, electric, and pneumatic technology and have driving mechanism property. Physical changes of the actuators result in "memorization" of a specific shape displaying significant hysteresis. Delays and inaccuracy of the motion control of actuators are the result of hysteresis behavior. The authors have presented geometrical implementation based numerical Preisach model for the hysteresis in SMA. This model is used in a PID control strategy. The genetic algorithm is used to derive optimal values of PID parameters in computer simulation. However, the obtained values did not provide sufficient control performance in the real SMA control (due to unknown factors including disturbances). In view of this, an adjustment of the PID parameters based on fuzzy logic is proposed for further improving the control performance.

In [205] it is mentioned that engineers and designers have to make right materials choice meeting product requirements, such as weight saving, higher product performance, and cost reduction. The goal of the research is to suggest a new, interval-valued intuitionistic fuzzy sets (IVIFSs) and multi attributive border approximation area comparison (MABAC) based approach. It is used to settle material selecting problems with incomplete weight data. The authors offer that polypropylene is the best for the automotive instrument panel and Co–Cr alloys-wrought alloy is the optimal variant for hip prosthesis. IVIF-MABAC and other relevant representative methods have been compared and it was concluded that alternative materials are in a good agreement with the before derived ones. This new approach can be used to solve other material selection problems with robustness and efficiency.

In [100] for selecting materials of an automotive instrument panel Fuzzy PROMETHEE (Preference Ranking Organization Method for Enrichment Evaluation) and PROMETHEE II (EXPROM2) methods are used. These methods are based on trapezoidal fuzzy interval numbers. The comparison of fuzzy PROMETHEE method with other three various fuzzy MCDM methods (fuzzy VIKOR, fuzzy TOPSIS, and fuzzy ELECTRE) is shown.

The fuzzy methods including fuzzy multicriteria approaches, fuzzy inference, fuzzy expert systems and other methods are successively used for such problems as automotive component material selection [96], piezoelectric material selection [25], material selection in the electronics industry [52], material selection in concurrent product design [215] and other problems.

[199] is devoted to fuzzy logic based material selection in an applied field. The author reviews the main methods for material selection including classical MADM methods, MODM methods, expert systems and justify use of fuzzy logic. The proposed approach is based on expert-driven fuzzy If-Then rules with inputs describing important characteristics as price, corrosion resistance, yield strength, toughness and others. The output of the rules is a performance index used to rank materials with respect to the characteristics. The approach is applied to various case studies including material selection for pressure vessel, turbine blade, drive shaft, mooring connection. The author use some simplifying techniques to reduce number of fuzzy rules. Approximately 20-40 candidate alloys are compared to choose the best alternative in each case study. For validation of the proposed fuzzy logic based approach, the comparison with classical SAW method is used. The comparison is based on analysis of minimal, maximal and average performance indexes produced by the classical and fuzzy approaches for each case study. The results of comparison show that two methods provide close results. The fuzzy method differentiates the candidate alloys better and, at the same time, the produced average indices are more stable in terms of deviation from the medium between min and max indices.

The main disadvantages of the both classical methods and existing fuzzy logic and soft computing approaches is the lack of the account for partial reliability of information related to material selection and synthesis. In [213] Zadeh proposed a concept of Z-number to account for fuzziness and partial reliability of real-world decision relevant information. The first approach for material selection problem under Z-number valued information is proposed in [31]. The problem of material selection is formulated as a MADM problem. Criteria values and weights measuring properties of candidate alloys and the related importance are characterized by partial reliability. The solution approach is based on aggregation of Z-number-valued information and Z-number ranking procedures. Application of the proposed approach to selection of an optimal titanium alloy on the basis of three criteria is considered.

2.2. Literature review on synthesis of materials with characteristics required

For a long time experimental approach was main method for material design. However, experimental approach has many drawbacks. With the development of the computing sciences, a new era of synthesis of alloys or different materials began. Scientists proposed and developed various approaches for the synthesis of new alloys which relies on phase diagrams, Thermo-Calc, machine learning, neural network and fuzzy concepts.

2.2.1. *Classical approaches*

Paper [106] is aimed to report experimental data on binary Ti-Al and ternary Ti-Al-X systems. Ti-Al binary phase diagram based on the observations, TiAl-X (X = Cr, MO and W) phase diagrams have been formed using the Thermo-Calc program. Results of the high temperature X-beam diffraction examination plainly show that the alpha phase is stable near melting point. Albeit some equivocal points still remain (composition and morphology may change at very high temperatures during observations), from the aftereffects of the high temperature X-beam diffraction, the Ti-Al binary phase diagram is reproduced qualitatively.

    Also in this paper ternary phase diagrams have been calculated for Ti-Al-0 at 1473 K, Ti-Al-MO at 1473 K, and Ti-Al-W at 1473 K, based on database [106].

In [22] authors presented Thermo-Calc Software's developments. From this paper it is clear that Thermo-Calc is a very useful software and database package. Generally, this database package includes all kinds of phase transformation calculations, phase diagram, phase equilibrium, and thermodynamic assessments. With Thermo-Calc application-oriented interface, many types of process simulations for metallurgy, material science, alloy design and development, geochemistry, semiconductors, any thermodynamic system in the fields of chemistry etc. could be performed. This software can be applied depending on the kind of database it is connected to.

Thermo-Calc is also sufficiently good software for solving problems in such processes as alloying, melting, solidification, refining, sintering, casting, reheating and in areas as heat treatment, annealing, surface treatments, sintering, corrosion as well as in the case of environmental issues. It is given a few examples of such solutions and application examples for material science such as Si-Al-O-N system. In this paper, results of the Scheil-Gulliver simulation in Thermo-Calc Software for the Al-Mg-Si system were also demonstrated [22].

Other modern material design method is FLAPW (full-potential linearized augmented plane wave) which also involves a collaboration experimental material science and computational approach. FLAPW is one such method that provides the requisite level of numerical accuracy, despite of complexity. Thus, this method accurately could predict new materials properties, describe the physics of the experiments, and be applicable to new and complex structures [198].

The modifications and extensions (along with others) described in [198] makes the FLAPW method practical and applicable to a large class of new complex materials. Also in this article the efficiency of the method by computations of the induced densities in external fields, magnetic coupling between core holes and valence states, and the intrinsic defects effect on the phase stability of Zr–Al alloys were illustrated. Analytical approaches to material design are finite elements method (FEM)[121,172,217], Analysis of Variance (ANOVA) based approach, and regression analysis[148].

In [24, 174, 83, 98] the authors consider composite material design as a linear programming problem. The decision variables of the problem are components (generic materials). The constraints are the desired properties (e.g. tensile strength) and coefficients of each constraint describe levels of this property for each component. The right hand side of the constraint is the minimal required property level. The objective function is the overall cost as the sum of the amount of generic materials multiplied by the unit costs. As can be seen, assumptions of additive and linear impacts of components to the property are assumed.

In [1] they use computer simulations to overcome difficulties in analysis of the designed materials that often restrict the use of physical experiments (e.g. restrictions on time and cost, and conditions of experiments).

2.2.2. Modern computational approaches

Despite that computer experiments help to facilitate material design approaches, they still are restricted much when are based on hard computational schemes. In view of this modern approaches including machine learning, big data and soft computing approaches become desired tools.

Machine learning approaches

Japanese scientists applied machine learning to predict material synthesis and design [184]. Density functional theory-based material data describing every possible element combinations were constructed and used to support vector machines. The properties of predicted material correspond to experimental data. Desired material properties based on material combinations are able to be predicted too. Flow between the material database and designing materials has become the bridge. This approach makes it possible to reveal undiscovered desired materials and targeted material mining using big data. Targeted material synthesis is carried out experimentally [184].

Up until now, candidate molecules for energetic materials have been screened using predictions from expensive quantum simulations and thermochemical codes. In [82] it is demonstrated that machine learning techniques can be used to predict the properties of CNOHF energetic molecules by using their molecular structures. Therefore, authors in this paper present a comprehensive comparison of machine learning models and several molecular featurization methods — sum over bonds, custom descriptors, Coulomb matrices, Bag of Bonds, and fingerprints. In this paper the assumption about importance of huge set of data for machine learning were challenged. To prove the opposite only 109 energetic compounds computed by Huang & Massa and others were used [82,109].

It is known that for finding new materials with best properties, decreasing the cost and time consumption and error experiments is one of the outstanding factor in materials science. In carrying out experiments and calculations on the materials with good properties data-driven machine learning tools have been used recently. Offer of the best dopant and its concentration for next time-dependent Ginzburg-Landau simulation is the goal of the experimental design. The time-dependent Ginzburg-Landau theory for shape memory alloys based computational problem was formulated in this experimental design and it showed effect and superelasticity of the physics of shape memory. It is required to find material to lower dissipation feature using Landau model for shape memory alloys in order to minimize the number of experiments [72]. [150] is devoted the potential of data-driven approaches and machine learning methods for future materials research. Machine learning, as a part of artificial intelligence, is known for a significant results in various fileds. Examples of machine learning methods and selected materials applications is given in Table 2.3.

Table 2.3. Supervised and unsupervised learning examples.

	Example Methods	Selected Materials Applications
Supervised learning	Regularized least squares Support vector machines Kernel ridge regression Neural networks Decision trees Genetic programming	Predict processing structure-property relationships; develop model Hamiltonians; predict crystal structures; classify crystal structures; identify descriptors
Unsupervised learning	k-Means clustering Mean shift theory Markov random fields Hierarchical cluster analysis Principal component analysis Cross-correlation	Analyze composition spreads from combinational experiments; analyze micrographs; identify descriptors; noise reduction in data sets

Big data approaches

Let us provide a short introduction about Big Data over Material science. In 2007, Turing Prize laureate Jim Gray celebrated four scientific paradigms [107]: empirical; theoretical; computational; data exploration or eScience(Big data).

Note that first paradigm includes natural phenomena based empirical science. Kernel of the next paradigm is models and generalizations. Computational branch of this scientific paradigm includes simulation of complex real-world problems.

Currently data exploration is being developed (eScience, Big Data Computing)) to integrate theory, practice and simulation. According to the fourth paradigm, the science-based intensification of data has begun to evolve. The development of the fourth paradigm is stimulated by large volumes of data.

The object of research in this area is large data (BIG DATA) and focused on extracting generalized knowledge from data. This concept reflects the idea of using, storing, analyzing, and retrieving data from a great deal of data collected at great speeds and from different sources.

Big data is making significant changes to all areas of science and engineering and is improving interaction among researchers.

Type and sources of materials science data become particularly heterogeneous compared with data encountered in other fields.

In paper by Ashley A. White the author demonstrates the future impact of big data on materials science [201]. To speed up materials discovery, researches are presently using computers more widely.

In [4] authors analyze the way data-driven techniques is used in deciphering processing/structure/property/performance relationships in materials, with examples of forward (property prediction) and inverse (materials discovery) models. Such analysis can noticeably improve cost-effective materials discovery as the aim of Materials Genome Initiative (MGI). Here it is shown that, adding data sciences to the other three paradigms of materials science, is important to deal successfully with big data.

Agrawal *et al.* [3] used the Japan National Institute of Material Science (NIMS) Mat Navi database [144] to develop models for prediction of fatigue strength of steel. Prediction accuracy is important for a number of applications due to the significant complexity of fatigue testing and serious consequences of its failures. Actually, fatigue usually leads to more than 90% of all mechanical failures of structural components [75].

The database mentioned above consist of composition and processing attributes of 18 spring steels, 48 carburizing steels, and 371 carbon and low-alloy steels. The materials informatics approach involves data preprocessing for consistency and model evaluation. The data preprocessing is done using domain knowledge, ranking-based feature selection, predictive modeling while the model evaluation — using leave-one-out cross-validation for prediction accuracy of various metrics. Most of the tested 12 predictive modeling techniques were able to obtain the result with R2 value of 0.98, and error rate of 4%, which is better than the previous research on fatigue strength prediction (R2=0.94). Other methods such as decision trees, neural networks, or regression obtained a value of R2=0.97.

Microstructure-related optimization problem based on data is considered in this paper to apply to a magnetoelastic Fe-Ga alloy for achieving improved elastic, plastic, and magnetostrictive characteristics.

Thus, big data based analytics has brought to the development of materials informatics, and it is of extreme importance for further development of the materials genome initiative. The considered workflow for materials informatics and the suggested applications have been successfully used to produce relationship for invertible PSPP tool. Currently, the area of integration computer science and material science, or by other words, materials informatics is still pretty much in its early stage of development. Collaborations integrating expertise from materials science and computer science, and developing a skilled workforce, are important to expand the available opportunities and allow continual discovery of new advanced materials.

Melissae Fellet noted that Big Data Analytics deliver materials science insights. Analysis of big data of materials patterns and structure help researchers to mine the data for hidden relationships search[90]. Design of new materials is complex process based on fusion of serendipity and difficult methodical work. Researchers perform time-consuming synthesis of new materials by using chemical knowledge and intuition to infer material performance. The materials were designed for powerful batteries, lightweight aircraft components, tough body armour, etc.

Traditional computer modelling of materials uses methods recognised with the year 1998 Nobel Prize in Chemistry of Walter Kohn and John Pople. They developed quantum mechanics-based algorithms to model molecules. This improves the calculation accuracy for molecular structure and chemical reactivity. Kohn and Pople developed emergent techniques of computational chemistry that provide good practical results.

These methods are effective to predict crystalline metals and metal oxides' structural and electronic properties. But these predictions are not always accurate for complex bulk materials. Predicting properties of bulk materials and their surfaces using current quantum mechanical methods requires lengthy calculations using supercomputers.

To improve the calculations, chemists are analyzing public databases of atomic, chemical and physical properties to find combinations that predict materials properties. They use big-data analytics tools to search for meaningful patterns in the large amounts of data. Although materials scientists does not have much data (compared to those of email providers or online stores), there is enough open-access data on atomic radius, electronegativity, bonding geometry and other properties, as well as the geometric and electronic structures. Theses materials databases are Materials Project (USA) and the Novel Materials Discovery Laboratory (Europe), among others. The Novel Materials Discovery Laboratory, a European Center of Excellence established in 2015, operates the world's largest computational materials science database.

In [206] the authors processed the materials properties database for selecting and designing high-temperature alloys for solid oxide fuel cell (or SOFC) applications. Also, this work considers the selection of alloy compositions and properties, which are relevant to the SOFC application. The alloys of interest included such high-temperature alloys as Co, Ni, and Fe base superalloys, as well as stainless steels and Cr base alloys. Hundreds of commercial compositions are produced in USA alone. Over 250 of these alloys are listed in the Compositions of High Temperature Alloy table. The down-selected compositions (about 130) with characteristics and applications are included. On the basis of down-selection of alloy compositions, important properties of materials related to the the functional requirements are listed in SOFC stacks.

The problem of materials design and the use of regression methods for large data are discussed in [140].

Among shape memory alloys, those with reduced dissipation or low hysteresis are of interest. Recently, there was success in theoretical prediction of material characteristics, such as inter-atomic distances, crystal structure, polarization, etc. However, the parameter space remains still very large after some natural reduction. At the same time, physical and chemical constraints make impossible realization theoretical findings. Usually, they form a database of calculated properties, which is then used for required materials search. As to multi component alloys these methods are not so effective. Unfortunately, there is a lack for methods combining statistical inference and the high-throughput approach.

The fusion of clustering and regression methods with optimization approaches provide a new opportunity for material discovery and design.

In [83] they discuss the challenges and opportunities associated with materials research. An information about 4 specific efforts of material science: Materials Project [186], Open Quantum Materials Database [155], expert database at the University of California, Santa Barbara and The University of Utah [187], and the Citrination platform [6]. These bases allow to aggregate, analyze, and visualize large amount of research data for free. The data may be used for machine learning and improvement of new materials discovery.

Material property databases built from literature data, and methods of data aggregation from literature are considered in [175]. Here authors consider manual aggregation of data for forming interactive databases to support interactive visualization of the original experimental data and additional metadata. The described databases include materials for thermoelectric energy conversion, and for Li-ion batteries electrodes.

There are very good open access databases in the crystallography field. One of them is the well-known Inorganic Crystal Structure Database (ICSD), managed by FIZ Karlsruhe. It includes over 180 000 entries on the crystal structures of metals, minerals, and other inorganic compounds [40]. The Cambridge Structural Database of the Cambridge Crystallography Data Centre is also a popular database. It includes small molecule organic and metal-organic crystal structures (more than 800 000 entries) [21]. The Crystallography Open Database (COD) include 120 000 entries of structures and a search infrastructure [73,106]. Pearson's Crystal Structure Database (274 000 entries) [193] and the Protein Databank for nucleic acids, and other complex materials [41].

In [142] it is given a database with approximately 61 materials and the properties including Chemical Properties, Dimensional Properties, Electrical Properties, Electrochemical Properties, Petroleum Properties, Solution Properties, Spectroscopic Properties, Surface Properties, Thermal and Thermodynamic Properties etc.

Chemical resistance database covers about 1200 material grades, it represents 226 types of materials consisting of thermoset resins, rubbers and other thermoplastics. After update, the size of the base was increased to 183,000 unique records obtained from published and other sources (commercial sources, journal papers, reports, and materials information datasheets).

Database on titanium alloys properties is given in [143,26].

The Novel Materials Discovery (NOMAD) Laboratory [188] manages the largest open-access database of all important codes of computational materials science. It can build several Big-Data Services to support materials science and engineering. Extracting hidden information from repositories of computational materials science, it is possible by using NOMaD.

The work [94] for the first time represents machine learning-based determination of viable new compound from true chemical white space, whereas no characterization was provided by promising chemistries. The authors consider an effective prediction model for materials properties, that may be easily accessible and useful for researchers.

In site http://thermoelectrics.citrination.com/#/ a large library and machine learning-based models are integrated to estimate a material's merits of being a candidate thermoelectric (e.g. beck coefficient, Resistivity , Thermal Conductivity, Band Gap properties are given).

Data sharing and the collaborative databases role is discussed in work [118]. The authors consider the topic of data reuse in the Materials

Genome Initiative (MGI). Especially, they consider the role of 3 computational databases (that rely on the density functional theory methods) for researchers. They also propose recommendations on data reuse technical aspects, discuss future fundamental challenges, including those of data sharing in MGI perspective [65,153,182,200,202,203]. They discuss perspective form of data sharing: the use of density functional theory databases formed by experimental groups and theory for wide applications of materials design. Note that, it is possible to compute material properties by using density functional theory, to analyze the electronic structure of a material on the basis of approximate solutions to Schrödinger's equation [53].

Fuzzy logic and Soft Computing approaches

The paradigms of soft computing include fuzzy logic [212,12], artificial neural networks [162], evolutionary computing, chaos theory and other algorithms. Each paradigm, has its own advantages and disadvantages. The use of fuzzy logic for modeling and prediction of properties allows to describe development process and interpret results better [31,62,63]. In turn, artificial neural networks have very good learning abilities that are useful for solving problems with complex data on material compositions [66].

Papers [78,136,168] show the necessity to account for non-linearity and uncertainty factors that characterize modeling of material design problems. This requires searching for new ways in formalization of systematic approaches to material design. These papers are devoted to the application of soft computing to deal with these factors.

The use of hybrid soft computing approaches [61,104] allows to achieve better results for material engineering due to fusion of advantages of different paradigms. The strategies applied are ANN-fuzzy models (57% works on material engineering, fuzzy-genetic and neuro-genetic (18%) and neuro-fuzzy-genetic (7%) approaches [152].

Nowadays, a huge amount of works devoted to application of fuzzy logic and soft computing exist. A systematic review of the use of fuzzy logic and soft computing approaches for material engineering is conducted in [69,152,176].

Authors in [68] used a new combining tool with which it is possible to model and optimize new alloys that simultaneously satisfy up to eleven physical criteria. To develop a new polycrystalline nickel-base superalloy with the optimal combination of cost, density, gamma-primary phase and sol-content, phase stability, durability, yield point, tensile strength, stress rupture, oxidation resistance and elongation, neural network was used.

The neural network-based materials design methods are used to predict a composition and treatments that are most likely to fulfill the multi-criteria targets [131]. At first, predictive models are constructed for each property, then, these models are used to calculate the probability that a proposed composition fulfills the target specification. Finally, search composition space for the alloy most likely to fulfill the specification.

Authors of [67] are discussing their result of work where they applied artificial intelligence tool to analyze a new molybdenum-base alloy. The experimental results obtained by neural network (Optimal composition (wt%) : Mo – base; Nb 5.7 ± 0.2; Ti 1.0 ± 0.1; C 0.20 ± 0.01; Zr 0.9 ± 0.1; Hf 9.0 ± 0.1; W 0.5 ± 0.2) alloy corresponded to the computational predictions and the cost, phase stability, precipitate content, yield stress, and hardness exceed other commercially Mo-base alloys for forging-die applications such as MHC (1.1wt% Hf, 0.1wt% C, balance Mo), TZC (1.2wt% Ti, 0.1wt% C, 0.3wt% Zr, base Mo), TZM (0.5wt% Ti, 0.02wt% C, 0.08wt% Zr, base Mo), and ZHM (1.2wt% Hf, 0.1wt% C, 0.4wt% Zr, base Mo).

Based on [8] it could be said Mo-Hf-Nb-Ti-Zr-W-C alloy which was designed by using neural network has the ideal properties to be used as a forging die for future high strength superalloys at the high temperatures 1000–1100°C.

In [183] they have developed a rule-based fuzzy logic model for predicting shear strength of Ni–Ti alloys specimens which were produced using powder metallurgy method. As input variables the authors selected processing time and temperature and designed a fuzzy model with two inputs and one output variable. Model accuracy is assessed by four statistical parameters. The results of this model and the artificial neural network (ANN) model have been compared and it was concluded that fuzzy rule-based model possesses better predicting capability. Less than 33% experimental data are required for the developed fuzzy model. The presented fuzzy model has higher accuracy and more economical performance and it can be used as a powerful tool in predicting shear strength of Ni–Ti alloys in powder metallurgy.

From literature it is known that traditional approach to deal with material synthesis based on experimental outcomes is used by scientists and practitioners during a long time. However, classical approach has several drawbacks and for eliminating of this flaws different methods were suggested. One of this method was investigated in [30]. In this paper they applied the fuzzy set theory to knowledge mining from big data on material characteristics. Author propose fuzzy clustering-generated If-Then rules as a basis for computer synthesis of new materials. For this approach fuzzy If-Then rules based model was proposed to predict properties of new materials.

This model is constructed on the basis of fuzzy clustering of big data on dependence between material composition and related properties. The motivation to use fuzzy model is inspired by necessity to construct an intuitively well-interpretable development strategy from imperfect and complex data.

Validity of the proposed approach is verified on an example of prediction properties of Ti-Ni alloy and Computer experiments of the proposed fuzzy model show its better performance as compared to physical experiments based analysis. [30]

The use of hybrid SC approaches provides a higher efficiency by combining advantages of basic SC methods. Let us mention that a growth of publication of SC application is observed in such well-known journals of material engineering field as *Journal of Alloys and Compounds*, *Materials and Design* and others. Below we will consider some of these publications.

In [189] they use synergy of Fuzzy logic and ANN for prediction of strength development of cements.

[190] is devoted to prediction of flank wear during end-milling process in framework of neuro-fuzzy methodology, particularly ANFIS. The obtained results exhibit 4% accuracy of prediction of flank wear behavior under various end-milling conditions.

In [86] they propose a hybrid scheme of application of GA and support vector regression (SVR) for prediction of zinc and steel atmospheric corrosion. GAs are used for computing the optimal hyper-parameters for SVR. It is shown that the performance of the proposed approach is higher than that of the ANN.

In [151] a method of design of knowledge base of fuzzy logic controller using GA is proposed. To compare the effectiveness of approach with that of a previous GA-fuzzy hybrid approach, a combination of prediction of power requirement and surface finish in grinding is used. The results show advantage of the proposed method.

[47] is devoted to application of the orthogonal design method, Fuzzy optimum method and ANN to the optimization and evaluation of the performance of the phosphate graphite mold. The optimum technology parameters as phosphoric acid percentage, Al_2O_3 percentage, drying temperature and drying time are determined by fuzzy multi-objective optimization. It is shown that the ANN can be used to form mono- and multi-objective models for the prediction of tests other than outside orthogonal test with higher accuracy. However, the results are worse for linear regression by the orthogonal method.

In [171] fuzzy logic and GA are used to find optimal solution to the multiobjective problem of recyclable materials selection. Case study on the actual conceptual design using computer aided design environment is demonstrated showing that the proposed method successfully can be applied concurrently during product design. Comparison of proposed method with Sustainability Express Solid Work is also presented. The proposed method can assist product designers to design a high recyclability product without ignoring technical perspectives.

İn [60] ANFIS model is used to describe the high-temperature deformation behavior of Ni-based superalloy. The inputs of the ANFIS model are deformation temperature, strain rate and true strain; the output is true stress. The optimal numbers and types of membership function for the input variables are found. The results show that the constructed ANFIS model is effective in predicting the considered behavior of the Ni-based superalloy.

In [191] ANFIS model is used to predict high temperature behavior of lead free solder alloy. As compared to strain-dependent Arrhenius type constitutive equation, the performance of the suggested ANFIS model is tested. Given the fitness function of well-trained ANFIS model, the model of hot processing parameters optimization was built using imperialist competitive algorithm (ICA). It is shown that the hybrid ANFIS and ICA approach provides a good alternative in optimization of processing parameters in hot deformation as compared to Prasad proposed dynamic materials model.

In [137] they apply the pattern recognition method based on the fuzzy set theory to the line shape analysis of the elastic peak electron spectroscopy (EPES) spectra recorded at Co, Pd and CoPd alloys. The motivation to use the fuzzy set theory is a complex character of electron interaction with a solid surface reflected in the EPES spectrum and its vicinity. The method is called the fuzzy k-nearest neighbour (fkNN) rule. It allows for qualitative analysis of the effects of the surface roughness, the texture and the grain size, and for quantitative identification of the surface composition. Some problems of the results, the limitations and sensitivity of the applied method, and the accuracy of the electron elastic cross-sections are discussed.

Main motivation of book [145] is that computational approaches and physical methods should be considered in a synergetic realm. In view of this such techniques as programming material behaviour, material design on an interdisciplinary basis, bio-inspired methods for material analysis and design and other methodologies are considered.

[167] covers synthesis of complex materials by using decomposition of precursor compounds, atomic layer deposition, and synthesis of different shapes of nanomaterials.

[7] provides introduction into application of soft computing (SC) concept and its constituents in materials design. The motivation to apply SC method is justified by complexity and high-level uncertainty of design and manufacturing affecting to material performance.

Analyzing a wide diversity of approaches to material selection and synthesis, one can observe a tendency to shift research efforts from physical experiments to systematic analysis based on mathematical models and computational schemes. The latter, in turn, evolutes from traditional analytical methods and computational schemes to modern approaches that are based on collaboration of fuzzy logic and soft computing, machine learning, big data and other new methods. The aim to apply fuzzy logic and soft computing methods is to improve research using the advantage of dealing with: imprecision of experimental data; partial reliability of experimental data, prediction results and expert opinions; uncertainty of material properties stemming from complex relationship between material components; a necessity to analyze, summarize, and reason with large amount of information of various types (numeric data, linguistic information, graphical information, geometric information, etc).

Fuzzy logic, Z-number theory and Soft computing methods have a good capability to effectively capture and process imprecise experimental data, that is interpret, classify, learn, and compute with them.

Z-number theory has a promising capability to account for fuzzy and partially reliable information due to its ability to fuse fuzzy computation and probabilistic arithmetic. Indeed, variability of experimental conditions, complex structure of materials, and imperfect expert knowledge demand to consider reliability of information on material behavior as very important one.

Uncertainty of material properties requires to combine FL and efficient learning methods such as ANNs, evolutionary algorithms and others to more adequately model and predict possible material behavior.

Fuzzy logic, Z-number theory and Soft computing may help to improve abilities of big data principles to deal with huge amount and variety of information. In this realm, fuzzy clustering, Neuro-fuzzy inference systems, intelligent databases, soft CBR, computational intelligence based KBs and information search algorithms provide bridge between complexity, imperfectness, qualitative nature of information and research techniques. Particularly, this may help to get intuitive general interpretation of material science results obtained by various techniques, and ways to get practical results would be then more evident.

Chapter 3

Fuzzy Material Selection Methodology

3.1. Factors affecting material selection

Before making decision for material selection, some questions such as mechanical properties, service requirement etc. should find answers. The questions for material selection can be presented as four general groups.

What properties are required?
The first group includes set of question about properties, such as mechanical properties (ductility, strength, stiffness, wear properties, hardness, toughness, fatigue resistance, etc.), chemical properties (request of environment where the material will be used), thermal properties (demands for heat capacity, linear coefficient of expansion, thermal conductivity etc.), electrical properties (requirement for conductor of electricity or electrical isolation etc.), magnetic properties (basically non-magnetic request or delicate either hard magnetic properties) and dimensional conditions (requirements of a particular size, good surface finish, flatness, have dimensional stability, etc.) are required?

What are the processing requirements and their implications for the choice of material?
This is a set of requests for processing during material selection. This includes cast processing, extrude processing, chemical treatment, mechanical treatment etc. Some special tools for producing and processing also could be required.

What is the availability of materials?

For different applications during material selection, availability implies issues as: whether a material is a local product, or it could be obtained from abroad; availability from only special suppliers, shape of raw materials etc.

What is the cost?

Financial requirement for material is one of the main factor in section problem. Cost of the raw material, cost implications of the process requirements, cost penalties for over specification are important questions which should find answers before selecting and design of new material [85].

Strength

The strength of a material is characterized with its ability to withstand the force applied without any failure. The structure, load of the material should be determined, the stress should be calculated.

Strength of the material can be tensile, compressive, shear or bending. It is necessary to find out which of the following are important: yield strength or ultimate strength.

One of the important strength properties is knit line strength used for injection molding. This property is met when two flow fronts come together. It is also called a weld line. In a knit line the strength is less than in a base material.

We can assess the strength on a force cross sectional area bases without considering the strength type. When choosing a material, the loads in those specific areas must be taken into account.

Stiffness

The other ability of the material to withstand an applied force without any deformation is the stiffness. Stiffness is the resistance of the object to the bending. It depends both on the bending modulus of the material and inertia moment of the structure. The bending ability of thermoplastic materials is high that is when they are often applied. It is easy to determine bending ability of thermoplastic materials and we must not forget that stiffness of an object depends highly on design too.

Sometimes it is difficult to find bending/flexural modulus data. This data of the material varies in different directions and fiber-reinforced materials are related to these materials. Availability of fiber alignment in the same orientation as the test specimen length is considered when preparing property data for reinforced materials.

Toughness

We can use a number of methods to assess strength & stiffness and also toughness. For quantifying toughness of thermoplastic materials, a lot of tests are used, these tests are very easy and can be carried out with few equipment. The complex test requires more advanced equipment. Cracks is the subject studied in the fracture mechanics. This is a field of mechanical engineering. For constructing bridges and buildings, we have to understand how cracks form in steel.

Environmental effects

Environmental effects should be considered in material selection. These effects are divided into two groups: reversible and irreversible. When exposing to a cold almost all materials expand. When applying at high temperature, they become more flexible. When applied in a cold, they get stiffer. By welding, some materials can soften and by drying out they return their original hardness. All these reversible changes have to be considered for material selection.

Temperature factor

When applying at a high temperature all thermoplastics become soften (or melt). Long term application of heat, even low one, will have detrimental effect on a thermoplastic material. This exposure to heat causes breakdown in polymer chains which brings to the lower molecular weight distribution and properties loss. Elasticity and toughness are the common losses.

While applying temperature degradation occurs and it varies. The use of additives as heat stabilizers can result in the reduce of degradation.

Chemical factor

Thermoplastics are also subjected to chemical attack: acids, bases, alcohols, gasolines, fuels, solvents-based cleaning solutions can influence them. But fats, oil, greases, lubricants, disinfectants are also chemicals. Some of these chemical compounds are found in nature but others are artificially synthesized.

H_2O (water) is also often considered. It is thought as inert material. But the materials as raw iron when subjected to exposure causes an immediate chemical reaction. Most thermoplastics do not enter into chemical reaction with water. They do not interact with water, but nylon adsorbs water. The absorption process can be reversible fully; it makes the material to swell and when it is used as plasticizer it gives the ability of toughness.

Radiation

Thermoplastics are undergone to radiation — another environmental factor. Sometimes radiation is thought as radioactivity. The "light" is the term made by electromagnetic waves. These waves are between 390 and 750 nm.

Time

The final and most critical factor is time. It results in polymer degradation. Environmental effects are evaluated by the application of time. The effect of long-term exposure in heat-aging tests is evaluated using function of time.

For assessment of long-term effect of exposure to an outdoor environment weather ability test are often used. Combination of temperature, chemical and radiation effects (measured daily, weekly, monthly, yearly) is addressed to these tests [135].

Above mentioned information is an outline or general factors which required for material selection. It is clear that all demands can't applied for every material. Each material has own specifications and special requests. For dental materials selection factors are illustrated in [73].

The selection of restorative dental material depends on some factors, such as the characteristics of the dentist, the patient, tooth itself and the material. Restorative dental material depends on three main factors:

1) Patient factors

2) Dentist factors

3) Material factors

Patient factors mean personal oral hygiene, prevention practices, oral habits, size of restorations, cooperation at time of placement etc.; dentist factors include clinical skill, size of preparation etc.; material factors surround factors such as technique sensitive, deterioration, appropriateness with the organism, strength, durability[73].

Stainless steels are most regularly selected and used in humid environment due to their resistance to aqueous corrosion; these kinds of steel are also widely utilized at elevated temperatures.

There is a multitude of characteristics affecting material selection for high temperature environment and a vast amount of steel brand is available, such as corrosion resistant brands or special steel brands developed for particular environment [132].

Depending on the working conditions, the demands on steels which will be used at high temperatures could be as follows:

• high creep strength

• high resistance of steel for elevated temperature corrosion and oxidation

- stability of microstructure

- high resistance to erosion-corrosion

From information described in [132] we can see that the author analyzes factors which affecting the mentioned particular demands during material selection for high temperature applications. In [132], the factors which affect to the particular demands are presented and analyzed as follows:

✓ The role of alloying elements
✓ The role of microstructure
✓ Stability of microstructure
✓ Operating conditions

The execution of a material in an aggressive water environment relies on the simplicity service, selection of materials, the type of working condition, corrosion control methods and design configurations [177]. The significance of adequate material choice is aggrandized in the case of renewable marine energy, given the destructive environment of the workplace. The chosen materials for every segment in a system must meet all execution necessities. The significant aspects to be assumed while choosing materials for revolving marine energy projects are high resistances to corrosion and bio fouling, strength, toughness, weld ability, machine ability, thermal conductivity and for cost effectiveness[199]. As summarizing all demands for this kind of material the author of PhD thesis [199] provides information given below:

Corrosion and Bio fouling
Due to the high corrosiveness of ocean environment and high risk of biofouling issues in this environment, the high resistances to corrosion and biofouling are utmost important mechanical demands in material selection for renewable ocean energy installations. Corrosion rate in ocean or in marine is reliant on temperature, pH of water, oxygen content, saltiness, water chemistry, galvanic interactions, alloy composition, biofouling, contamination, fluid velocity, geometry, alloy

surface films, heat transfer and surface roughness. All mentioned factors could be gathered into three general classes, biological, chemical and physical [122]. Biological organisms of seawater can influence physical properties of materials. The membranes of alive bodies which can merge to the surfaces of materials in marine conditions repress diffusion. This also can harm defensive layers. Bio organisms can create conditions on the surface of materials which is much more different than conditions of the main environments. In some cases, bio organisms may cause responses not predicted thermodynamically. Resistivity to corrosion and bio fouling resistivity of metals are complex and change cardinally, in various conditions.

Strength and Fatigue
Because of the cyclic nature and magnitude of wave loading, a great part of the resolving of fatigue and fracture problems has been increased by issues encountered in the marine environment [169]. Actually all segments of a projected scheme will have big value of loading, also will have some cyclic loading.

Strength and resistance from high cycle failure are vital traits for any component of system. Dynamic loadings are particularly critical in the marine condition, where they are constantly present. Elements that should be considered and examined are weight burdens, hydrodynamic burdens, the likelihood of hydrogen embrittlement, high cycle fatigue load behavior, fatigue-oxidation relation, fracture toughness and dynamic reaction of the structure to loading of the materials [44].

Weldability and Machinability
Weldability and machinability are critical parameters in any material selection task, and considerably more so in new applications, such as renewable ocean energy, where most segments won't be mass fabricated at first. The requests of fabrication are vital in any marine related task and effect the cost of the undertaking straightforwardly [169]. Thus, fabrication should be considered as a material property and as a variable affecting expense.

Thermal Conductivity and Thermal Expansion

Thermal conductivity and thermal expansion are other important properties of material which cannot be overlooked during material selection process. Some segments demand a material that can quickly dispel heat. In this case the system will not overheat and will function properly. Most renewable ocean energy systems require pipes with good insulation where fluids can maintain the correct temperature. For example, a deep water pipe which is used to carry cold water in the OTEC (Ocean thermal energy conversion) process. Control of material expand or contract in systems in which temperatures are variate drastically is very important so that segments of system keep the right orientation and fit [85].

Cost Effectiveness

A project ought to be cost effective to be able to achieve success. Startup price in comparison to the running life and fee of maintenance of a project is a number one consideration while material selecting [87]. Alloy surcharge rates may be used to help estimate value, but the price of materials is constantly fluctuating because of financial variations. The recent price history of the metals utilized in Ni (nickel) alloys and corrosion resistant stainless steels have fluctuated extensively. From first quarter 2006 to first quarter 2009 the price of nickel jumped from $0.15 per gram to over $0.50 consistent with gram after it fallen back to $0.09 [22]. Same oscillation have observed with other metals such as Co (cobalt) and Mo (molybdenum). The charge of these metals is driven by means of the world financial system and isn't possible to be expecting.

3.2.   Fuzzy Big database on candidate materials (alloys)

As it is noted in [43], Big Data is the term for a "collection of data sets so large and complex that it becomes difficult to process using on-hand database management tools or traditional data processing applications".

The major differences between traditional data and big data are related to structures of data. Today Data Science sounds similar to new concept of Big Data. But these are different means. Big data consists of voluminous amounts of unstructured, semi-structured or structured data, used to extract meaningful insights from large data sets. Data Science combines statistical, mathematical, programming and problem-solving techniques, application of mentioned techniques for better strategic decision-making.

Big data radically change all industries and change human behavior. This environment depend on the result of an information age. The dedication of scientific and popular journals to Big Data issues, and the publication of new academic journals covering scientific and theoretical problems of Big data since 2014, indicate that this area is a very serious scientific direction. Landscape of Big Data is given below (Fig. 3.1) (see https://www.forbes.com/sites/davefeinleib).

Looking at the development history of data analysis, we see that, yet at the end of 70s of the last century data management and analysis technology — database management systems [69] are developed and thereby the "database" concept is established. However, as a result of the increase in the volume of data, mainframe computers could not demonstrate adequacy for storage and processing information. From structure viewpoint all data are divided into the following types (Fig. 3.2).

Further, the problem of "parallel databases" has been addressed [173]. The architecture of this system is based on the use of clusters (in a cluster each computer consists of processor, memory, and disk). Until the end of the 1990s, the "parallel database system" was very popular. However, as the range of Internet services grows, the problem of storing and processing large data has also increased. In problem solving, computational architecture requires fundamental changes and expandable processing mechanisms.

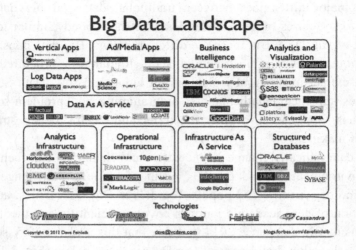

Fig. 3.1. Landscape of Big Data.
(https://www.forbes.com/sites/davefeinleib/2012/06/19/the-big-data-landscape/#
753c686a35e6).

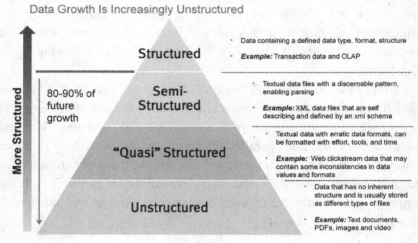

Fig. 3.2. Types of data.

Google company has created Google File System [95] and MapReduce [71] software platform for management and analysis of Big Data on the Internet.

Apache Hadoop and Hadoop Distributed File System open source coding software [101,102], NoSQL databases were also developed, on the basis of large data technologies.

Big Data technology has been used in clustering issues, particularly in determining the rankings of web pages. At the same time, it overwhelms the weaknesses of data warehousing systems and makes it possible to obtain the necessary information by using more in-depth analytical tools [102]. Fragment of the Big Table or Hbase is given in Fig. 3.3.

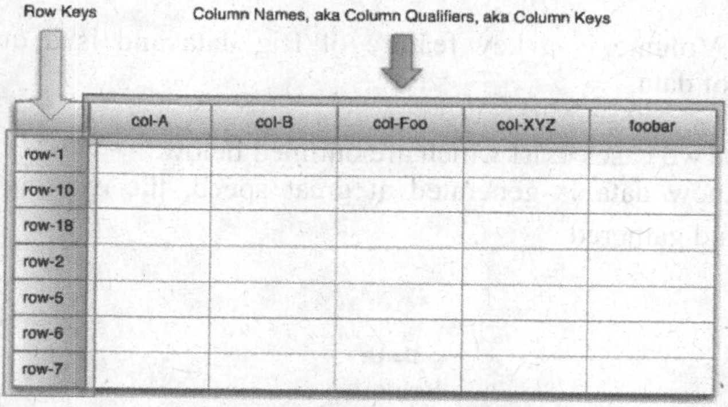

Fig. 3.3. Big table.

There are many studies on the history and explanation of the Big data term [74,141]. The big data term was first introduced in 1998 by John Mei, a computer science expert from the US Silicon Graphics computer company. In 2000 year, a professor at the University of Pennsylvania, Francis Diebold, one of the famous researchers in Big data, published a related study in an academic environment [74], Berkeley University professor Klifford Linch gained popularity following a scientifically-researched study.

Big data concept reflects the idea of using, storing, analyzing, and retrieving data from a great deal of data collected at great speeds and from different sources.

The general features for describing the big data are divided into five basic categories (Fig. 3.4)[134]:

- Volume
- Velocity
- Variety
- Verasity
- Value.

In general these features constitute the basic concept of Big data technologies and these characteristics have been interpreted as follows:

Volume. Volume is a key feature of Big data and is a quantitative indicator of data.

Velocity. Two cases exist which are outlined below.

First, new data is generated at great speed, the existing ones are updated and gathered.

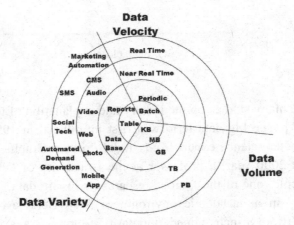

Fig. 3.4. Three basic categories of Big Data.

Second, as the volume increases, too much speed is required for processing. Speed is estimated in terms of data processing time and is explained by the fact that existing processing technologies have the ability to analyze data in real time.

Variety. Most data comes from different sources (emails, social networks, websites, sensors, etc.) in different formats and uses different indexing schemes. It's not an easy task to simply collect and combine them and make them fit for analysis.

Based on the reliability of the data, IBM is pleased to announce that the fourth "V" (veracity). Oracle also incorporated the fifth "V" — the value of BD.

Verasity. The truth is that the quality of data (full, incomplete, contradictory, etc.) is understood. The quality of the data can vary greatly, which can affect the outcome of the analysis.

Value. The data should be worth creating. If Big data does not create value, it turns into "dump trash". Continuous keeping of Big data by the business sector is due to the value added. Therefore, this factor is considered as a marketing feature. Because the value of the information is determined by how we use it. It is also worth mentioning that the number of "Vs" numbers has been increasing recently.

The following are the basics of Big data:

- -Big Data Architecture
- -Big data management
- -Big Data Modeling
- -Big Data Analytics
- -Big Data Toolkits
- -Big Data Open Platforms
- -Big Data as a Service
- -Big Data in Business Performance Management
- -Big Data Analytics in e-Government and Society
- -Visualization
- -Security.

Big data architecture. At present, there is no broad and well-accepted architecture for Big Data's analytics. Today in literature exist Hadoop, MapReduce, NoSQL as the architectures of Big Data. Architecture of the Hadoop platform is given in Fig. 3.5.

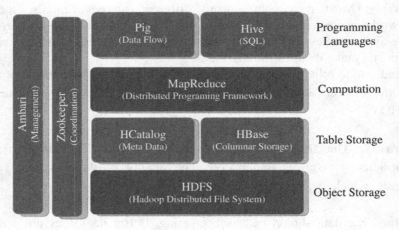

Fig. 3.5. Hadoop platform.

The major functional components of the Big data architecture include:

1) Data Extraction
2) Data Stream Processing
3) Information Extraction,
4) Management of Data Quality (Uncertainty)
5) Data Integration
6) Data Analysis
7) Data Distribution
8) Data Storage
9) Metadata management
10) Data lifecycle management
11) Privacy

MapReduce architecture of the Big data has the following form (Fig. 3.6):

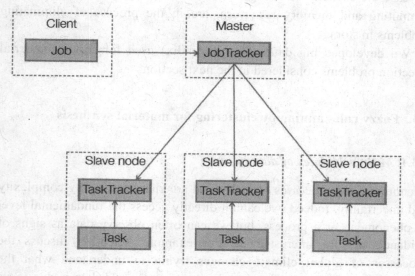

Fig. 3.6. MapReduce architecture.

It is unclear how the optimal architecture of analytical systems should be used for simultaneous processing of real-time data. At present, Big data technologies enable migration between information devices in solving the storage problem [103,123].

1) DAS (Direct Attach Storage, direct connection),
2) NAS (Network Attached Storage, Network Connection),
3) SAN (Storage Area Networks, data storage network),
4) HSM (Hierarchical Storage Management, Hierarchical Data Management),
5) ILM (Information Life-Cycle Management, Life Cycle Management)

These storage archives of the data have shortcomings and limitations. Recently, the use of Grid and Cloud computing[138] technologies to increase the capacity of storage devices, clustering and virtualization of computing and memory resources, are in the process of eliminating problems in storage.

We developed big data base (Appendix) used for solving material selection problems considered in the next sections.

3.3. Fuzzy rules mining by clustering for material synthesis

3.3.1. *Main principles of data mining*

Phenomena and processes of real-world are characterized by complexity and uncertainty. Indeed, we cannot directly access the fundamental level of phenomena or a process, but we can often observe data as signs of evidence we are interested in. For example, scientists discuss the processes of global climate changes trying to understand what the underlying reasons are. The complexity of real-world data is due to its multidimensional essence such that one often deals with a set of interrelated characteristics. In new materials design, one tries to understand a pattern of several characteristics as toughness, weldability, yield strength etc as induced by a pattern of the material components. The problem is that direct analytical study is too complex, and thus one tries to uncover this dependence by analyzing a set of experimental data to arrive at desired knowledge. However, here a researcher meets the other factor — uncertainty of real world phenomena. This is due to measurement errors, influence of unknown factors, variability of data, incomplete and imprecise data, qualitative and partially reliable experts opinion that we have to deal with due to absence of representative data etc. Thus, we have to pass the hard way from data to knowledge. In view of this we shortly describe the principal concepts which represent three levels of understanding: data, information, and knowledge.

Data are of a large variety of signs including facts, numbers, color intensities etc that reflect evidence of the object under study.

Data becomes *information* if the context of the study is known, and when some associations and relationships within this data are uncovered.

Knowledge can be considered as the principal rules, relations and dependencies that underlie existence of these data. Knowledge represents the properties of the relationships such as sensitivity, robustness, stability, optimality, etc.

Therefore, the study of the complex processes requires us to pass from data to information and knowledge, from purely numerical and quantitative signs to qualitative patterns, from surface to the fundamentals. This is what data mining is from conceptual point of view.

Let us provide some definitions of data mining in the existing literature.

Data mining is the analysis of (often large) observational data sets to find unsuspected relationships and to summarize the data in novel ways that are both understandable and useful to the data owner[105].

Data mining is the automated process of discovering interesting (non-trivial, previously unknown, insightful and potentially useful) information or patterns, as well as descriptive, understandable, and predictive models from (large-scale) data[147].

Data mining is of multidisciplinary structure. It involves methods of such fields as databases, statistics, machine learning, pattern recognition, visualization, neural networks, fuzzy logic and others.

Generally, data mining includes the following stages: 1) finding key dependencies between data; 2) validate the found dependencies in new subsets of data; and 3) predict new findings on new datasets based on the validated knowledge.

At first, it is needed to understand that data is collected by *measurement,* which is generally a mapping of characteristic intensities to symbolic form. As a rule, data entity Xi is represented in a vector form $Xi=(xi1,xi2,...,xin)$ where components are encoded intensities of characteristics considered.

Usually, data mining is based on determining *similarity* between data entities. This is needed to study how data are grouped within data set. Conceptually, similarity of two data entities Xi and Xj increases when the *distance* between them decreases. Various existing distance measures for vectors are used as Euclidean distance, Chebyshev metrics, etc. The similarity measure is then defined as a monotonically decreasing function of distance measure.

Sometimes, it is convenient to *transform* data into a form more suitable for study. As an example, the use of logarithmic scale can be considered.

Data may be in different *forms*. The simplest form is a table with rows being data entities (objects) of the same type. When different types of objects are considered (e.g. related tables of employees and departments), we deal with multirelational data. The other main types are *strings*, *image data,* and *hierarchical data.*

Data mining depends on data *quality*. Quality of individual data entities and quality of a collection of data should be considered. Individual data entity may include measurement errors, low reliability and other distortions from reality. Quality of collection of data relates to whether this collection reflects the whole picture of the phenomenon considered (for example, representative sample).

The above mentioned relates to data themselves. The second that is important is data mining tasks. These mainly include classification, clustering, regression, pattern discovery, retrieval by content. Solving data mining task is based on the use of some *algorithm*. The key components of algorithm are: *model structure* (e.g. decision tree, neural network etc), *score function* that measures the quality of the model (e.g. squared error), *optimization or search method* (e.g. gradient search or evolutionary optimization), and *data management* technique used to handle data efficiently.

In this study we consider fuzzy If-Then rules mining from experimental data which relate alloy composition to alloy properties [30].

In general, fuzzy rules are derived from data by using fuzzy clustering and other learning methods. Data-driven fuzzy If-Then rules based provide intuitively interpretable and mathematically consistent models of knowledge discovered from complex data. We will describe the main methods of fuzzy rules mining.

3.3.2. *Fuzzy rules mining from big database of materials by clustering*

3.3.2.1. *Fuzzy K-means clustering algorithm*

The classical K-means algorithm produces crisp (non-fuzzy) clusters. Any object (vector x_i) belongs or does not belong to a particular cluster. The fuzzy K-means algorithm [55] determines a degree u_{ij} to which a vector x_i belongs to Cluster j, j=1,...,k. This degree is determined on the basis of the distance between x_i and the cluster center C_j.

The fuzzy K-means is based on the search for such u_{ij} and C_j that minimizes the following score function:

$$J = \sum_{j=1}^{k} \sum_{i=1}^{N} u_{ij}^{m} \left\| x_i - C_j \right\|$$

(3.1)

subject to

$$\sum_{j=1}^{k} u_{ij} = 1$$

(3.2)

m is the fuzzifier parameter.
The algorithm is described below.
1) Choose initial values of the cluster centers C_j and the value of ε. Set iteration number p=1.

2) Compute the degree of membership u_{ij} of x_i in jth cluster. For example, if $a_{ij} = e^{\left(-\|x_i - C_j\|^2\right)}$, one might use $u_{ij} = \dfrac{a_{ij}}{\sum\limits_{j=1}^{k} a_{ij}}$

3) Replace C_j with the fuzzy mean of all of the points for Cluster j: $C_j = \dfrac{\sum\limits_{i=1}^{N} u_{ij}^m x_i}{\sum\limits_{i=1}^{N} u_{ij}^m}$

4) If $\left\| C_j(p) - C_j(p-1) \right\| \leq \varepsilon$, then Stop. Otherwise, set p=p+1 and go to step 2.

Example. Let the following two-dimensional numeric data be given (Fig. 3.7):
For simplicity, we will consider clustering of these data into two clusters by using classical (non-fuzzy) K-means method. According to the algorithm of K-means clustering, at first (step 1) we randomly chose the initial values of centroids:

$$C_1 = (36.6, 27.14), \ C_2 = (69.14, 55.14).$$

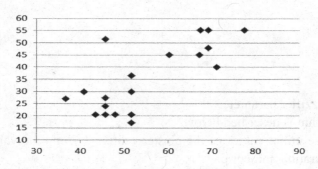

Fig. 3.7. Two-dimensional data.

Next, we computed Euclidean distance of each data point to these centroids and assigned the data points to the closest cluster (step 2). At step 3, the cluster centers were computed as the mean points of the clusters:

$$C_1 = (46.14, 25.38), \ C_2 = (65.93, 49.39).$$

Membership of each data point was again determined and the recomputed centroids did not change, $\left\| C_j(3) - C_j(2) \right\| = 0$. This implies that the clusters were formed (Fig. 3.8).

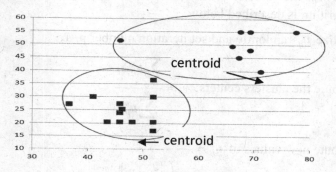

Fig. 3.8. The clusters obtained by using K-means algorithm.

3.3.2.2. *Fuzzy C-means algorithm*

Fuzzy C-means is also known as soft K-means. The fuzzy C-means algorithm [42] determines a degree u_{ij} to which a vector x_i belongs to Cluster j, j=1,…,k. This degree is determined on the basis of the distance between x_i and the cluster center C_j. The problem clustering of data $X = \{x_1, x_2, …, x_n\}$ into c fuzzy clusters is described as a minimization problem for determination of clusters centers:

$$J_m = \sum_{i=1}^{n} \sum_{j=1}^{c} \left\| u_{ij}^m x_i - v_j \right\|^2 \rightarrow \min \tag{3.3}$$

subject to

$$0 < \sum_{i=1}^{n} u_{ij} < n,$$ (3.4)

$$\sum_{i=1}^{c} u_{ij} = 1$$ (3.5)

v_j is the center of *j*th cluster to be found, c is the number of clusters given in advance, u_{ij} are membership degrees, $\|\cdot\|^2$ is the Euclidean distance, m is the value of fuzzifier which defines fuzziness of clusters. The algorithm is described below.

1) Initialize u_{ij} randomly and set iteration number p=1.

2) Compute the clusters centers: $v_j = \dfrac{\sum_{i=1}^{N} u_{ij}^m x_i}{\sum_{i=1}^{N} u_{ij}^m}$

3) Compute new values of $u_{ij} = \dfrac{1}{\sum_{k=1}^{c} \left(\dfrac{\|x_i - v_j\|}{\|x_i - v_k\|} \right)^{\frac{2}{m-1}}}$

4) If $\sum_{i=1}^{n} \sum_{j=1}^{c} \left\| u_{ij}^m(p) - u_{ij}^m(p-1) \right\| \leq \varepsilon$, then stop. Otherwise, set p=p+1 and go to step 2.

Example. Consider an application of fuzzy c-means clustering to construction of fuzzy rules on the basis of complex experimental data on alloy design. These data contain information on relation between alloy composition and its properties (Table 3.1). To extract knowledge from imperfect and complex data we use fuzzy c-means clustering.

By using fuzzy c-means clustering 5 fuzzy clusters are obtained from these multidimensional data. A fuzzy cluster represents a fuzzy rule that describes relation between the inputs and outputs. Thus, five fuzzy rules are obtained, three of them are shown below.

IF x_1 is Medium and x_2 is Medium and x_3 is Medium
THEN y_1 is Low and y_2 is Low and y_3 is Very High,

IF x_1 is Low and x_2 is Very high and x_3 is High
THEN y_1 is Low and y_2 is High and y_3 is High,

IF x_1 is High and x_2 is Low and x_3 is Very low
THEN y_1 is Very high and y_2 is Medium and y_3 is Low.

Table 3.1. Ti-Ni alloy composition big data fragment.

Inputs			Outputs		
Composition		Test temperature	Characteristics		
Ti, %) y_2 (Ni,%)		T, C	z_1 (convent. ultimate strength, MPa)	z_2 (convent. yield streng y_1 th, MPa)	z_3 (unit elongation, %)
49,8	50,2	−196	1260	410	40
49,8	50,2	20	970	150	55
49	51	20	940	550	62
49	51	200	1050	560	28

The linguistic terms used in the If-Then rules are described by trapezoidal fuzzy numbers as follows. Inputs: for x_1, Low=(48.75, 8.94, 9.06, 9.26), Medium=(48.97, 49.36, 49.6, 49.99), High=(49.16, 49.46, 49.65, 49.96); for x_2,Low=(50.04,50.35,50.54,50.84), Medium= (50.05,50.46,50.72, 51.13), Very High=(50.74,50.94,51.06,51.25); for x_3:Very Low=(−307.3,−222.3,−168,−83.02), Medium=(−104.9, −25.11, 25.87, 105.7), High=(−38.58, 42.52, 94.35, 175.4). Outputs: for

y_1: Low=(817.2, 868, 947.5, 998.6), Very High=(1128, 1223, 1284, 1380); for y_2: Low=(6.528, 119.2, 191.2, 303.9), Medium=(265.2, 316.7, 370.6, 422.1), High=(421.7, 520.4, 583.4, 682.1); for y_3: Low=(16.8, 30.8, 39.7, 53.7), High=(41.98, 50.22, 55.48, 63.72), Very High=(38.05, 51.24, 59.67, 72.86).

3.3.2.3. Adaptive Network Based Fuzzy Inference System

Another approach to fuzzy rules mining is the construction and learning of neural network (NN) to perform fuzzy inference. A typical model of this kind is adaptive network based fuzzy inference system (ANFIS)[119].

For simplicity, consider Sugeno fuzzy inference system with two inputs x and y and one output z:

Rule 1: If x is A₁ and y is B₁, then $f_1 = p_1 x + q_1 y + r_1$;
Rule 2: If x is A₂ and y is B₂, then $f_2 = p_2 x + q_2 y + r_2$.

ANFIS model that implements fuzzy reasoning is shown in Fig. 3.9.

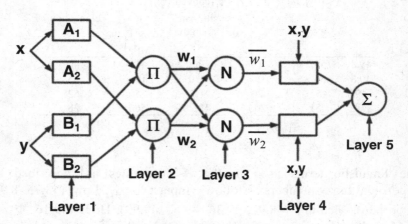

Fig. 3.9. ANFIS architecture.

Let us describe the function of each layer in Fig. 3.8.

Layer 1. The layer adaptive nodes i with node functions:

$$O_{1,i} = \mu_{A_i}(x), \text{ for } i = 1, 2, \quad O_{1,i} = \mu_{B_{i-2}}(y), \text{ for } i = 3, 4, \tag{3.6}$$

$O_{1,i}$ computes a membership degree of a fuzzy set $(A_1, A_2, B_1, \text{ or } B_2)$. For the fuzzy sets typical forms of membership functions can be used. For example:

$$\mu_A(x) = \frac{1}{1 + \left| \dfrac{x - c_i}{a_i} \right|^{2b}} \tag{3.7}$$

where a_i, b_i, c_i are parameters referred to as premise parameters.

Layer 2. The layer includes nonadaptive nodes performing the product of the incoming signals to compute the activation degree of ith rule:

$$O_{2,i} = w_i = \mu_{A_i}(x)\mu_{B_i}(y), i = 1, 2. \tag{3.8}$$

In general, any T-norm operator can be used.

Layer 3. The layer includes nonadaptive nodes which compute normalized activation degrees of the rules:

$$O_{3,i} = \bar{w}_i = \frac{w_i}{w_1 + w_2}, i = 1, 2. \tag{3.9}$$

Layer 4. This layer includes adaptive nodes with a node function

$$O_{4,i} = \bar{w}_i f_i = \bar{w}_i \left(p_i x + q_i y + r_i \right), \tag{3.10}$$

where $\bar{w}_i$ is an output of layer 3 and $\{p_i, q_i, r_i\}$ are the node parameters referred to as consequent parameters.

Layer 5. The layer includes nonadaptive node labeled to compute the overall output as the convex combination of inputs:

$$overall\ output = O_{5,1} = \sum_i \overline{w}_i f_i = \frac{\sum_i w_i f_i}{\sum_i w_i} \tag{3.11}$$

Fuzzy rules mining based on ANFIS requires the use of an NN learning algorithm to adjust parameters of adaptive nodes in Layers 1 and 4. The Hybrid learning algorithm (BackPropagation Learning for Parameter Premises and Learning to Parameter Consequent Recursive Least Square Estimator) is one of the efficient learning algorithms to be applied [119].

3.4. Decision making for material selection by fuzzy inference

3.4.1. *Statement of the problem of multiattribute decision making on alloy selection*

Let a set of n alloys (alternatives) be given, $F = \{f_1, f_2, ..., f_n\}$. Every alternative $f_i, i = 1, ..., n$ is characterized by m criteria $C_j, j = 1, ..., m$ (mechanical properties, electrical properties etc). The problem is to choose the best alloy. We consider this problem under Z-valued information because decision-relevant information is characterized by partial reliability. All the criteria evaluations and weights $W_j, j = 1, ..., m$ are described by Z-numbers. The problem is described by a decision matrix (Table 3.2):

Table 3.2. Decision matrix.

	C_1	C_2	C_3	$\cdots$	C_m
	w_1	w_2	w_3		w_m
f_1	f_{11}	f_{12}	f_{13}	$\cdots$	f_{1m}
f_2	f_{21}	f_{22}	f_{23}	$\cdots$	f_{2m}
f_3	f_{31}	f_{32}	f_{33}	$\cdots$	f_{3m}
$\vdots$	$\vdots$	$\vdots$	$\vdots$	$\vdots$	$\vdots$
f_n	f_{n1}	f_{n2}	f_{n3}	$\cdots$	f_{nm}

$f_{ij} = (A_{ij}, B_{ij}), i = 1,...,n, j = 1,...,m$ are Z-number valued criteria evaluations. The considered problem of multiattribute choice is to determine the best alloy:

Find $f^* \in F$ such that $f^* \succ f_i$, $\forall f_i \in F$ where $\succ$ is a preference relation.

For solving the considered problem we suggest several approaches based on computation with Z-numbers and human-oriented ranking of Z-numbers. These approaches are outlined in the next sections.

3.4.2. Multiattribute decisions on selection of titanium alloys on the basis of the Z-number-valued weighted arithmetic mean

In this section we propose an approach to solving the problem formulated in Section 3.4.1 by using aggregation of Z-valued criteria evaluations. As an aggregating operator, Z-number valued weighted arithmetic mean (ZWAM) operator is used. The values of ZWAM operator are ranked by using FPO principle Pessimism-Optimism degree based comparison of Z-numbers [8]. The necessary definitions are given below.

Definition 3.1. *Z-number valued weighted arithmetic mean of discrete Z-numbers* [20]. Let a Z-valued vector $Z = (Z_1, Z_2, ..., Z_n)$ be given. The Z-number valued weighted arithmetic mean (ZWAM) operator $M()$ assigns to any vector Z a unique Z-number $Z_M = M(Z_1, Z_2, ..., Z_n) = (A_M, B_M)$:

$$M(Z_1, Z_2, ..., Z_n) = \frac{1}{n} \sum_{i=1}^{n} Z_i.$$

Definition 3.2. *Fuzzy Pareto optimality (FPO) principle based comparison of Z-numbers* [8]. For Z-numbers $Z_1 = (A_1, B_1)$ and $Z_2 = (A_2, B_2)$ total degrees of optimality $do(Z_1)$ and $do(Z_2)$ are determined. Z_1 is considered higher than Z_2 if $do(Z_1) > do(Z_2)$.

Definition 3.3. *Pessimism-Optimism degree based comparison of Z-numbers* [8]. In order to improve FPO-based comparison of Z-numbers a degree of pessimism $\beta \in [0,1]$ is submitted by a human observer to adjust the results obtained by the FPO approach. Given $do(Z_j) \le do(Z_i)$, we define for two Z-numbers Z_1 and Z_2:

$$r(Z_i, Z_j) = \beta do(Z_j) + (1 - \beta) do(Z_i) \qquad (3.12)$$

Then

$$\left.\begin{array}{l} Z_i > Z_j \ \text{iff} \ r(Z_i, Z_j) > \dfrac{1}{2}(do(Z_i) + do(Z_j)) \\[2mm] Z_i < Z_j \ \text{iff} \ r(Z_i, Z_j) < \dfrac{1}{2}(do(Z_i) + do(Z_j)) \\[2mm] \text{and} \\[1mm] Z_i = Z_j \ \text{otherwise} \end{array}\right\} \qquad (3.13)$$

The algorithm for applying the proposed approach to the considered problem is as follows.

Step 1. Scaling of Z-number-valued criteria evaluations.

Step 2. Aggregation of scaled evaluations by using Z-valued weighted arithmetic mean according to Definition 3.1.

Step 3. Ranking of Z-numbers by using the FPO approach and pessimism degree (Definition 3.2).

Example [199]. A set of alloys includes three alloys created by the author: Ti12Mo2Sn alloy (f_1), Ti12Mo4Sn alloy (f_2), Ti12Mo6Sn alloy (f_3). The choice criteria: Strength Level, Plastic Deformation Degree, Tensile strength. Due to partial reliability and imprecision of information on the criteria, Z-numbers-based formalization is used (Table 3.3).

Table 3.3. Z-number valued information on alloys characteristics.

	Strength Level, MPa	Plastic Deformation Degree,%	Tensile Strength, MPa
Ti12Mo2Sn	((490,510,530), (0.94,0.95,0.96))	((30,35,40), · (0.94,0.95,0.96))	((850,910,970), (0.94,0.95,0.96))
Ti12Mo4Sn	((550,595,640), (0.9,0.935,0.97))	((25,27.5,30), (0.9,0.935,0.97))	((815,865,915), (0.9,0.935,0.97))
Ti12Mo6Sn	((705,718,730), (0.91,0.935,0.96))	((16,20,25), (0.91,0.935,0.96))	((896,976,1056), (0.91,0.935,0.96))

Experts' opinion based information on criteria importance weights is also represented by Z-numbers $V_i, i = 1,...,3$:

$$V_1 = ((0.4,0.5,0.6),(0.95,0.97,0.98)),$$

$$V_2 = ((0.25,0.3,0.35),(0.95,0.97,0.98)),$$

$$V_3 = ((0.05,0.2,0.35),(0.95,0.97,0.98)).$$

Let us create the scaled decision matrix given information in Table 3.3 and codebooks in Tables 3.4,3.5,3.6:

$$D_{3\times3} = \begin{Vmatrix} & C_1 & C_2 & C_3 \\ f_1 & (very\,low, very\,sure) & (high, very\,sure) & (low\,average, very\,sure) \\ f_2 & (below\,average, very\,sure) & (average, very\,sure) & (low, very\,sure) \\ f_3 & (very\,high, very\,sure) & (low, very\,sure) & (above\,average, very\,sure) \end{Vmatrix}$$

Table 3.4. The codebook for A parts of Z-number-valued criteria evaluations.

Linguistic term	Fuzzy number
Very low	(0.01,0.1,0.15)
Low	(0.15,0.2,0.25)
Low average	(0.2,0.3,0.4)
Below average	(0.3,0.4,0.5)
Average	(0.4,0.5,0.6)
Above average	(0.5,0.6,0.7)
High average	(0.6,0.7,0.8)
High	(0.7,0.8,0.9)
Very high	(0.8,0.9,1)

Table 3.5. The codebook for A parts of criteria importance weights.

Linguistic term	Fuzzy number
Very Low	(0.01,0.1,0.2)
Low	(0.1,0.2,0.2)
Average	(0.2,0.3,0.4)
High	(0.4,0.5,0.6)
Very High	(0.6,0.7,0.8)

Table 3.6. The codebook for B parts of criteria evaluations and importance weights.

Linguistic term	Fuzzy number
Almost Sure	(0.6,0.7,0.8)
Sure	(0.7,0.8,0.9)
Very sure	(0.8,0.9,1)

For example, $D_{n \times m}$ shows that if we choose the 1st alternative then the value of Strength Level will be (very low, very sure), Plastic Deformation Degree will be (high, very sure), Tensile strength will be (low average, very sure).

Now, according to Step 2 (see Section 3.4.2) we compute ZWAM by using Definition 1:

$$M(Z_{11}, Z_{12}, Z_{13}) = V_1 Z_{11} + V_2 Z_{12} + V_3 Z_{13} = (A_1, B_1)$$

$$M(Z_{21}, Z_{22}, Z_{23}) = V_1 Z_{21} + V_2 Z_{22} + V_3 Z_{23} = (A_2, B_2)$$

$$M(Z_{31}, Z_{32}, Z_{33}) = V_1 Z_{31} + V_2 Z_{32} + V_3 Z_{33} = (A_3, B_3)$$

The Z-number-valued criteria evaluations $M(Z_{i1}, Z_{i2}, Z_{i3}) = (A_i, B_i)$, $i = 1, ..., 3$ for alloys are given below:

$A_1 = 0/0.15 + 0.4/0.2 + 1/0.34 + 0.4/0.437 + 0/0.57$,

$B_1 = 0/0.96 + 0.5/0.968 + 1/0.97 + 0.5/0.972 + 0/0.974$.

$A_2 = 0/19 + 0.5/0.26 + 1/0.4 + 0.5/0.52 + 0/0.65$,

$B_2 = 0/0.85 + 0.5/0.875 + 1/0.9 + 0.5/0.925 + 0/0.95$.

$A_3 = 0/0.36 + 0.4/0.45 + 1/0.62 + 0.4/0.74 + 0/0.895$,

$B_3 = 0/0.85 + 0.5/0.875 + 1/0.9 + 0.5/0.925 + 0/0.95$.

Graphical representation of the obtained Z-numbers is given in Figs. 3.10.-3.12.

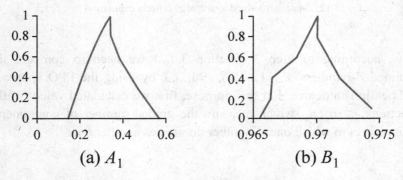

(a) A_1 (b) B_1

Fig. 3.10. Z-number valued aggregated criteria evaluation for f_1.

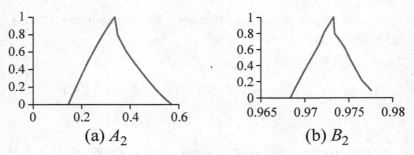

Fig. 3.11. Z-number valued aggregated criteria evaluation for f_2.

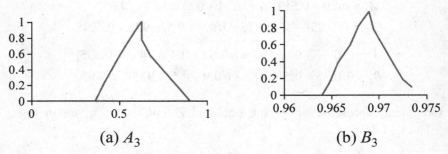

Fig. 3.12. Z-number valued aggregated criteria evaluation for f_3.

Now, according to Step 3 (Section 3.4.2) we need to compare the obtained Z-numbers $Z_i = (A_i, B_i)$, $i = 1,...,3$ by using the FPO approach and pessimism degree. For this purpose, first we calculated values of the functions n_b, n_e, n_w which measure the graded number of components with respect to which one Z-number dominates another one:

$$n_b(Z_1, Z_2) = 0, \ n_b(Z_2, Z_1) = 0.1, \ n_e(Z_1, Z_2) = 1,$$

$$n_e(Z_2, Z_1) = 1.9, n_w(Z_1, Z_2) = 0, \ n_w(Z_2, Z_1) = 0,$$

$$n_b(Z_1, Z_3) = 0, \ n_b(Z_3, Z_1) = 0.54, \ n_e(Z_1, Z_3) = 1,$$

$$n_e(Z_3, Z_1) = 1.5, \ n_w(Z_1, Z_3) = 1, \ n_w(Z_3, Z_1) = 0,$$

$$n_b(Z_2, Z_3) = 0.1, \ n_b(Z_3, Z_2) = 0.26, \ n_e(Z_2, Z_3) = 0.9,$$

$$n_e(Z_3, Z_2) = 0.74, \ n_w(Z_2, Z_3) = 1, \ n_w(Z_3, Z_2) = 0.$$

Next, a function d is calculated which measures degree of dominance of one Z-number over another one:

$$d(Z_1, Z_2) = 0, d(Z_1, Z_3) = 0,$$

$$d(Z_2, Z_1) = 1, d(Z_2, Z_3) = 0,$$

$$d(Z_3, Z_2) = 1; \ d(Z_3, Z_1) = 1.$$

The obtained optimality degrees for the Z-numbers are $do(Z_1) = 0$, $do(Z_2) = 0$, $do(Z_3) = 1$.

Finally, we adjust FPO-based ranking by using pessimism-optimism degrees. We consider only Z- $Z_2 = (A_2, B_2)$ and $Z_3 = (A_3, B_3)$ (Z_1 is the worst as $d(Z_1, Z_2) = 0, d(Z_1, Z_3) = 0$). Let $\beta = 0.4$. For this case we have:

$$r(Z_3, Z_2) = 0.6 > \frac{1}{2}(0 + 1) = 0.5. \ \text{Therefore,} \ Z_3 > Z_2.$$

Thus, the best alternative is Alloy 3.

3.4.3. *Multiattribute decisions on selection of alloys for pressure vessel on the basis of the VIKOR method*

In this section we propose solving of the problem in Section 3.4.1 by using the VIKOR method under Z-information. The VIKOR method is one of the most famous and effective decision approaches [2, 59, 64, 139, 154, 194, 208, 209]. In this approach multiattribute alternatives are compared by using two important measures — utility measure and regret measure. The algorithm of application of the VIKOR method under Z-information is given below.

Step 1. Calculate positive point f_j^* and negative point f_j^- (for each criteria):

$$f_j^* = \max_i(f_{ij}), \quad j = 1,...,m \tag{3.14}$$

$$f_j^- = \min_i(f_{ij}), \quad j = 1,...,m \tag{3.15}$$

Step 2. Calculate the values of regret measure $R_i = (A_{R_i}, B_{R_i})$:

$$R_i = \max_j \left[w_j \frac{\left(f_j^* - f_{ij}\right)}{\left(f_j^* - f_j^-\right)} \right] i = 1,...,n \tag{3.16}$$

Step 3. Calculate the values of utility measure $S_i = (A_{S_i}, B_{S_i})$:

$$S_i = \sum_{j=1}^n \left[w_j \frac{\left(f_j^* - f_{ij}\right)}{\left(f_j^* - f_j^-\right)} \right] i = 1,...,n \tag{3.17}$$

Step 4. Compute the Z-valued VIKOR index $Q_i = (A_{Q_i}, B_{Q_i})$:

$$Q_i = \left[v \frac{(S_i - S^-)}{(S^* - S^-)} + (1-v) \frac{(R_i - R^*)}{(R^* - R^-)} \right], \tag{3.18}$$

Here $S^* = \max_i S_i$, $S^- = \min_i S_i$, $R^* = \max_i R_i$, $R^- = \min_i R_i$ and $v \in [0,1]$ is introduced as the weight of the maximum group utility.

Step 5. Sort the values (R_i, S_i, Q_i) in ascending form and get three ranking lists.

Step 6: Propose the alternative f^1 as a compromise solution, which is ranked as the best by the values of VIKOR index Q_i (minimum) if the following two conditions are satisfied:

C1. Acceptable advantage:

$$Q(f^2) - Q(f^1) \geq \frac{1}{n-1} \qquad (3.19)$$

where f^2 is the alternative with the second position in the ranking list by VIKOR index Q_i, n is the number of alternatives.

C2. Acceptable stability in decision making: Alternative f^1 must also be the best ranked S or/and R.

If one of the conditions is not satisfied, then a set of compromise solutions is proposed :

- If only condition C2 is not satisfied, alternatives f^1 and f^2 are compromise solutions;

- If condition C1 is not satisfied and f^N is determined by the relation $Q(f^N) - Q(f^1) < \dfrac{1}{m-1}$ for maximum N (the positions of these alternatives are "in closeness"), so alternatives $f^1, f^2, ..., f^N$ are compromise solutions.

Example. Selection of an alloy for pressure vessel by using the VIKOR method under Z-information. Assume that the following alternatives are considered for pressure vessel: f_1-alloy 825; f_2-alloy 59; f_3-alloy 625, f_4-alloy 718. Each alternative is evaluated by 4 criteria: C_1- PREN, C_2-yield strength, C_3- weldability, C_3-impact strength. The decision matrix of Z-valued scaled criteria evaluations of the alternatives is given below in Table 3.7.

Table 3.7. Z-number values decision matrix.

	C_1	C_2
f_1	$(0.28;0.31;0.34)(0.5;07;1)$	$(0.22;0.24;0.27)(0.5;07;1)$
f_2	$(0.66;0.74;0.81)(0.5;0.7;1)$	$(0.28;0.31;0.34)(0.5;07;1)$
f_3	$(0.46;0.51;0.56)(0.3;0.5;0.7)$	$(0.38;0.42;0.46)(0.3;0.5;0.7)$
f_4	$(0.29;0.32;0.35)(0.3;0.5;0.7)$	$(0.73;0.82;0.9)(0.3;0.5;0.7)$
	C_3	C_4
f_1	$(0.53;0.59;0.64)(0.5;0.7;1)$	$(0.27;0.31;0.34)(0.5;0.7;1)$
f_2	$(0.42;0.47;0.51)(0.5;0.7;1)$	$(0.74;0.82;0.91)(0.5;0.7;1)$
f_3	$(0.42;0.47;0.51)(0.3;0.5;0.7)$	$(0.33;0.37;0.4)(0.3;0.5;0.7)$
f_4	$(0.42;0.47;0.51)(0.3;0.5;0.7)$	$(0.27;0.31;0.34)(0.3;0.5;0.7)$

For simplicity, we consider numeric values of criteria weights: $w_1 = 0.47$, $w_2 = 0.12$, $w_3 = 0.23$, $w_4 = 0.18$. Let us solve the considered problem by the VIKOR method under Z-information.

At first step, we determine the positive point and the negative point for every criteria:

For C_1 $f_{i1}^* = (0.66;0.74;0.81)(0.5;0.7;1)$; $f_{i1}^- = (0.29;0.32;0.35)(0.3;0.5;0.7)$

For C_2 $f_{i2}^* = (0.73;0.82;0.9)(0.3;0.5;0.7)$; $f_{i2}^- = (0.22;0.24;0.27)(0.5;07;1)$

For C_3 $f_{i3}^* = (0.53;0.59;0.64)(0.5;0.7;1)$; $f_{i3}^- = (0.42;0.47;0.51)(0.3;0.5;0.7)$

For C_4 $f_{i4}^* = (0.74;0.82;0.91)(0.5;0.7;1)$; $f_{i4}^- = (0.27;0.31;0.34)(0.3;0.5;0.7)$

At the second step we calculate the regret measure as follows.

for f_{11} :

$$w_j \frac{\left(f_{ij}^+ - f_{ij}^+\right)}{\left(f_{ij}^+ - f_{ij}^-\right)} = 0.47 \cdot \frac{((0.66\,0.74\,0.81)(0.5\,0.7\,1) - (0.28\,0.31\,0.34)(0.5\,0.7\,1))}{((0.66\,0.74\,0.81)(0.5\,0.7\,1) - (0.29\,0.32\,0.35)(0.3\,0.5\,0.7))}$$

$$= 0.47 \cdot \frac{(0.32\,0.43\,0.53)(0.3\,0.53\,0.94)}{(0.31\,0.42\,0.52)(0.22\,0.42\,0.7)} = 0.47 \cdot ((0.62\,1.02\,1.71)(0.1\,0.27\,0.67))$$

$$= (0.29\,0.48\,0.8)(0.1\,0.27\,0.67)$$

for f_{12} :

$$w_j \frac{\left(f_{ij}^+ - f_{ij}^+\right)}{\left(f_{ij}^+ - f_{ij}^-\right)} = 0.12 \cdot \frac{((0.73\,0.82\,0.9)(0.3\,0.5\,0.7) - (0.22\,0.24\,0.27)(0.5\,0.7\,1))}{((0.73\,0.82\,0.9)(0.3\,0.5\,0.7) - (0.22\,0.24\,0.27)(0.5\,0.7\,1))}$$

$$= 0.12 \cdot \frac{(0.46\,0.58\,0.68)(0.2\,0.4\,0.66)}{(0.46\,0.58\,0.68)(0.2\,0.4\,0.66)} = 0.12 * (0.68\,1\,1.48)(0.2\,0.28\,0.5)$$

$$= (0.08\,0.12\,0.18)(0.2\,0.28\,0.5)$$

for f_{13} :

$$w_j \frac{\left(f_{ij}^+ - f_{ij}^+\right)}{\left(f_{ij}^+ - f_{ij}^-\right)} = 0.23 \cdot \frac{((0.53\,0.59\,0.64)(0.5\,0.7\,1) - (0.53\,0.59\,0.64)(0.5\,0.7\,1))}{((0.53\,0.59\,0.64)(0.5\,0.7\,1) - (0.42\,0.47\,0.51)(0.3\,0.5\,0.7))}$$

$$= 0.23 \cdot \frac{(-0.11\,0\,0.11)(0.44\,0.58\,0.94)}{(0.02\,0.12\,0.22)(0.23\,0.4\,0.7)} = 0.23 \cdot ((-1.27\,0\,1.27)(0.3\,0.46\,0.78))$$

$$= (-1.27\,0\,1.27)(0.3\,0.46\,0.78)$$

for f_{14}:

$$w_j \frac{\left(f_{ij}^+ - f_{ij}^+\right)}{\left(f_{ij}^+ - f_{ij}^-\right)} = 0.18 \cdot \frac{((0.74\,0.82\,0.91)(0.5\,0.7\,1) - (0.27\,0.31\,0.34)(0.5\,0.7\,1))}{((0.74\,0.82\,0.91)(0.5\,0.7\,1) - (0.27\,0.31\,0.34)(0.3\,0.5\,0.7))}$$

$$= 0.18 \cdot \frac{((0.4\,0.51\,0.64)(0.37\,0.55\,0.93))}{((0.4\,0.51\,0.64)(0.29\,0.45\,0.69))} = 0.18 \cdot ((0.63\,1\,1.6)(0.24\,0.35\,0.66))$$

$$= (0.11\,0.18\,0.29)(0.24\,0.35\,0.66)$$

So, for f_1,
$$R_1 = (0.29\,0.48\,0.8)(0.1\,0.27\,0.67).$$

Analogously we computed the regret measures for all alternatives:

$$R_2 = (0.02\,0.23\,2.53)(0.22\,0.32\,0.67),$$
$$R_3 = (0.02\,0.23\,2.53)(0.22\,0.28\,0.55),$$
$$R_4 = (0.02\,0.23\,2.53)(0.22\,0.28\,0.55).$$

At the third step we calculate the utility measures for all alternatives:

$$S_1 = (-0.79\,0.78\,2.54)(0.01\,0.04\,0.24);$$
$$S_2 = (-0.31\,0.33\,3)(0\,0.04\,0.32);$$
$$S_3 = (0.26\,0.73\,3.5)(0.01\,0.05\,0.15);$$
$$S_4 = (0.31\,0.88\,3.66)(0.01\,0.03\,0.18).$$

At the fourth step we compute VIKOR index for all alternatives Q_i. For this, at first we obtain

$$R^+ = (0.02\,0.23\,2.53)(0.22\,0.32\,0.67);$$
$$R^- = (0.29\,0.48\,0.8)(0.1\,0.27\,0.67);$$

and

$$S^+ = (0.31\,0.88\,3.66)(0.01\,0.03\,0.18);$$
$$S^- = (-0.79\,0.78\,2.54)(0.01\,0.04\,0.24).$$

So, the VIKOR index for each alternative is as follows:

$$Q_1 = (-17.5 \quad 0 \quad 17.5)(0 \quad 0.02 \quad 0.09);$$
$$Q_2 = (-18.73 \quad -1.75 \quad 23.45)(0 \quad 0.0007 \quad 0.007);$$
$$Q_3 = (-15.88 \quad 0.25 \quad 25.95)(0 \quad 0.0007 \quad 0.03);$$
$$Q_4 = (-15.98 \quad 1 \quad 26.75)(0.06 \quad 0.24 \quad 0.32).$$

At the fifth step we sort values of (R_i, S_i, Q_i) from minimum to maximum by ranking Z-numbers on the basis of FPO principle (Table 3.8):

Table 3.8. Ranking of (R_i, S_i, Q_i) measures.

ranking values of regret measure R_i	*ranking values of utility measure S_i*	*ranking values of Vikor index Q_i*
Alternative f_1 vs. Alternative f_2: $do(f_1) = 0$, $do(f_2) = 1$,	Alternative f_1 vs. Alternative f_2: $do(f_1) = 0$, $do(f_2) = 1$,	Alternative f_1 vs. Alternative f_2: $do(f_1) = 1$, $do(f_2) = 0.11$,
Alternative f_3 vs. Alternative f_2: $do(f_3) = 0$, $do(f_2) = 1$,	Alternative f_3 vs. Alternative f_2: $do(f_3) = 0.9$, $do(f_2) = 1$,	Alternative f_3 vs. Alternative f_2: $do(f_3) = 1$, $do(f_2) = 0$,
Alternative f_3 vs. Alternative f_1: $do(f_3) = 1$, $do(f_1) = 0$,	Alternative f_3 vs. Alternative f_1: $do(f_3) = 1$, $do(f_1) = 0.6$,	Alternative f_3 vs. Alternative f_1: $do(f_3) = 0.45$, $do(f_1) = 1$,
Alternative f_4 vs. Alternative f_2 $do(f_4) = 0$, $do(f_2) = 1$,	Alternative f_4 vs. Alternative f_2 $do(f_4) = 1$, $do(f_2) = 0.9$,	Alternative f_4 vs. Alternative f_2 $do(f_4) = 1$, $do(f_2) = 0$,
Alternative f_4 vs. Alternative f_1 $do(f_4) = 1$, $do(f_1) = 0$,	Alternative f_4 vs. Alternative f_1 $do(f_4) = 1$, $do(f_1) = 0.5$,	Alternative f_4 vs. Alternative f_1 $do(f_4) = 1$, $do(f_1) = 0$,
Alternative f_4 vs. Alternative f_3 $do(f_4) = 1$, $do(f_3) = 1$,	Alternative f_4 vs. Alternative f_3 $do(f_4) = 1$, $do(f_3) = 0$,	Alternative f_4 vs. Alternative f_3 $do(f_4) = 1$, $do(f_3) = 0$,

The sorted values of (R_i, S_i, Q_i) are shown in Table 3.9.

Table 3.9. The sorted values of (R_i, S_i, Q_i).

R_i	S_i	Q_i
f_1	f_1	f_2
f_3, f_4	f_3	f_3
f_2	f_2	f_1 :
	f_4	f_4

According to the VIKOR method, f_2 and f_3 are compromise solutions, but f_2 is preferable.

3.4.4. *Decision making on alloy selection for drive shaft by using Z-valued If-Then rules*

Alloy selection process rely on comparison in terms of desired alloy characteristics. Due to complexity and uncertainty of problems of alloy selection, one of an adequate solution approach may be based on the use of Z-number valued If-Then rules. Z-Rules may describe dependence between alloy characteristics $X_1, ..., X_m$ and overall performance index of alloy Y.

Assume that Z-rules base is as follows.

$$\textit{If } X_1 \textit{ is } Z_{X_1,1} = (A_{X_1,1}, B_{X_1,1}) \textit{ and}, ..., \textit{ and } X_m \textit{ is } Z_{X_m,1} = (A_{X_m,1}, B_{X_m,1})$$
$$\textit{then } Y \textit{ is } Z_Y = (A_{Y,1}, B_{Y,1})$$
$$\textit{If } X_1 \textit{ is } Z_{X_1,2} = (A_{X_1,2}, B_{X_1,2}) \textit{ and}, ..., \textit{ and } X_m \textit{ is } Z_{X_m,2} = (A_{X_m,2}, B_{X_m,2})$$
$$\textit{then } Y \textit{ is } Z_Y = (A_{Y,2}, B_{Y,2})$$

*If X_1 is $Z_{X_1,n} = (A_{X_1,n}, B_{X_1,n})$ and,..., and X_m is $Z_{X_m,n} = (A_{X_m,n}, B_{X_m,n})$
then Y is $Z_Y = (A_{Y,n}, B_{Y,n})$*

Thus, given Z-valued information on characteristics $X_1^i, ..., X_m^i$, $i = 1, 2$ of two alternative alloys, one can compute the corresponding performance indices Y^i, $i = 1, 2$ on the basis of reasoning within the Z-rules. Then, by comparing Z-numbers Y^1 and Y^2, the best alloy can be found.

The proposed approach consists of the following steps.

Given alloy characteristics $Z'_{X_1} = (A'_{X_1}, B'_{X_1})$ and,..., and $Z'_{X_m} = (A'_{X_m}, B'_{X_m})$ compute the performance index Z'_{Y^i}, $i = 1, 2$ by using linear interpolation:

$$Z'_{Y^i} = \sum_{j=1}^{n} w_j Z_{Y^i,j} = \sum_{j=1}^{n} w_j (A_{Y^i,j}, B_{Y^i,j}) \tag{3.20}$$

where $Z_{Y_i,j}$ is the Z-valued consequent of the jth rule, $w_j = \dfrac{\rho_j}{\sum\limits_{k=1}^{n} \rho_k}$,

$j = 1, ..., n$; $k = 1, ..., n$ are coefficients of linear interpolation, n is the number of Z-rules. ρ_j is defined as follows.

$$\rho_j = \min_{i=1,...,m} S(Z'_{X_i}, Z_{X_i,j}) \tag{3.21}$$

where S is the similarity index. ρ_j computes jth rule activation degree. Similarity S can be defined as

$$S(Z'_{X_i}, Z_{X_i,j}) = \frac{1}{1 + D(Z'_{X_i}, Z_{X_i,j})} \tag{3.22}$$

Distance D between Z_1 and Z_2 is defined as [19]

$$D(Z_1, Z_2) = \frac{1}{n+1} \sum_{k=1}^{n} \left\{ \left| a_{1\alpha_k}^L - a_{2\alpha_k}^L \right| + \left| a_{1\alpha_k}^R - a_{2\alpha_k}^R \right| \right\}$$

$$+ \frac{1}{m+1} \sum_{k=1}^{m} \left\{ \left| b_{1\alpha_k}^L - b_{2\alpha_k}^L \right| + \left| b_{1\alpha_k}^R - b_{2\alpha_k}^R \right| \right\}$$

where $a_{i,\alpha}^L = \min A_i^\alpha$, $a_{i,\alpha}^R = \max A_i^\alpha$, $b_\alpha^L = \min B^\alpha$, $b_\alpha^R = \max B^\alpha$. Finally, the computed performance indices Z_{Y^i}' are compared. For comparison, the approach based on the FPO principle (Section 3.4.2) can be used.

Example. Let us consider a problem of selection of the best alloy for drive shaft [199]. A knowledge base of 26 Z-rules describing relation between such characteristics as *hardness*, X_1, *strength*, X_2, *machinability*, X_3, *toughness*, X_4 and the overall performance index Y is given below.

If X_1 is (E, H), X_2 is (E, H), X_3 is (E, H), X_4 is (E, M) THEN Y is (E, H),
If X_1 is (E, H), X_2 is (E, H), X_3 is (E, H), X_4 is (B, H) THEN Y is (G, M),
If X_1 is (E, H), X_2 is (E, H), X_3 is (G, M), X_4 is (E, H) THEN Y is (E, H),
If X_1 is (E, H), X_2 is (E, H), X_3 is (G, M), X_4 is (G, M) THEN Y is (G, M),
If X_1 is (E, H), X_2 is (E, H), X_3 is (B, H), X_4 is (G, M) THEN Y is (A, M),
If X_1 is (E, H), X_2 is (E, H), X_3 is (B, H), X_4 is (B, H) THEN Y is (B, H),
If X_1 is (E, H), X_2 is (G, M), X_3 is (E, H), X_4 is (E, H) THEN Y is (E, H),
If X_1 is (E, H), X_2 is (G, M), X_3 is (E, H), X_4 is (G, M) THEN Y is (G, M),
If X_1 is (E, H), X_2 is (G, M), X_3 is (G, M), X_4 is (G, M) THEN Y is (G, M),
If X_1 is (E, H), X_2 is (G, M), X_3 is (G, M), X_4 is (B, H) THEN Y is (A, M),
If X_1 is (E, H), X_2 is (G, M), X_3 is (B, H), X_4 is (G, M) THEN Y is (A, M),
If X_1 is (E, H), X_2 is (G, M), X_3 is (B, H), X_4 is (B, H) THEN Y is (B, H),
If X_1 is (G, M), X_2 is (E, H), X_3 is (E, H), X_4 is (E, H) THEN Y is (E, H),
If X_1 is (G, M), X_2 is (E, H), X_3 is (E, H), X_4 is (B, H) THEN Y is (A, M),
If X_1 is (G, M), X_2 is (E, H), X_3 is (G, M), X_4 is (G, M) THEN Y is (G, M),
If X_1 is (G, M), X_2 is (E, H), X_3 is (G, M), X_4 is (B, H) THEN Y is (A, M),
If X_1 is (G, M), X_2 is (E, H), X_3 is (B, H), X_4 is (G, M) THEN Y is (A, M),
If X_1 is (G, M), X_2 is (E, H), X_3 is (B, H), X_4 is (B, H) THEN Y is (B, H),
If X_1 is (G, M), X_2 is (G, M), X_3 is (E, H), X_4 is (G, M) THEN Y is (G, M),

If X_1 is (G,M), X_2 is (G,M), X_3 is (E,H), X_4 is (B,H) THEN Y is (A,M),

If X_1 is (G,M), X_2 is (G,M), X_3 is (G,M), X_4 is (G,M) THEN Y is (A,M),

If X_1 is (G,M), X_2 is (G,M), X_3 is (G,M), X_4 is (B,H) THEN Y is (B,H),

If X_1 is (G,M), X_2 is (G,M), X_3 is (B,H), X_4 is (G,M) THEN Y is (B,H),

If X_1 is (G,M), X_2 is (G,M), X_3 is (B,H), X_4 is (B,H) THEN Y is (T,H),

If X_1 is (B,H), X_2 is (B,H), X_3 is (B,H), X_4 is (B,H) THEN Y is (T,H),

If X_1 is (B,H), X_2 is (B,H), X_3 is (G,M), X_4 is (B,H) THEN Y is (T,H).

The codebooks for the used linguistic terms are given in Tables 3.10-3.15.

Table 3.10. The encoded linguistic terms for X_1-Hardness.

#	Linguistic term	Fuzzy number
1	Bad	$\left\{ \dfrac{1}{100} \quad \dfrac{1}{120} \quad \dfrac{0}{150} \right\}$
2	Good	$\left\{ \dfrac{0}{180} \quad \dfrac{1}{220} \quad \dfrac{1}{250} \quad \dfrac{0}{270} \right\}$
3	Excellent	$\left\{ \dfrac{0}{300} \quad \dfrac{1}{320} \quad \dfrac{1}{350} \right\}$

Table 3.11. The encoded linguistic terms for X_2-Strength.

#	Linguistic term	Fuzzy number
1	Bad	$\left\{ \dfrac{1}{0} \quad \dfrac{1}{50} \quad \dfrac{0}{100} \right\}$
2	Good	$\left\{ \dfrac{0}{250} \quad \dfrac{1}{300} \quad \dfrac{1}{400} \quad \dfrac{0}{450} \right\}$
3	Excellent	$\left\{ \dfrac{0}{550} \quad \dfrac{1}{600} \quad \dfrac{1}{1000} \right\}$

Table 3.12. The encoded linguistic terms for X_3-Machinability.

#	Linguistic term	Fuzzy number
1	Bad	$\left\{\frac{1}{1}\ \frac{1}{1.2}\ \frac{0}{1.5}\right\}$
2	Good	$\left\{\frac{0}{2.3}\ \frac{1}{2.7}\ \frac{1}{3.3}\ \frac{0}{3.7}\right\}$
3	Excellent	$\left\{\frac{0}{4.3}\ \frac{1}{4.7}\ \frac{1}{5}\right\}$

Table 3.13. The encoded linguistic terms for X_4-Toughness.

#	Linguistic term	Fuzzy number
1	Bad	$\left\{\frac{1}{0}\ \frac{1}{100}\ \frac{0}{120}\right\}$
2	Good	$\left\{\frac{0}{250}\ \frac{1}{300}\ \frac{1}{400}\ \frac{0}{450}\right\}$
3	Excellent	$\left\{\frac{0}{550}\ \frac{1}{650}\ \frac{1}{1000}\right\}$

Table 3.14. The encoded linguistic terms for Y.

#	Linguistic term	Fuzzy number
1	Terrible	$\left\{\frac{1}{0}\ \frac{1}{5}\ \frac{0}{7}\right\}$
2	Bad	$\left\{\frac{0}{10}\ \frac{1}{15}\ \frac{1}{25}\ \frac{0}{30}\right\}$
3	A	$\left\{\frac{0}{40}\ \frac{1}{45}\ \frac{1}{55}\ \frac{0}{60}\right\}$
4	Good	$\left\{\frac{0}{70}\ \frac{1}{75}\ \frac{1}{85}\ \frac{1}{90}\right\}$
5	Excellent	$\left\{\frac{0}{95}\ \frac{1}{100}\ \frac{1}{105}\right\}$

Table 3.15. The encoded linguistic terms for reliability.

#	Linguistic term	Fuzzy number
1	Low	$\left\{ \dfrac{0}{1} \quad \dfrac{1}{0} \quad \dfrac{1}{0.3} \quad \dfrac{0}{0.4} \right\}$
2	Medium	$\left\{ \dfrac{0}{0.3} \quad \dfrac{1}{0.4} \quad \dfrac{1}{0.6} \quad \dfrac{0}{0.7} \right\}$
3	High	$\left\{ \dfrac{0}{0.6} \quad \dfrac{1}{0.7} \quad \dfrac{1}{1} \quad \dfrac{0}{1} \right\}$

Assume that it is needed to choose the best alloy among two alloys with the following characteristics:

Alloy 1:

$$X_1 \text{ is } ((270 \quad 280 \quad 290 \quad 300), (0.5 \quad 0.6 \quad 0.7 \quad 0.8)),$$
$$X_2 \text{ is } ((400 \quad 450 \quad 500 \quad 550), (0.5 \quad 0.6 \quad 0.7 \quad 0.8)),$$
$$X_3 \text{ is } ((1.5 \quad 1.6 \quad 1.7 \quad 1.8), (0.7 \quad 0.8 \quad 0.9 \quad 1)),$$
$$X_4 \text{ is } ((110 \quad 120 \quad 130 \quad 140), (0.7 \quad 0.8 \quad 0.9 \quad 1))$$

Alloy 2:

$$X_1 \text{ is } ((250 \quad 270 \quad 290 \quad 300), (0.7 \quad 0.8 \quad 0.9 \quad 1)),$$
$$X_2 \text{ is } ((450 \quad 460 \quad 470 \quad 480), (0.7 \quad 0.8 \quad 0.9 \quad 1)),$$
$$X_3 \text{ is } ((4.0 \quad 4.1 \quad 4.2 \quad 4.3), (0.5 \quad 0.6 \quad 0.7 \quad 0.8)),$$
$$X_4 \text{ is } ((200 \quad 210 \quad 230 \quad 240), (0.5 \quad 0.6 \quad 0.7 \quad 0.8))$$

By using the codebooks in Tables 3.10-3.15, the following linguistic approximation can be used:

Alloy 1: X_1 is (E, M), X_2 is (G, M), X_3 is (B, H), X_4 is (B, H)

Alloy 2: X_1 is (G, H), X_2 is (G, H), X_3 is (E, M), X_4 is (G, M)

In order to determine the best alloy, we need to compute the performance indices $Y_i, i = 1, 2$ using linear interpolation of the Zs and to compare the indices.

Let us consider computation of performance index Y_1, computation of Y_2 is analogous. To compute Y_1, at first we compute similarity (3.22) of current inputs (characteristics of alloy 1) with the inputs of the Z rules. The obtained results are given below.

For 1 rule:
$S((270 \quad 280 \quad 290 \quad 300), (0.5 \quad 0.6 \quad 0.7 \quad 0.8), E(H)) = 0.013;$
$S((400 \quad 450 \quad 500 \quad 550), (0.5 \quad 0.6 \quad 0.7 \quad 0.8), E(H)) = 0.002;$
$S((1.5 \quad 1.6 \quad 1.7 \quad 1.8), (0.7 \quad 0.8 \quad 0.9 \quad 1), E(H)) = 0.159;$
$S((110 \quad 120 \quad 130 \quad 140), (0.7 \quad 0.8 \quad 0.9 \quad 1), E(H)) = 0.0009$

For 2 rule:
$S((270 \quad 280 \quad 290 \quad 300), (0.5 \quad 0.6 \quad 0.7 \quad 0.8), E(H)) = 0.013;$
$S((400 \quad 450 \quad 500 \quad 550), (0.5 \quad 0.6 \quad 0.7 \quad 0.8), E(H)) = 0.002;$
$S((1.5 \quad 1.6 \quad 1.7 \quad 1.8), (0.7 \quad 0.8 \quad 0.9 \quad 1), E(H)) = 0.159;$
$S((110 \quad 120 \quad 130 \quad 140), (0.7 \quad 0.8 \quad 0.9 \quad 1), B(H)) = 0.008$

For 3 rule:
$S((270 \quad 280 \quad 290 \quad 300), (0.5 \quad 0.6 \quad 0.7 \quad 0.8), E(H)) = 0.013;$
$S((400 \quad 450 \quad 500 \quad 550), (0.5 \quad 0.6 \quad 0.7 \quad 0.8), E(H)) = 0.002;$
$S((1.5 \quad 1.6 \quad 1.7 \quad 1.8), (0.7 \quad 0.8 \quad 0.9 \quad 1), G(M)) = 0.265;$
$S((110 \quad 120 \quad 130 \quad 140), (0.7 \quad 0.8 \quad 0.9 \quad 1), E(H)) = 0.0009$

For 4 rule:
$S((270 \quad 280 \quad 290 \quad 300), (0.5 \quad 0.6 \quad 0.7 \quad 0.8), E(H)) = 0.013;$
$S((400 \quad 450 \quad 500 \quad 550), (0.5 \quad 0.6 \quad 0.7 \quad 0.8), E(H)) = 0.002;$
$S((1.5 \quad 1.6 \quad 1.7 \quad 1.8), (0.7 \quad 0.8 \quad 0.9 \quad 1), G(M)) = 0.265;$
$S((110 \quad 120 \quad 130 \quad 140), (0.7 \quad 0.8 \quad 0.9 \quad 1), G(M)) = 0.003$

For 5 rule:
$S((270 \quad 280 \quad 290 \quad 300), (0.5 \quad 0.6 \quad 0.7 \quad 0.8), E(H)) = 0.013;$
$S((400 \quad 450 \quad 500 \quad 550), (0.5 \quad 0.6 \quad 0.7 \quad 0.8), E(H)) = 0.002;$

$S((1.5 \quad 1.6 \quad 1.7 \quad 1.8), (0.7 \quad 0.8 \quad 0.9 \quad 1), B(H)) = 0.526;$
$S((110 \quad 120 \quad 130 \quad 140), (0.7 \quad 0.8 \quad 0.9 \quad 1), G(M)) = 0.003$

For 6 rule:
$S((270 \quad 280 \quad 290 \quad 300), (0.5 \quad 0.6 \quad 0.7 \quad 0.8), E(H)) = 0.013;$
$S((400 \quad 450 \quad 500 \quad 550), (0.5 \quad 0.6 \quad 0.7 \quad 0.8), E(H) = 0.002;$
$S((1.5 \quad 1.6 \quad 1.7 \quad 1.8), (0.7 \quad 0.8 \quad 0.9 \quad 1), E(H)) = 0.526;$
$S((110 \quad 120 \quad 130 \quad 140), (0.7 \quad 0.8 \quad 0.9 \quad 1), B(H)) = 0.008$

For 7 rule:
$S((270 \quad 280 \quad 290 \quad 300), (0.5 \quad 0.6 \quad 0.7 \quad 0.8), E(H)) = 0.013;$
$S((400 \quad 450 \quad 500 \quad 550), (0.5 \quad 0.6 \quad 0.7 \quad 0.8), G(M) = 0.005;$
$S((1.5 \quad 1.6 \quad 1.7 \quad 1.8), (0.7 \quad 0.8 \quad 0.9 \quad 1), E(H)) = 0.159;$
$S((110 \quad 120 \quad 130 \quad 140), (0.7 \quad 0.8 \quad 0.9 \quad 1), E(H)) = 0.0009$

For 8 rule:
$S((270 \quad 280 \quad 290 \quad 300), (0.5 \quad 0.6 \quad 0.7 \quad 0.8), E(H)) = 0.013;$
$S((400 \quad 450 \quad 500 \quad 550), (0.5 \quad 0.6 \quad 0.7 \quad 0.8), G(M) = 0.005;$
$S((1.5 \quad 1.6 \quad 1.7 \quad 1.8), (0.7 \quad 0.8 \quad 0.9 \quad 1), E(H)) = 0.159;$
$S((110 \quad 120 \quad 130 \quad 140), (0.7 \quad 0.8 \quad 0.9 \quad 1), G(M)) = 0.003$

For 9 rule:
$S((270 \quad 280 \quad 290 \quad 300), (0.5 \quad 0.6 \quad 0.7 \quad 0.8), E(H)) = 0.013;$
$S((400 \quad 450 \quad 500 \quad 550), (0.5 \quad 0.6 \quad 0.7 \quad 0.8), G(M) = 0.005;$
$S((1.5 \quad 1.6 \quad 1.7 \quad 1.8), (0.7 \quad 0.8 \quad 0.9 \quad 1), G(M)) = 0.265;$
$S((110 \quad 120 \quad 130 \quad 140), (0.7 \quad 0.8 \quad 0.9 \quad 1), G(M)) = 0.003$

For 10 rule:
$S((270 \quad 280 \quad 290 \quad 300), (0.5 \quad 0.6 \quad 0.7 \quad 0.8), E(H)) = 0.013;$
$S((400 \quad 450 \quad 500 \quad 550), (0.5 \quad 0.6 \quad 0.7 \quad 0.8), G(M) = 0.005;$
$S((1.5 \quad 1.6 \quad 1.7 \quad 1.8), (0.7 \quad 0.8 \quad 0.9 \quad 1), G(M)) = 0.265;$
$S((110 \quad 120 \quad 130 \quad 140), (0.7 \quad 0.8 \quad 0.9 \quad 1), B(H)) = 0.008$

For 11 rule:
$S((270 \quad 280 \quad 290 \quad 300), (0.5 \quad 0.6 \quad 0.7 \quad 0.8), E(H)) = 0.013;$
$S((400 \quad 450 \quad 500 \quad 550), (0.5 \quad 0.6 \quad 0.7 \quad 0.8), G(M) = 0.005;$
$S((1.5 \quad 1.6 \quad 1.7 \quad 1.8), (0.7 \quad 0.8 \quad 0.9 \quad 1), B(H)) = 0.526;$

$S((110 \quad 120 \quad 130 \quad 140),(0.7 \quad 0.8 \quad 0.9 \quad 1), G(M)) = 0.003$

For 12 rule:

$S((270 \quad 280 \quad 290 \quad 300),(0.5 \quad 0.6 \quad 0.7 \quad 0.8), E(H)) = 0.013;$
$S((400 \quad 450 \quad 500 \quad 550),(0.5 \quad 0.6 \quad 0.7 \quad 0.8), G(M) = 0.005;$
$S((1.5 \quad 1.6 \quad 1.7 \quad 1.8),(0.7 \quad 0.8 \quad 0.9 \quad 1), B(H)) = 0.526;$
$S((110 \quad 120 \quad 130 \quad 140),(0.7 \quad 0.8 \quad 0.9 \quad 1), B(H)) = 0.008$

For 13 rule:

$S((270 \quad 280 \quad 290 \quad 300),(0.5 \quad 0.6 \quad 0.7 \quad 0.8), G(M)) = 0.011;$
$S((400 \quad 450 \quad 500 \quad 550),(0.5 \quad 0.6 \quad 0.7 \quad 0.8), E(H) = 0.002;$
$S((1.5 \quad 1.6 \quad 1.7 \quad 1.8),(0.7 \quad 0.8 \quad 0.9 \quad 1), E(H)) = 0.159;$
$S((110 \quad 120 \quad 130 \quad 140),(0.7 \quad 0.8 \quad 0.9 \quad 1), E(H)) = 0.0009$

For 14 rule:

$S((270 \quad 280 \quad 290 \quad 300),(0.5 \quad 0.6 \quad 0.7 \quad 0.8), G(M)) = 0.011;$
$S((400 \quad 450 \quad 500 \quad 550),(0.5 \quad 0.6 \quad 0.7 \quad 0.8), E(H) = 0.002;$
$S((1.5 \quad 1.6 \quad 1.7 \quad 1.8),(0.7 \quad 0.8 \quad 0.9 \quad 1), E(H)) = 0.159;$
$S((110 \quad 120 \quad 130 \quad 140),(0.7 \quad 0.8 \quad 0.9 \quad 1), B(H)) = 0.008$

For 15 rule:

$S((270 \quad 280 \quad 290 \quad 300),(0.5 \quad 0.6 \quad 0.7 \quad 0.8), G(M)) = 0.011;$
$S((400 \quad 450 \quad 500 \quad 550),(0.5 \quad 0.6 \quad 0.7 \quad 0.8), E(H) = 0.002;$
$S((1.5 \quad 1.6 \quad 1.7 \quad 1.8),(0.7 \quad 0.8 \quad 0.9 \quad 1), G(M)) = 0.264;$
$S((110 \quad 120 \quad 130 \quad 140),(0.7 \quad 0.8 \quad 0.9 \quad 1), G(M)) = 0.003$

For 16 rule:

$S((270 \quad 280 \quad 290 \quad 300),(0.5 \quad 0.6 \quad 0.7 \quad 0.8), G(M)) = 0.011;$
$S((400 \quad 450 \quad 500 \quad 550),(0.5 \quad 0.6 \quad 0.7 \quad 0.8), E(H) = 0.002;$
$S((1.5 \quad 1.6 \quad 1.7 \quad 1.8),(0.7 \quad 0.8 \quad 0.9 \quad 1), G(M)) = 0.265;$
$S((110 \quad 120 \quad 130 \quad 140),(0.7 \quad 0.8 \quad 0.9 \quad 1), B(H)) = 0.008$

For 17 rule:

$S((270 \quad 280 \quad 290 \quad 300),(0.5 \quad 0.6 \quad 0.7 \quad 0.8), G(M)) = 0.011;$
$S((400 \quad 450 \quad 500 \quad 550),(0.5 \quad 0.6 \quad 0.7 \quad 0.8), E(H) = 0.002;$
$S((1.5 \quad 1.6 \quad 1.7 \quad 1.8),(0.7 \quad 0.8 \quad 0.9 \quad 1), B(H)) = 0.526;$
$S((110 \quad 120 \quad 130 \quad 140),(0.7 \quad 0.8 \quad 0.9 \quad 1), G(M)) = 0.003$

For 18 rule:

$S((270 \quad 280 \quad 290 \quad 300),(0.5 \quad 0.6 \quad 0.7 \quad 0.8), G(M)) = 0.011;$
$S((400 \quad 450 \quad 500 \quad 550),(0.5 \quad 0.6 \quad 0.7 \quad 0.8), E(H)) = 0.002;$
$S((1.5 \quad 1.6 \quad 1.7 \quad 1.8),(0.7 \quad 0.8 \quad 0.9 \quad 1), B(H)) = 0.526;$
$S((110 \quad 120 \quad 130 \quad 140),(0.7 \quad 0.8 \quad 0.9 \quad 1), B(H)) = 0.008$

For 19 rule:

$S((270 \quad 280 \quad 290 \quad 300),(0.5 \quad 0.6 \quad 0.7 \quad 0.8), G(M)) = 0.011;$
$S((400 \quad 450 \quad 500 \quad 550),(0.5 \quad 0.6 \quad 0.7 \quad 0.8), G(M) = 0.005;$
$S((1.5 \quad 1.6 \quad 1.7 \quad 1.8),(0.7 \quad 0.8 \quad 0.9 \quad 1), E(H)) = 0.159;$
$S((110 \quad 120 \quad 130 \quad 140),(0.7 \quad 0.8 \quad 0.9 \quad 1), G(M)) = 0.003$

For 20 rule:

$S((270 \quad 280 \quad 290 \quad 300),(0.5 \quad 0.6 \quad 0.7 \quad 0.8), G(M)) = 0.011;$
$S((400 \quad 450 \quad 500 \quad 550),(0.5 \quad 0.6 \quad 0.7 \quad 0.8), G(M) = 0.005;$
$S((1.5 \quad 1.6 \quad 1.7 \quad 1.8),(0.7 \quad 0.8 \quad 0.9 \quad 1), E(H)) = 0.159;$
$S((110 \quad 120 \quad 130 \quad 140),(0.7 \quad 0.8 \quad 0.9 \quad 1), B(H)) = 0.008$

For 21 rule:

$S((270 \quad 280 \quad 290 \quad 300),(0.5 \quad 0.6 \quad 0.7 \quad 0.8), G(M)) = 0.011;$
$S((400 \quad 450 \quad 500 \quad 550),(0.5 \quad 0.6 \quad 0.7 \quad 0.8), G(M)) = 0.005;$
$S((1.5 \quad 1.6 \quad 1.7 \quad 1.8),(0.7 \quad 0.8 \quad 0.9 \quad 1), G(M)) = 0.265;$
$S((110 \quad 120 \quad 130 \quad 140),(0.7 \quad 0.8 \quad 0.9 \quad 1), G(M)) = 0.003$

For 22 rule:

$S((270 \quad 280 \quad 290 \quad 300),(0.5 \quad 0.6 \quad 0.7 \quad 0.8), G(M)) = 0.011;$
$S((400 \quad 450 \quad 500 \quad 550),(0.5 \quad 0.6 \quad 0.7 \quad 0.8), G(M)) = 0.005;$
$S((1.5 \quad 1.6 \quad 1.7 \quad 1.8),(0.7 \quad 0.8 \quad 0.9 \quad 1), G(M)) = 0.265;$
$S((110 \quad 120 \quad 130 \quad 140),(0.7 \quad 0.8 \quad 0.9 \quad 1), B(H)) = 0.008$

For 23 rule:

$S((270 \quad 280 \quad 290 \quad 300),(0.5 \quad 0.6 \quad 0.7 \quad 0.8), G(M)) = 0.011;$
$S((400 \quad 450 \quad 500 \quad 550),(0.5 \quad 0.6 \quad 0.7 \quad 0.8), G(M) = 0.005;$
$S((1.5 \quad 1.6 \quad 1.7 \quad 1.8),(0.7 \quad 0.8 \quad 0.9 \quad 1), B(H)) = 0.526;$
$S((110 \quad 120 \quad 130 \quad 140),(0.7 \quad 0.8 \quad 0.9 \quad 1), G(M)) = 0.003$

For 24 rule:

$S((270 \quad 280 \quad 290 \quad 300), (0.5 \quad 0.6 \quad 0.7 \quad 0.8), G(M)) = 0.011;$

$S((400 \quad 450 \quad 500 \quad 550), (0.5 \quad 0.6 \quad 0.7 \quad 0.8), G(M)) = 0.005;$

$S((1.5 \quad 1.6 \quad 1.7 \quad 1.8), (0.7 \quad 0.8 \quad 0.9 \quad 1), B(H)) = 0.526;$

$S((110 \quad 120 \quad 130 \quad 140), (0.7 \quad 0.8 \quad 0.9 \quad 1), B(H)) = 0.008$

For 25 rule:

$S((270 \quad 280 \quad 290 \quad 300), (0.5 \quad 0.6 \quad 0.7 \quad 0.8), B(H)) = 0.004;$

$S((400 \quad 450 \quad 500 \quad 550), (0.5 \quad 0.6 \quad 0.7 \quad 0.8), B(H)) = 0.001;$

$S((1.5 \quad 1.6 \quad 1.7 \quad 1.8), (0.7 \quad 0.8 \quad 0.9 \quad 1), B(H)) = 0.526;$

$S((110 \quad 120 \quad 130 \quad 140), (0.7 \quad 0.8 \quad 0.9 \quad 1), B(H)) = 0.008$

For 26 rule:

$S((270 \quad 280 \quad 290 \quad 300), (0.5 \quad 0.6 \quad 0.7 \quad 0.8), B(H)) = 0.004;$

$S((400 \quad 450 \quad 500 \quad 550), (0.5 \quad 0.6 \quad 0.7 \quad 0.8), B(H)) = 0.001;$

$S((1.5 \quad 1.6 \quad 1.7 \quad 1.8), (0.7 \quad 0.8 \quad 0.9 \quad 1), G(M)) = 0.265;$

$S((110 \quad 120 \quad 130 \quad 140), (0.7 \quad 0.8 \quad 0.9 \quad 1), B(H)) = 0.008.$

Second, we computed activation degrees of the rules by using (3.21). Some of the results are shown below:

$$\rho_1 = \min(0.01, 0.002, 0.16, 0.0009) = 0.0009;$$
$$\rho_1 = \min(0.01, 0.002, 0.16, 0.008) = 0.002;$$

$$\rho_{26} = \min(0.003, 0.001, 0.26, 0.008) = 0.001.$$

On the basis of the activation degrees we computed the coefficients of linear interpolation:

$$w_1 = \frac{\rho_1}{\sum_{j=1}^{26} \rho_j} = 0.01, \quad w_2 = \frac{\rho_2}{\sum_{j=1}^{26} \rho_j} = 0.03, ..., \quad w_{26} = \frac{\rho_{26}}{\sum_{j=1}^{26} \rho_j} = 0.02;$$

The resulting output Z'_{Y^1} is computed by using (3.20) as follows:

$$Z'_{y1} = 0.01 * E(H) + 0.03 * G(M) + 0.01 * E(H) + 0.03 * G(M) + 0.03 * A(M)$$
$$+ 0.03 * B(H) + 0.01 * E(H) + 0.04 * G(M) + 0.04 * G(M) + 0.08 * G(M)$$
$$+ 0.04 * G(M) + 0.08 * B(H) + 0.01 * E(H) + 0.03 * A(M) + 0.03 * G(M)$$
$$+ 0.03 * A(M) + 0.03 * A(M) + 0.03 * B(H) + 0.04 * G(M) + 0.08 * A(M)$$
$$+ 0.04 * A(M) + 0.08 * B(H) + 0.04 * B(H) + 0.08 * T(H) + 0.02 * T(H)$$
$$+ 0.02 * T(H) = (33.16 \quad 37.59 \quad 46.7 \quad 50)(0.007 \quad 0.02 \quad 0.14 \quad 0.15)$$

The resulting output Z'_{y2} is

$$Z'_{y2} = 0.01 * E(H) + 0.03 * G(M) + 0.01 * E(H) + 0.03 * G(M) + 0.03 * A(M)$$
$$+ 0.03 * B(H) + 0.01 * E(H) + 0.07 * G(M) + 0.07 * G(M) + 0.05 * G(M)$$
$$+ 0.07 * G(M) + 0.05 * B(H) + 0.01 * E(H) + 0.03 * A(M) + 0.03 * G(M)$$
$$+ 0.03 * A(M) + 0.03 * A(M) + 0.03 * B(H) + 0.07 * G(M) + 0.05 * A(M)$$
$$+ 0.07 * A(M) + 0.05 * B(H) + 0.07 * B(H) + 0.05 * T(H) + 0.02 * T(H)$$
$$+ 0.02 * T(H) = (35.8 \quad 37.1 \quad 41.53 \quad 54.42)(0.11 \quad 0.41 \quad 0.73 \quad 0.74)$$

Now, we need to compare the Z-numbers Z'_{y1}, Z'_{y2} by using the FPO principle. The obtained results are $do(Z'_{y1}) = 0.04, do(Z'_{y2}) = 1$. Thus, the best alloy is Alloy 2.

3.5. Material selection methodology on the basis of fuzzy expert systems

3.5.1. *Expert System ESPLAN*

Expert systems are important and wide class of knowledge-based systems which are used in solving real-world problems in various fields.

The ESPLAN shell allows to construct fuzzy If-Then rules based fuzzy expert systems for various applications. The main functions of

ESPLAN includes: building module-oriented structures and knowledge bases segmentation; representation of fuzzy values; compositional inference with possibility measures; arithmetic operations with fuzzy numbers; realization of simple user-machine dialogue; the use of a confidence degree for any rule; call of external programs; data interchange using file system. The flowchart of the expert system shell ESPLAN is shown in Fig. 3.13.

The antecedent of each If-Then rule contains logical connectives like $\begin{Bmatrix} = \\ \neq \end{Bmatrix}$ <linguistic value> named elementary antecedent.

The consequent of the rule is a list of imperatives, among which may be some operator-functions (i.e. input and output of objects' values, operations with segments of a knowledge base, etc). A confidence degree $Cf \in [0,100]$ can be used for each rule.

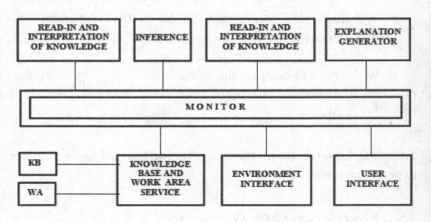

Fig. 3.13. Expert system shell ESPLAN.

Linguistic values are described by membership functions. The subsystem of fuzzy arithmetic provides automatic interpretation of linguistic values like "approximately A", "less than A", "more than A", "middle", "much", "high", "low", "near...", "from ... to..." and so on. The trapezoidal fuzzy numbers are used:

less than A: $(0, I, A - Z, Z)$

approximately A: (Z, A, A, Z)

more than a : $(Z, A + Z, S, 0)$

neutral:

much : $(Z, S - Z, S, 0)$

etc

where I and S are lower and upper bounds of universe, $Z = (S - I)/5$.

ESPLAN shell system has a lot of automatic interpretable linguistic values which are represented by using trapezoidal fuzzy numbers:

little more <X> from <X> to <Y> strictly less <X>

large less <X> <X> -:- <Y> strictly more <X>

middle about <X>

Everywhere linguistic values are allowed, membership function may be obviously determined in simplificated Modified LR-format (trapezoidal fuzzy number) :

mf(<left deviation>,<left peak>,<right peak>,<right deviation>)

User may define his own linguistic values by using the following statement :

LINGV(<object name>,<linguistic value>,<left deviation>,<left peak>,

<right peak>,<right deviation>).

The fuzzy If-Then rules are of described as:

$$R^k: IF \; x_1 \; is \; \tilde{A}_{k1} \; and \; x_2 \; is \; \tilde{A}_{k2} \; and \ldots and \; x_m \; is \; \tilde{A}_{km} \; THEN \qquad (3.23)$$

$$u_{k1} \; is \; \tilde{B}_{k1} \; and \; u_{k2} \; is \; \tilde{B}_{k2} \; and \ldots and \; u_{k1} \; is \; \tilde{B}_{k1}, \quad k = \overline{1, K}$$

where $x_i, i = \overline{1, m}$ and $u_j, j = \overline{1, l}$ are total input and local output variables (crisp or fuzzy variables), $\tilde{A}_{ki}, \tilde{B}_{kj}$ are fuzzy sets, and k is the number of rules, (tilde denotes type-1 fuzzy set).

Let us shortly describe the inference mechanism. Given current inputs, activation degrees of If-Then rules in the knowledge base are computed. Net consequents are computed for the rules activation degrees of which exceed some threshold. The assigned value of the object is also complemented by a numeric confidence degree.

The algorithm of inference mechanism is as follows.

1. First the objects are evaluated, i.e. every w_i object has appropriate value defined as (v_k, cf_k), where v_k is linguistic value, $cf \in [0,1000]$ is confidence degree of the value v_k. Then it is needed to compute:

$$r_{jk} = Poss\left(\tilde{v}_k \, / \, \tilde{a}_{jk}\right) \cdot cf_k,, \text{ if the sign is "="}$$

or

$$r_k = \left(1 - Poss\left(\tilde{v}_k \, \middle| \, \tilde{a}_{jk}\right)\right) cf_k,, \text{ if the sign is "} \neq \text{"}.$$

Poss is defined as

$$Poss\left(\tilde{v} \, \middle| \, \tilde{a}\right) = \max_u \min\left(\mu_{\tilde{v}}(u), \mu_{\tilde{a}}(u)\right) \in [0,1] \; \tau_j = \min\left(r_{jk}\right)$$

a_{jk}- current linguistic value (j is index of the rule, k is index of fuzzy relation)

2. For each rule, calculate

$$R_j = \left(\min_j r_{jk}\right) * CF_j \, / \, 100.$$

The user assigns the threshold (π) and $R_j \geq \pi$ is checked. If the condition holds true, then the consequent part of rule is calculated.

3. The evaluated w_i objects have S_i values [12]:

$$w_i, \left(v_i^1, cf_i^1 \right), \ldots, \ldots, \left(v_i^{S_i}, cf_i^{S_i} \right)$$

The consequents of rules are aggregated into the average:

$$\bar{v}_i = \frac{\sum\limits_{n=1}^{S_i} v_i^n \cdot cf_i^n}{\sum\limits_{n=1}^{S_i} cf_i^n}$$

$$IF\ x_1 = \tilde{a}_1^j\ AND\ x_2 = \tilde{a}_2^j\ AND \ldots THEN\ y_1 = \tilde{b}_1^j\ AND\ y_2 = \tilde{b}_2^j\ AND \ldots$$

$$IF \ldots THEN\ Y_1 = AVRG(y_1)\ AND\ Y_2 = AVRG(y_2)\ AND \ldots$$

This model has a built-in function AVRG which calculates the average value. This function simplifies the implementation of compositional inference with possibility measures. As a possibility measure, here a confidence degree is used. So, the compositional relation is given as a set of rules like

$$IF\ x_1 = \tilde{A}_1^j\ AND\ x_2 = \tilde{A}_2^j \ldots THEN\ y_1 = \tilde{B}_1^j\ AND\ y_2 = \tilde{B}_2^j\ AND,$$

where j is a number of a rule. After all these rules have been executed (with different truth degrees) the next rule (rules) ought to be executed:

$$IF\ THEN\ Y_1 = AVRG(y_1)\ AND\ Y_2 = AVRG(y_2)\ AND \ldots$$

Using this model one may construct hypotheses. Such system contains the rules:

$$IF < \text{condition}_j > THEN\ X = \tilde{A}_j\ CONFIDENCE\ cf_j$$

Here "$X = \tilde{A}_j$" is a hypothesis that the object X takes the value $\tilde{A}_j$. Using some preliminary information, this system generates elements $X = \left(\tilde{A}_j, R_j \right)$, where R_j is a truth degree of jth rule. In order to account the hypothesis (i.e. to estimate the truth degree that X takes the value A_j the recurrent Bayes-Shortliffe formula generalized for the case of fuzzy hypotheses, is used:

$$P_0 = 0$$

$$P_j = P_{j-1} + cf_j \, Poss\left(\tilde{A}_0 \, / \, \tilde{A} \right)\left(1 - \frac{P_{j-1}}{100} \right)$$

This formula is realized as a built-in function BS :

$$\text{IF END THEN } P = BS\left(X, \tilde{A}_0 \right).$$

3.5.2. Statement of the problem

Let us consider solving material selection problem for Turbine Blade by using fuzzy expert system ESPLAN.

The basic problem is to evaluate the performance index of alloys given fuzzy values of characteristics: Density, Weldability, Corrosion, Toughness, Strength. Expert opinion based description of dependence between performance index and the characteristics can be expressed in the form of (3.23) as:

IF Density(D) = good AND Weldability (W)= excellent AND Corrosion(C)=good AND Toughness(T)= good AND Strength(S)=good THEN Performance(P)=good

IF Density(D) = good AND Weldability (W)= excellent AND Corrosion(C)=bad AND Toughness(T)= bad AND Strength(S)=bad THEN Performance(P)=terrible

IF Density(D) = good AND Weldability (W)= good AND Corrosion(C)=bad AND Toughness(T)= bad AND Strength(S)=bad THEN Performance(P)=terrible

IF Density(D) = excellent AND Weldability (W)= excellent AND Corrosion(C)= good AND Toughness(T)= good AND Strength(S)= good THEN Performance(P)=excellent

For instance, object= "density", I=minimum=2, S=maximum=10, and linguistic term="good" is $(1.5, 2.75, 3.25, 1.5)$.

In this context we define all the basic objects and linguistic terms according to ESPLAN shell. The fragment of representation of the object and linguistic terms is given below in Fig. 3.14.

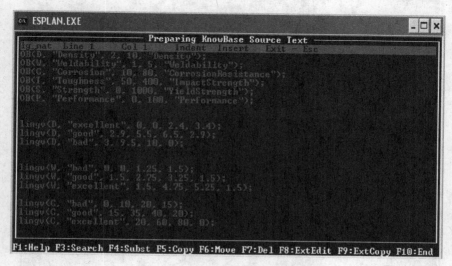

Fig. 3.14. Basic objects and linguistic terms.

Fragments of the preparation of the knowledge base by using ESPLAN shell are illustrated in Figs. 3.15 and 3.16.

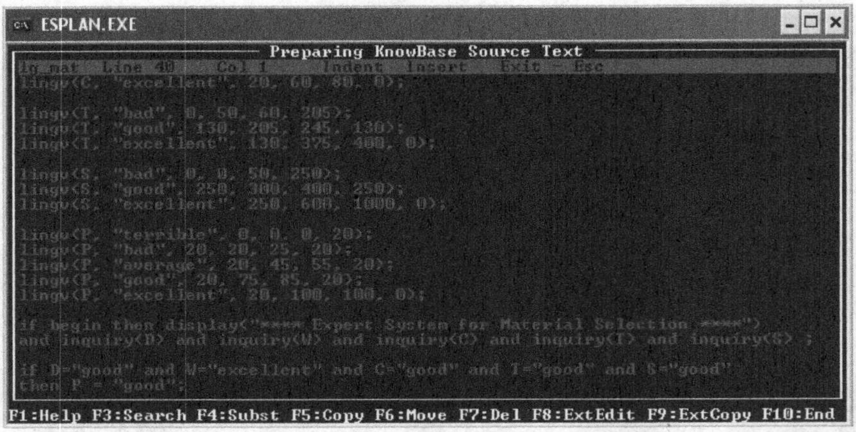

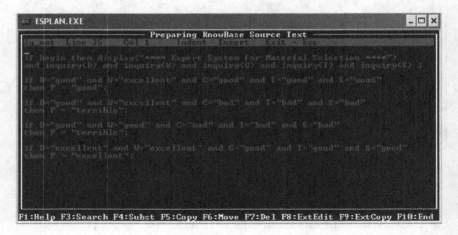

Fig. 3.15. Fragment of the preparation of the knowledge base.

Fig. 3.16. Fragment of the preparation of the knowledge base.

Let us consider computation of performance index of alloys on the basis of the given fuzzy rules in ESPLAN shell.

Test 1. *IF Density(D) = good AND Weldability (W)= excellent AND Corrosion(C)=bad AND Toughness(T)= bad AND Strength(S)=good THEN*
Define Performance(P) =?

The considered fuzzy values of characteristics are entered to the expert system as initial data (Fig. 3.17). The obtained result is represented in Figs. 3.18-3.21.

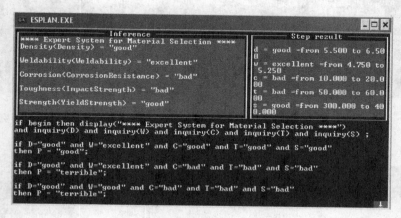

Fig. 3.17. Entering data as initial data.

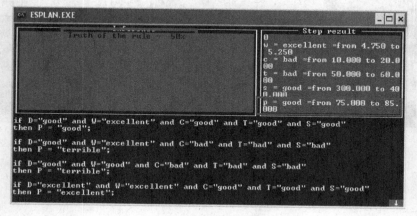

Fig. 3.18. Computation of the result.

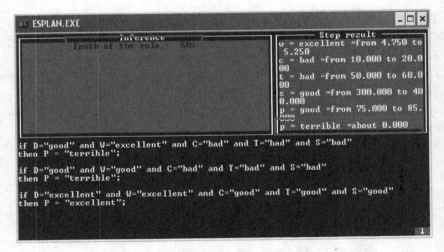

Fig. 3.19. Computation of the result (*Continued*).

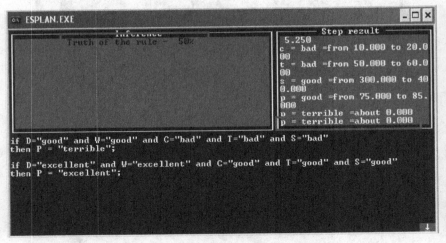

Fig. 3.20. Computation of the result (*Continued*).

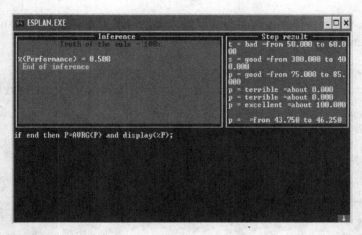

Fig. 3.21. The obtained result is P = from 43.750 to 46.250 with confidence degree 0.5.

Test 1(result). *IF Density(D) = good AND Weldability (W)= excellent AND Corrosion(C)=bad AND Toughness(T)= bad AND Strength(S)=good THEN*

Defined Performance(P) = from 43.750 to 46.250

Test 2. *IF Density(D) = excellent AND Weldability (W)= excellent AND Corrosion(C)=good AND Toughness(T)= bad AND Strength(S)=good THEN* **Define Performance(P) =?**

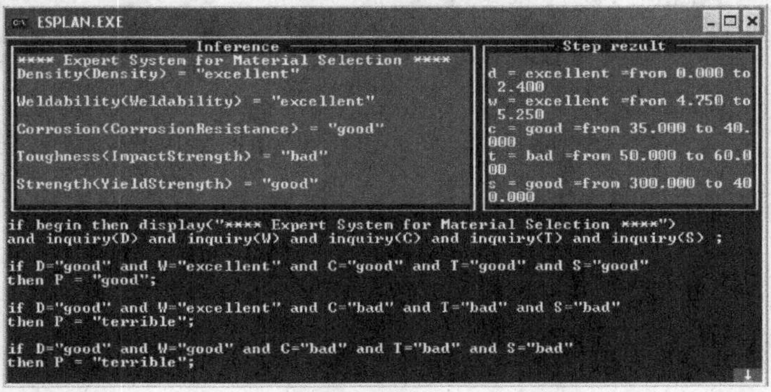

Fig. 3.22. Initial data.

The following entered data (Fig. 3.22) and the obtained result are represented below Figs. 3.23-3.26.

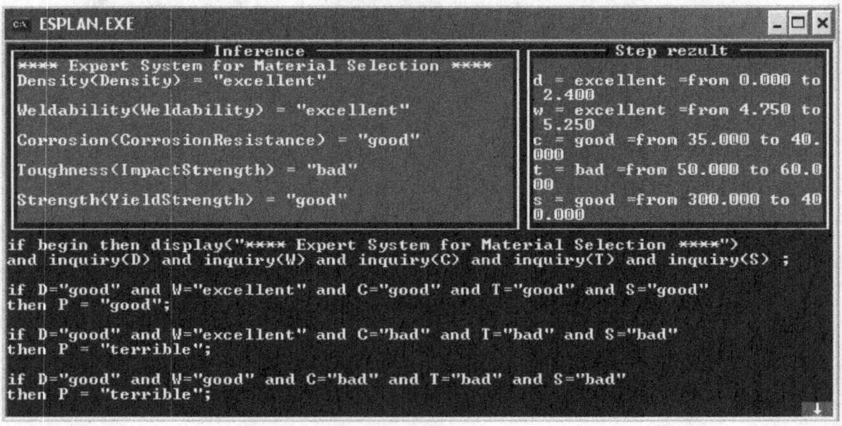

Fig. 3.22. (*Continued*).

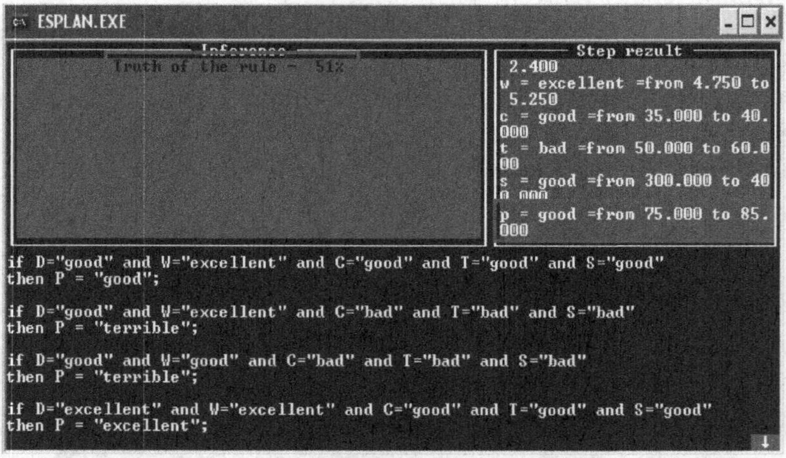

Fig. 3.23. Computation of the result.

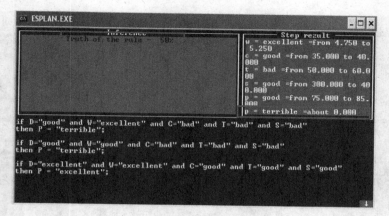

Fig. 3.24. Computation of the result (*Continued*).

Test 2(result). *IF Density(D) = excellent AND Weldability (W)= excellent AND Corrosion(C)=good AND Toughness(T)= bad AND Strength(S)=good THEN* **Defined Performance(P) = from 45.690 to 48.138**

The results are shown in Figs. 3.25, 3.26.

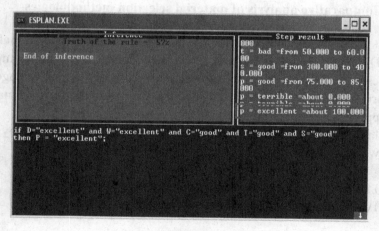

Fig. 3.25. Computation of the result (*Continued*).

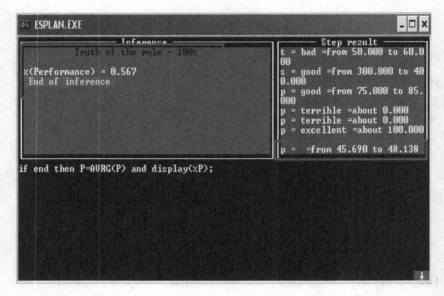

Fig. 3.26. Obtained result P = from 45.690 to 48.138 with confidence degree 0.567.

3.6. Comparative analysis of material selection methodologies

As it was mentioned in Chapter 2, multi-criteria decision-making (MCDM) is used for selection of new materials with complex application, and when each material has a competitive advantage in performance criteria [114]. In this section we try to shortly systematize the approaches to material selection overviewed in Section 2.1.

Mainly, the material selection problems are characterized by the following aspects:

1) the use of both quantitative and qualitative criteria
2) difficulties of assignment of criteria weights

3) scaling problems

4) imperfect decision relevant information.

In order to address the first three aspects, several methods such as AHP method, modified digital logic (MDL) method, Z-transformation method and others are applied [89, 129, 178, 214]. These methods are based on systematic procedures that increase reliability of results. However, they are characterized by intensive involvement of a decision maker and some of them may not be practical when dealing with a large number of criteria.

In order to escape these complexities to some extent and achieve better tradeoff between efficiency and computational complexity, other existing methods can be used including TOPSIS, EXPROM, CORPAS and VIKOR. EVAMIX and CORPAS methods are practically effective methods to account for various factors and requirements including ordinal and cardinal choice criteria [58].

VIKOR method is characterized by relatively higher performance than several existing methods in solving material selection problems [57]. This method allows to determine optimal and compromise (near-optimal) solutions.

In order to achieve additional performance, combination of the existing methods such as a combination of the TOPSIS method [116] and the objective weighting method, TOPSIS and AHP methods and other alternative approaches are used.

In order to resolve the fourth aspect of real-world material selection problems, it is needed to account for imprecision and partial reliability of information on criteria evaluations and criteria weights. In order to account for imprecision, fuzzy extensions of VIKOR, TOPSIS, EXPROM2 and ELECTRE are applied [96,100].

The modern view on combination of fuzzy and probabilistic uncertainties involves use of Z-numbers. This allows to account for partial reliability of information on material characteristics stemming from subjective evaluations, incompleteness of data, complex relationships of characteristics, etc [31].

Chapter 4

Intelligent System for Synthesis of Materials with Characteristics Required

4.1. Statement of material synthesis problem

Assume that big data on smart materials sourced from experiments is available. These big data describe relationship between alloy composition and its characteristics (Table 4.1).

Table 4.1. Big data of relationship between alloy composition and its characteristics.

Experiment	Alloy composition (in %)		Conditions		Alloy characteristics		
#	Metal1, y_1	... Metal n, y_n	Cond.1 ...	Cond.l	Char. 1, z_1	...	Char. m, z_m
1	y_{11}	... y_{1n}	T_{11}	... T_{1l}	z_{11}	...	z_{1m}
s	y_{s1}	... y_{sn}	T_{s1}	... T_{sl}	z_{s1}	...	z_{sm}

The problem is to extract knowledge based model from considered data and to find an alloy composition which provides a predefined alloy characteristics. The problem is solved as follows [30].

First, fuzzy clustering of the big data is applied to determine fuzzy clusters $C_1, C_2, ..., C_K$.

149

Second, fuzzy IF-THEN rules based model is constructed from $C_1, C_2, ..., C_K$:

$$IF\ y_1\ is\ A_{k1}\ and\ ,...,and\ y_n\ is\ A_{kn}\ THEN\ z_1\ is\ B_{k1}\ and\ ,...,$$
$$and\ z_m\ is\ B_{km},\ k = 1,...,K$$

Third, fuzzy inference is implemented on the basis of the fuzzy IF-THEN rules to compute optimal values $B'_1, ..., B'_m$ of alloy characteristics $z_1, ..., z_m$. We propose to implement fuzzy inference by using linear interpolation (see Section 3.4.4). Optimal values $B'_1, ..., B'_m$ are found as those closed to the ideal vector of characteristics $B^* = (B_1^*, ..., B_m^*)$.

4.2. Z-clustering of materials data

4.2.1. *State-of-the-art*

With the explosive development of knowledge discovery from data, a key issue that can significantly affect the predefined generalization performance of resulting knowledge became the study of the reliability issue in knowledge discovery.

Reliability problems in knowledge discovery often arise when user deals with data drawn from too small sample or uncertain, incomplete, partially reliable database. Indeed real-world information in large and big data sets is often partially reliable due to partial reliability of data, restricted confidence, etc. There are different approaches for knowledge extraction from data, such as expert driven and data driven.

The most popular technique in this trend is association rule mining using clustering approach to transform data available into knowledge. K-means, fuzzy C-means, model-based clustering methods and others are most commonly used methods in this trend.

Clustering is very important unsupervised technique in data mining. It is efficient for large data analysis and knowledge discovery. Given a data set $X = \{x_1, x_2, ..., x_N\} \subset R^q$, the clustering technique partitions X into C clusters such that data element within a cluster posses high similarity. Clustering is usually classified as hard clustering and soft clustering [45,97,161].

In hard partition-based clustering, crisp sets of data elements are used. In contrast, soft clustering uses gradual assessment of membership of data elements in clusters. In general, hard clustering may be viewed as a special case of soft clustering [196]. Soft clustering can be categorized into probabilistic clustering and fuzzy clustering. When a data element's membership in a cluster is represented by probability, the corresponding clustering is called probabilistic clustering [45]. When a membership of a data element in a cluster is fuzzy membership, the corresponding clustering is called fuzzy clustering [42,45]. A variety of soft clustering methods exist; they basically are devoted to probabilistic clustering [45,117,204] or fuzzy clustering [42,157]. The main representations of probabilistic clustering are Expectation–Maximization method, probabilistic d-clustering, probabilistic exponential d-clustering, etc.

Fuzzy clustering includes type-1 clustering (FCM, PCM, PFCM, KFCM, etc.) [42,125,126], type-2 clustering (T2FCM, KT2FCM) [13,18,125,159], and intuitionistic clustering (IFCM etc.) [54,216].

Unfortunately, in all existing clustering methods reliability of processing information and resulting knowledge is not taken into consideration.

Reliability of knowledge discovery from data set by clustering approach is related to bimodal distribution, e.g. mix of possibility and probability distributions [9,20,213]. The main representative of bimodal distributions is the Z-number concept.

Indeed, as it is shown in [161,196] the relationship between fuzzy concept and probabilistic concept should be rather collaborative than exclusive. However, up to date, there is no paper that deals with combination of fuzzy clustering and probabilistic clustering. The use of concept of Z-number may build the bridge between probabilistic and fuzzy clustering approaches and give possibility to estimate reliability of resulting knowledge obtained from data set.

In this study the concept of Z-number is used for clustering of large data sets with reliability of discovered knowledge.

Two approaches to clustering of data are considered in this section. The first approach is based on new compound objective function optimization. The second approach is based on the theorem on relations between monotonic Type-2 fuzzy sets and Z-numbers [9,17]. Differential

Evolution Optimization (DEO) method is used to derive clusters in both approaches.

A numerical example is given that proves validity of the proposed methods.

Definition 4.1. *Bimodal distribution* **[213].** Let X be a real-valued variable taking values in a finite set, U={u_1,...,u_n}. X can be associated with a possibility distribution, μ, and a probability distribution, p, expressed as:

$$\mu = \mu_1 / u_1 + \cdots + \mu_n / u_n,$$
$$p = p_1 \setminus u_1 + \cdots + p_n \setminus u_n.$$

where μ_i / u_i implies that $\mu_i, i = 1,...,n$, is the possibility that X=u_i. Similarly, p_i / u_i implies that p_i is the probability that X=u_i.

The possibility distribution, μ, may be combined with the probability distribution, p, through what is referred to as confluence:

$$\mu : p = (\mu_1, p_1) / u_1 + \cdots + (\mu_n, p_n) / u_n.$$

Distributions μ and p are compatible if the centroids of μ and p are coincident, that is,

$$\sum_{i=1}^{n} u_i p_i = \frac{\sum_{i=1}^{n} u_i \mu_i}{\sum_{i=1}^{n} \mu_i}.$$

This condition is referred to as compatibility condition [213].

Definition 4.2. *Z-valuation and Z-information* **[213].** A Z-valuation is an ordered triple of the form (X, A, B), and (A, B) is a Z-number. Equivalently, a Z-valuation (X, A, B), is a Z-restriction on X,

$$(X,A,B) \rightarrow X \text{ is } (A,B).$$

A collection of Z-valuations is referred to as Z-information.

Definition 4.3. *Differential Evolution Optimization.* Differential Evolution (DE) is an evolutionary optimization method very suitable for numerical processing. As many of its counterparts it is a global search method, does not pose any constraints (convexity, continuity, differentiability, etc.) on function to optimize. Additionally, DE is characterized by fast convergence and wide customization flexibility to include different search strategies, constraints on variables, multiple-objectives, fuzzy processing and others. DE has been efficient in solving a large variety of problems such as image recognition, clustering, optimization etc.

DE algorithm uses randomly generated initial population, differential mutation, probability crossover, and selection operators. The main idea of the algorithm is to extract distance and direction of information for search directly from the population. The algorithm is described in details in [13].

Definition 4.4. *Type-2 fuzzy clustering* [13]. In the FCM-like family of fuzzy clustering, the fuzzification coefficient m (fuzzifier) plays a visible role as it directly translates into the shape (geometry) of resulting fuzzy clusters. Most frequently the value of fuzzifier m is set to 2. However, to get the quality cluster partition it may be worthy to consider a range of values. This led to the fuzzy type-2 clustering idea (see references in [13,18]), where they consider an interval valued fuzzifier $[m_L, m_R]$ instead a crisp value as in the traditional FCM. The interval memberships $[\underline{u}_{ij}, \overline{u}_{ij}]$ of vector $\mathbf{x}_i$ to cluster c_i can be computed as follows:

$$\underline{u}_{ij} = \min\left(\frac{1}{\sum_{l=1}^{c}\left(d_{ij}/d_{il}\right)^{2/(m_L-1)}}, \frac{1}{\sum_{l=1}^{c}\left(d_{ij}/d_{il}\right)^{2/(m_R-1)}}\right),$$

$$\overline{u}_{ij} = \max\left(\frac{1}{\sum_{l=1}^{c}\left(d_{ij}/d_{il}\right)^{2/(m_L-1)}}, \frac{1}{\sum_{l=1}^{c}\left(d_{ij}/d_{il}\right)^{2/(m_R-1)}}\right).$$

$$(4.1)$$

The interval cluster positions can be expressed as follows:

$$\tilde{c}_j = [c_j^L, c_j^R] = \sum_{u_{1j}} \cdots \sum_{u_{nj}} 1 \Bigg/ \frac{\sum_{i=1}^{n} x_i u_{ij}^m}{\sum_{i=1}^{n} u_{ij}^m} \tag{4.2}$$

where m switches from m_L to m_R as shown above.

The value of *m* has a direct impact on clustering quality. In order to account for fuzziness in the input data researchers proposed General Type-2 (GT2) FCM algorithm, which allows linguistic expression of the fuzzifier value. The resulting cluster membership functions can be implemented using the α-planes theorem (see references in [13,18]).

4.2.2. *Z-clustering using a new compound function*

Assume that data set D is given and consists of N data points:

$$D = \{x_1, x_2, \ldots, x_N\} \subset R^q.$$

It is needed to partition D into C clusters $c_j, j = \overline{1, C}$. Clusters c_j are described by Z-numbers: $c_j = (A_j, B_j)$.

It is needed to assign points to clusters in the sense that the membership of a data point x in a cluster c_j is given as a fuzzy membership degree and probability value. Formally, the problem is formulated as a multicriterial optimization problem as follows [11].

$$J = (J_m, J_p)$$
$$= \left(\sum_{i=1}^{N} \sum_{j=1}^{C} U_{ij}^m \|x_i - c_j\|^2, \sum_{i=1}^{N} \sum_{j=1}^{C} (\|x_i - c_j\| p_j(x_i))^2 \right) \to \min \tag{4.3}$$

where

$$U_{ij}^m = \frac{1}{\sum_{k=1}^{C} \left(\frac{\|x_i - c_j\|}{\|x_i - c_k\|} \right)^{\frac{2}{m-1}}} \tag{4.4}$$

$$c_j^m = \frac{\sum\limits_{i=1}^{N} U_{ij}^m \cdot x_i}{\sum\limits_{i=1}^{N} U_{ij}^m}, \tag{4.5}$$

$$U_j(x_i) = \frac{(p_j(x_i))^2}{\|x_i - c_j\|}, \tag{4.6}$$

$$c_j^p = \sum_{i=1}^{N} \left(\frac{U_j(x_i)}{\sum\limits_{i=1}^{N} U_j(x_i)} \right) \cdot x_i, \tag{4.7}$$

$$\sum_{i=1}^{N} p_j(x_i) = 1, \tag{4.8}$$

$$p_j(x_i) \geq 0, \tag{4.9}$$

$$\frac{\sum\limits_{i=1}^{N} U_{ij}^m \cdot x_i}{\sum\limits_{i=1}^{N} U_{ij}^m} = \sum_{i=1}^{N} \left(\frac{U_j(x_i)}{\sum\limits_{i=1}^{N} U_j(x_i)} \right) \cdot x_i. \tag{4.10}$$

Thus, for each data point $x \in D$ we need to compute the distance $\|x_i - c_j\|$, membership degree that x is in c_j, a probability that x is member of c_j.

The use of gradient-based optimization for clustering algorithms upon (FCM is the case) suffer from some disadvantages. In particular, a global minimum may not be found. In view of this, the use of DE algorithm or another population-based algorithm is more adequate.

Solving of problems (4.3)-(4.10) provides clusters characterized by bimodal distribution. Indeed, each cluster is a fusion of membership degrees $U_{ij}^m(x_i)$ and distribution of probabilities $p_j(x_i)$: (U_{ij}^m, p_j). Let us denote a fuzzy part of the bimodal distribution as $A_j(x_i) = U_{ij}^m(x_i)$. Then, the probability measure as a reliability of A_j is computed as

$$P(A_j) = \sum_{i=1}^{N} U_{ij}^m(x_i) \cdot p_j(x_i) \tag{4.11}$$

4.2.3. Z-rule base construction using general fuzzy type-2 clustering

Generalization of Zadeh's extension principle to Z-numbers given in [17] is outlined below.

Let $F : U_1 \times ... \times U_n \to U$ be a function, and for each $i = 1, ..., n$ let $X_i = (\mu_i, v_i)$ be a Z-number, where $\mu_i(x)$ are membership function and v_i are an expert's confidence degrees defined on the universal set U_i. By the result $f(X_1, ..., X_n)$ of applying the function $f(x_1, ..., x_n)$ to the Z-numbers $X_1, ..., X_n$, we mean a function that assigns, to each $v \in [0,1]$, the value

$$\mu_v(y) = \max\{\min(\mu_1(x_1), ..., \mu_n(x_n)) :$$
$$y = f(x_1, ..., x_n) \ and \ v_i(x_i) \geq v \ for \ all \ i\}$$

It is known that if instead of crisp value $\mu(x)$ we use a function that assigns to $\mu(x) \in [0,1]$ a degree $d(\mu(x), x)$, we get type-2 fuzzy set. To each value v we assign a degree $\mu_v(x)$. Consequently, the result of applying data processing to Z-number is a type-2 fuzzy set. The type-2 fuzzy sets obtained by this approach have an additional property, namely monotonicity property [17]. Type-2 fuzzy set $d(\mu(x), x)$ is monotonic if $\mu < \mu'$ implies $d(y, \mu) \geq d(y, \mu')$. This result is described in the following theorem.

Representation Theorem [17]. Every monotonic type-2 fuzzy set $d(y, \mu)$ can be represented as a result of applying an appropriate data processing algorithm $y = f(x_1, ..., x_n)$ to some Z-numbers $X_1, ..., X_n$.

Proof of this theorem is given in [17].

So, every monotonic type-2 fuzzy set can be represented as a result of applying data processing to Z-numbers.

Assume that for every data element from data set, the set of fuzzy type-1 membership degrees of any data point to each of the clusters is $\{\mu_1(x),...,\mu_c(x)\}$. Let's consider a case where the secondary membership function of these data elements is described as a normal distribution Gaussian function. Type-2 membership values can be defined as [207]

$$d_{ik} = \mu_{ik} e^{-\frac{1}{2}\left(\frac{p_{ik}-1}{p_{ik}}\right)^2}, \; i=1,2...,N, \; k=1,2,...,c,$$ (4.12)

where p_{ik} is membership degree of kth data element being a member of the ith corresponding cluster.

This approach to Z-clustering is based on implementation of fuzzy type-2 clustering [13,18] and determination of $p_{ik} = p_k(x_i)$ using (4.11). Then one can obtain reliability of resulting clusters as follows:

$$P_k = \sum_{i=1}^{N} \mu_k(x_i) p_k(x_i)$$

Example. Consider the following two-dimensional data (Fig. 4.1).

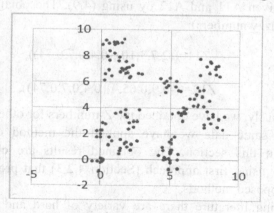

Fig. 4.1. Two-dimensional data.

We applied the approach outlined in Section 4.2.2 to construct Z-valued clusters for these data (with fuzzifier m=2). We have obtained

4 Z-valued clusters, each cluster is composed of membership function, A (fuzzy part) and probability distributions (reliability part). For example, one of the Z-clusters is given below (Fig. 4.2).

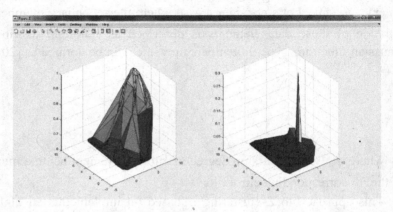

Fig. 4.2. Z-valued cluster: Membership function, A and probability distribution, p.

For this two-dimensional Z-cluster we have obtained two Z-numbers $Z11=(A11,B11)$ and $Z12=(A12,B12)$. The first components A11 and A12 are obtained as two projections, B11 and B12 (reliability parts) are computed given A11 and A12 by using (4.9). The obtained results (as triangular fuzzy numbers):

$$Z11=((2,7.3,10),(0.4,0.7,0.74)),$$

$$Z12=((-0.9,0.65,4)(0.4,0.7,0.74)).$$

Analogously, we have obtained the Z-numbers for other clusters.

For the same data we have applied the method of Z-clustering described in this section. The obtained results are close to results obtained by using first approach (Section 4.2.3) that proves validity of the both proposed methods.

In existing literature there are variety of hard and soft clustering methods such as the deterministic, probabilistic and fuzzy clustering. Unfortunately, in all existing clustering methods reliability of processing information and resulting knowledge is not taken into consideration. In this study for the first time we propose two approaches to soft clustering problem for large data set based on Z-information concept which takes into account reliability of obtained results. The first approach is based on new compound objective function optimization by using DEO. The second approach is based on the theorem on relations between monotonic Type-2 fuzzy sets and Z-numbers [9,17]. A numerical example is given that proves validity of the proposed methods.

4.3. Synthesis of new materials

4.3.1. *Synthesis of Ti-Ni-Pd alloys with given characteristics*

A problem of computational synthesis of Ti-Ni-Pd alloy with predefined characteristics is considered. A big data fragment describing dependence alloy composition and the corresponding characteristics is shown in Table 4.2:

Table 4.2. A big data fragment on Ti-Ni-Pd alloy composition [93].

Composition			Transformation temperatures			
x_1 (Ni,%)	x_2 (Ti,%)	x_3 (Pd,%)	y_1(martensitic finish temperature, K)	y_2(martensitic start temperature, K)	y_3(austenitic finish temperature, K)	y_4(austenitic start temperature, K)
41	50	9	322.3	329.4	341.3	331.2
39	50	11	318.2	335.7	347.6	334.7
29	50	21	406.4	424.5	440.3	426.6
20	50	30	515.3	533.8	546.8	534.9

A problem of computational synthesis is related to determination of alloy composition with corresponding values of the characteristics close to the target values:

$$z_1 = (302.3), z_2 = (323.3), z_3 = (347.1), z_4 = (331.3)$$

Thus, $B^* = (B_1^*, B_2^*, B_3^*) = ((302.3), (323.3), (347.1), (331.3))$ can be considered as an ideal solution.

In order to describe relationship between alloy composition and the characteristics values, the fuzzy IF-THEN rules were obtained by using FCM clustering of the considered big data:

IF Ni is L and Pd is A2

THEN M_f is A and M_s is A and A_s is a and A_f is A

IF Ni is A and Pd is A1

THEN M_f is L2 and M_s is L2 and A_f is L2 and A_s is L2

IF N_i is H2 and P_d is L1

THEN M_f is VL and M_s is VL and A_s is L and A_f is VL

IF Ni is H1 and Pd is L2

THEN M_f is L1 and M_s is L1 and A_f is L1 and A_s is L1

IF Ni is VH and Pd is VH

THEN M_f is H and M_s is H and A_f is VH and A_s is VH

The codebooks for inputs are shown in Tables 4.3 and 4.4.

Table 4.3. Codebook for input 1, Ni.

#	Linguistic value	TFN	
1.	Very Low (VL)	(3, 3, 13.5)	(1)
2.	Low (L)	(3, 13.5, 24)	(2)
3.	Average (A)	(13.5, 24, 34.5)	(3)
4.	High (H)	(24, 34.5, 45)	(4)
5.	Very High (VH)	(34.5, 45, 45)	(5)

Table 4.4. Codebook for input 2, Pd.

#	Linguistic value	TFN	
1.	Very Low (VL)	(3, 3, 13.75)	(1)
2.	Low (L)	(3, 13.75, 24.5)	(2)
3.	Average (A)	(13.75, 24.5, 35.25)	(3)
4.	High (H)	(24.5, 35.25, 46)	(4)
5.	Very High (VH)	(35.25, 46, 46)	(5)

The linguistic approximation of the inputs are shown in Tables 4.5-4.6.

Table 4.5. Linguistic terms for input 1, Ni.

#	Linguistic value	TFN
1.	Very Low(VL)	(−11.24, 3.977, 19.2)
2.	Low (L)	(6.709, 18.6, 30.48)
3.	Average (A)	(14.53, 24.7, 34.86)
4.	High 1 (H1)	(21.16, 39.33, 57.51)
5.	High 2 (H2)	(20.88, 30.73, 40.59)

Table 4.6. Linguistic terms for input 2, Pd.

#	Linguistic value	TFN
1.	Average 1 (A1)	(21.28, 30.03, 38.78)
2.	Average 2 (A2)	(15.9, 24.9, 33.9)
3.	Low 1 (L1)	(−6.899, 10.58, 28.06)
4.	Low 2 (L2)	(9.962, 19.04, 28.13)
5.	Very High (VH)	(28.8, 43.21, 57.62)

The codebooks for the outputs are shown in Tables 4.7-4.10.

Table 4.7. Linguistic terms for output 1, Mf.

#	Linguistic value	TFN
1.	Average (A)	(394.8, 502.1, 609.5)
2.	Low 1 (L1)	(359.2, 451.3, 543.5)
3.	Very Low (VL)	(199.3, 322.3, 445.2)
4.	Low 2 (L2)	(294.4, 386.8, 479.2)
5.	Very High (VH)	(475.4, 674.5, 873.5)

Table 4.8. Linguistic terms for output 2, Ms.

#	Linguistic value	TFN
1.	Average (A)	(417.4, 523.8, 630.2)
2.	Low 1 (L1)	(369.6, 463.1, 556.6)
3.	Very Low (VL)	(221.4, 338.8, 456.2)
4.	Low 2 (L2)	(306.8, 400.4, 494)
5.	Very High (VH)	(532.2, 717.8, 903.5)

Table 4.9. Linguistic terms for output 3, As.

#	Linguistic value	TFN
1.	Average (A)	(414.3, 527.4, 640.5)
2.	Low 1 (L1)	(374.6, 466.5, 558.4)
3.	Very Low (VL)	(246.3, 354.8, 463.3)
4.	Low 2 (L2)	(319.1, 409, 498.9)
5.	Very High (VH)	(536.5, 730.6, 924.7)

Table 4.10. Linguistic terms for output 4, Af.

#	Linguistic value	TFN
1.	Average (A)	(420.5, 537.7, 654.9)
2.	Low 1 (L1)	(360.5, 471.1, 581.6)
3.	Very Low (VL)	(214.5, 344, 473.6)
4.	Low 2 (L2)	(301.9, 406.6, 511.3)
5.	Very High (VH)	(599.2, 771, 982.8)

The constructed fuzzy model will be used to determine an input vector $A' = (A'_1, ..., A'_n)$ that induces the corresponding output vector $B' = (B'_1, ..., B'_m)$ maximally close to the ideal solution $B^* = (B^*_1, B^*_2, B^*_3)$. We have found that the fuzzy optimal output vector B' induced by the fuzzy input vector $A' = (A'_1, A'_2, A'_3) = (19.5, 50.5, 30)$ is $B' = (B'_1, B'_2, B'_3, B'_4) = ((347.78), (364.86), (382.17), (375.22))$. It is the closest vector to the considered ideal fuzzy vector $B^* = ((302), (323), (347), (313))$. The distance is $D(B', B^*) = 94$. The fuzzy model-based results for Ti-Ni-Pd shows that the optimal alloy composition is: Ni is about 19%, Ti is about 51%, Pd is about 30%. The obtained characteristics: $M_f = 347.78$, about $M_s = 364.86$, about $A_f = 382.17$, and $A_s = 375.22$.

4.3.2. Synthesis of TiNiPt alloys with given characteristics

A problem of computational synthesis of Ti-Ni-Pd alloy with predefined characteristics is considered. A big data fragment describing dependence alloy composition and the corresponding characteristics is shown in Table 4.11:

Table 4.11. Transformation temperatures of Ti-Ni-Pt alloy [191].

Composition			Transformation temperatures	
x_1 (Ni,%)	x_2 (Ti,%)	x_3 (Pt,%)	y_1(martensitic start temperature, K)	y_2(austenitic start temperature, K)
30	50	20	539	544
20	50	30	833	867
15	50	35	953	1023
.				
.				
.				
10	50	40	1173	1123

The following fuzzy IF-THEN rules were obtained by using FCM clustering of the considered big data:

If x_1 is VL and x_3 is VH THEN y_1 is VH and y_2 is VH
If x_1 is H2 and x_3 is L1 THEN y_1 is VL and y_2 is VL
If x_1 is A and x_3 is L3 THEN y_1 is L2 and y_2 is L2
If x_1 is L and x_3 is H THEN y_1 is H and y_2 is H
If x_1 is H1 and x_3 is L2 THEN y_1 is L1 and y_2 is L

The codebooks for inputs are shown in Tables 4.12-4.13.

Table 4.12. Codebook for input 1, x_1.

#	Linguistic value	TFN	
1.	Very Low (VL)	(5, 5, 13.75)	(1)
2.	Low (L)	(5, 13.75, 22.5)	(2)
3.	Average (A)	(13.75, 22.5, 31.25)	(3)
4.	High (H)	(22.5, 31.25, 40)	(4)
5.	Very High (VH)	(31.25, 40, 40)	(5)

Table 4.13. Codebook for input 2, x_3.

#	Linguistic value	TFN	
1.	Very Low (VL)	(10, 10, 18.75)	(1)
2.	Low (L)	(10, 18.75, 27.5)	(2)
3.	Average (A)	(18.75, 27.5, 36.25)	(3)
4.	High (H)	(27.5, 36.25, 45)	(4)
5.	Very High (VH)	(36.25, 45, 45)	(5)

The codebooks for the used inputs linguistic terms are shown in Tables 4.14-4.15.

Table 4.14. Linguistic terms for input 1, Ni.

#	Linguistic value	TFN
1.	Very Low (VL)	(−7.578, 7.535, 22.65)
2.	High 1 (H1)	(25.98, 35.17, 44.35)
3.	Average (A)	(19.27, 26.33, 33.39)
4.	Low (L)	(8.109, 17.64, 27.17)
5.	High 2 (H2)	(21.67, 30.06, 38.48)

Table 4.15. Linguistic terms for input 2, Pt.

#	Linguistic value	TFN
1.	Very High (VH)	(27.18, 42.47, 57.75)
2.	Low 1 (L1)	(5.859, 14.84, 23.82)
3.	Low 2 (L2)	(14.14, 21.78, 29.42)
4.	High (H)	(22.63, 32.36, 42.08)
5.	Low 3 (L3)	(13.71, 19.75, 26.18)

The codebooks for the used outputs are shown in Tables 4.16-4.17.

Table 4.16. Codebook for output 1, y_1.

#	Linguistic value	TFN	
1.	Very Low (VL)	(363, 363, 565.5)	(1)
2.	Low (L)	(363, 565.5, 768)	(2)
3.	Average (A)	(565.5, 768, 970.5)	(3)
4.	High (H)	(768, 970.5, 1173)	(4)
5.	Very High (VH)	(970.5, 1173, 1173)	(5)

Table 4.17. Codebook for output 2, y_2.

#	Linguistic value	TFN	
1.	Very Low (VL)	(373, 373, 585.5)	(1)
2.	Low (L)	(373, 585.5, 798)	(2)
3.	Average (A)	(585.5, 798, 1010.5)	(3)
4.	High (H)	(798, 1010.5, 1223)	(4)
5.	Very High (VH)	(1010.5,1223, 1223)	(5)

By using the procedures applied in the previous case (Section 4.3.1) we have found that the fuzzy optimal output vector B' induced by the fuzzy input vector $A' = (A_1', A_2', A_3') = (40, 50, 10)$ is $B' = ((479.68), (488))$. It is the closest vector to the considered ideal fuzzy vector $B^* = ((363), (373))$. The distance between them is $D(B', B^*) = 164$. The fuzzy model-based results show that the desired alloy composition is: Ti is about 50%, Ni is about 37%, Pt is about 13% and the obtained characteristics are about $M_s = 479.6828$, about $A_s = 488.1005$.

4.3.3. Synthesis of TiNiZr alloys with given characteristics

A fragment of the big data on relationship between composition of alloy and transformation temperatures is given in Table 4.18:

Table 4.18. A fragment of the big data on Ti-Ni-Zr alloy composition [93].

Composition			Transformation temperatures	
x_1 (Ni,%)	x_2 (Ti,%)	x_3 (Zr,%)	y_1 (austenitic finish temperature, K)	y_2 (austenitic start temperature, K)
49.5	49.5	1	388.9	358.3
49.5	47.5	3	395.8	355.6
49.5	40.5	10	428.2	401.8
49.5	35.5	15	505.9	483.4

The following fuzzy IF-THEN rules were obtained by using FCM clustering of the considered big data:

If x_2 is VL and x_3 is VH THEN y_1 is VH and y_2 is H
If x_2 is H and x_3 is L THEN y_1 is L and y_2 is L
If x_2 is L and x_3 is H THEN y_1 is H and y_2 is A

The codebooks for the inputs are given in Tables 4.19-4.20.

Table 4.19. Codebook for input 1, x_2.

#	Linguistic value	TFN	
1.	Very Low (VL)	(26, 26, 31.875)	(1)
2.	Low (L)	(26, 31.875, 37.75)	(2)
3.	Average (A)	(31.875,37.75,43.625)	(3)
4.	High (H)	(37.75, 43.625, 49.5)	(4)
5.	Very High (VH)	(43.625, 49.5, 49.5)	(5)

Table 4.20. Codebook for input 2, x_3.

#	Linguistic value	TFN	
1.	Very Low (VL)	(1, 1, 6.75)	(1)
2.	Low (L)	(1, 6.75, 12.5)	(2)
3.	Average (A)	(6.75, 12.5, 18.25)	(3)
4.	High (H)	(12.5, 18.25, 24)	(4)
5.	Very High (VH)	(18.25, 24, 24)	(5)

The codebooks for the linguistic terms are shown in Tables 4.21-4.22.

Table 4.21. Linguistic terms for input 1, Ti.

#	Linguistic value	TFN
1.	Very Low (VL)	(18.12, 28.21, 38.29)
2.	Low (L)	(26.9, 34.36, 41.82)
3.	High (H)	(22.81, 43.04, 63.28)

Table 4.22. Linguistic terms for input 2, Zr.

#	Linguistic value	TFN
1.	Very High (VH)	(12.09, 22.03, 31.97)
2.	High (H)	(8.41, 16.27, 24.14)
3.	Low (L)	(−12.61, 7.047, 26.7)

The codebooks for the used outputs are shown in Tables 4.23–4.24.

Table 4.23. Codebook for output 1, y_1.

#	Linguistic value	TFN	
1.	Very Low (VL)	(240, 240, 331.6)	(1)
2.	Low (L)	(240, 331.6, 423.2)	(2)
3.	Average (A)	(331.6, 423.2, 514.8)	(3)
4.	High (H)	(423.2, 514.8, 606.4)	(4)
5.	Very High (VH)	(514.8, 606.4, 606.4)	(5)

Table 4.24. Codebook for output 2, y_2.

#	Linguistic value	TFN	
1.	Very Low (VL)	(312, 312, 406)	(1)
2.	Low (L)	(312, 406, 500)	(2)
3.	Average (A)	(406, 500, 594)	(3)
4.	High (H)	(500, 594, 688)	(4)
5.	Very High (VH)	(594, 688, 688)	(5)

The codebooks for the used linguistic terms are shown in Tables 4.25-4.26.

Table 4.25. Linguistic terms for output 1, Ms.

#	Linguistic value	TFN
1.	Very High (VH)	(445.2, 596.7, 748.3)
2.	High (H)	(358.2, 469.9, 581.5)
3.	Low (L)	(217.3, 375.9, 534.6)

Table 4.26. Linguistic terms for output 2, As.

#	Linguistic value	TFN
1.	High (H)	(428.2, 637.3, 846.5)
2.	Average (A)	(366, 494.7, 623.4)
3.	Low (L)	(221.3, 374.9, 528.5)

We have found that the fuzzy optimal output vector B' induced by the fuzzy input vector $A' = (A'_1, A'_2, A'_3) = (50, 44, 7)$ is $B' = ((394), (377))$. It is the closest vector to the considered ideal fuzzy vector $B^* = ((240), (312))$. The distance is $D(B', B^*) = 167$. The fuzzy model-based results for Ti-Ni-Zr shows that the optimal alloy composition is: Ti is 'about 43.5%', Ni is 'about 49.5%', Zr is 'about 7%'. The obtained characteristics: A_f is 'about 393.8644', A_s 'is about 377.1977'.

4.3.4. Computational synthesis of TiNiHf alloys with given characteristics

A fragment of the big data on relationship between composition of Ni-Ti-Hf alloy and transformation temperatures is available (Table 4.27):

Table 4.27. A fragment of the big data on Ni-Ti-Hf alloy composition [106].

Composition			Transformation temperatures			
x_1 (Ni,%)	x_2 (Ti,%)	x_3 (Hf,%)	y_1(martensitic finish temperature, K)	y_2(martensitic start temperature, K)	y_3(austenitic finish temperature, K)	y_4(austenitic start temperature, K)
49.8	46.2	4	325,5	358.8	406,8	368,5
49.8	44.2	6	329,0	363,9	421,4	381.3
49,8	35,2	15	451,0	480,0	530,9	512,0
49,8	30.2	20	546,4	573,1	610,6	595,8

The If-Then rules obtained by using FCM method:

If x_2 is Very High and x_3 is Very Low THEN y_1 is Very Low and y_2 is Very Low and y_3 is Very Low and y_4 is Very Low

If x_2 is Low and x_3 is High THEN y_1 is Average and y_2 is Average and y_3 is Average and y_4 is Average

If x_2 is Average and x_3 is Average THEN y_1 is Low and y_2 is Low and y_3 is Low and y_4 is Low

If x_2 is Very Low and x_3 is Very High THEN y_1 is Very High and y_2 is Very High and y_3 is Very High and y_4 is Very High
The codebooks of inputs are shown in Tables 4.28-4.29.

Table 4.28. Codebook for input 1, Ti.

#	Linguistic value	TFN	
1.	Very Low (VL)	(30, 30, 34.05)	(1)
2.	Low (L)	(30, 34.05, 38.1)	(2)
3.	Average (A)	(34.05, 38.1, 42.15)	(3)
4.	High (H)	(38.1, 42.15, 46.2)	(4)
5.	Very High (VH)	(42.15, 46.2, 46.2)	(5)

Table 4.29. Codebook for input 2, Hf.

#	Linguistic value	TFN	
1.	Very Low (VL)	(4, 4, 8)	(1)
2.	Low (L)	(4, 8, 12)	(2)
3.	Average (A)	(8, 12, 16)	(3)
4.	High (H)	(12, 16, 20)	(4)
5.	Very High (VH)	(16, 20, 20)	(5)

The codebooks for the used terms are shown in Tables 4.30–4.39.

Table 4.30. Linguistic terms for input 1, Ti.

#	Linguistic value	TFN
1.	Very High (VH)	(35.64, 44.96, 54.29)
2.	Low (L)	(29.99, 34.79, 39.59)
3.	Average (A)	(33.76, 39.35, 44.93)
4.	Very Low (VL)	(24.77, 30.16, 35.55)

Table 4.31. Linguistic terms for input 2, Hf.

#	Linguistic value	TFN
1.	Very Low (VL)	(-4.111, 5.24, 14.59)
2.	High (H)	(10.94, 15.56, 20.17)
3.	Average (A)	(5.237, 10.82, 16.41)
5.	Very High (VH)	(14.69, 19.95, 25.21)

Table 4.32. Codebook for output 1, y_1.

#	Linguistic value	TFN	
1.	Very Low (VL)	(329, 329, 383.35)	(1)
2.	Low (L)	(329, 383.35, 437.7)	(2)
3.	Average (A)	(383.35, 437.7, 492.05)	(3)
4.	High (H)	(437.7, 492.05, 546.4)	(4)
5.	Very High (VH)	(492.05, 546.4, 546.4)	(5)

Table 4.33. Codebook for output 2, y_2.

#	Linguistic value	TFN
1.	Very Low (VL)	(363.9, 363.9,416.2) (1)
2.	Low (L)	(363.9, 416.2, 468.5) (2)
3.	Average (A)	(416.2, 468.5, 520.8) (3)
4.	High (H)	(468.5, 520.8, 573.1) (4)
5.	Very High (VH)	(520.8, 573.1, 573.1) (5)

Table 4.34. Codebook for input 3, y_3.

#	Linguistic value	TFN
1.	Very Low (VL)	(421.4, 421.4, 468.7) (1)
2.	Low (L)	(421.4, 468.7, 516) (2)
3.	Average (A)	(468.7, 516, 563.3) (3)
4.	High (H)	(516, 563.3, 610.6) (4)
5.	Very High (VH)	(563.3, 610.6, 610.6) (5)

Table 4.35. Codebook for output 4, y_4.

#	Linguistic value	TFN
1.	Very Low (VL)	(381.3, 381.3, 434.925)
2.	Low (L)	(381.3, 434.925, 488.55)
3.	Average (A)	(434.925, 488.55, 542.175)
4.	High (H)	(488.55, 542.175, 595.8)
5.	Very High (VH)	(542.175, 595.8, 595.8)

Table 4.36. Linguistic terms for output 1, Mf.

#	Linguistic value	TFN
1.	Very Low (VL)	(254, 329.2, 404.5)
2.	Average (A)	(366.7, 436.9, 507.1)
3.	Low (L)	(324.9, 379.3, 433.8)
5.	Very High (VH)	(416.6, 522.5, 628.4)

Table 4.37. Linguistic terms for output 2, Ms.

#	Linguistic value	TFN
1.	Very Low (VL)	(288, 363.3, 438.5)
2.	Average (A)	(400.7, 467.6, 534.4)
3.	Low (L)	(344.2, 407.4, 470.5)
5.	Very High (VH)	(447.3, 548.6, 649.9)

Table 4.38. Linguistic terms for output 3, As.

#	Linguistic value	TFN
1.	Very Low (VL)	(341.8, 416.2, 490.6)
2.	Average (A)	(431.9, 496.6, 561.2)
3.	Low (L)	(390.5, 455.3, 520.2)
5.	Very High (VH)	(486.6, 588.5, 691)

Table 4.39. Linguistic terms for output 4, Af.

#	Linguistic value	TFN
1.	Very Low (VL)	(272.7, 378.1, 483.6)
2.	Average (A)	(451, 511.5, 571.9)
3.	Low (L)	(375.8, 446.2, 516.5)
5.	Very High (VH)	(502.6, 590, 677.4)

We have found that the fuzzy optimal output vector B' induced by the fuzzy input vector $A' = (A_1', A_2', A_3') = (49.8, 46.2, 4)$ is $B' = ((351.3), (384.9), (434.85), (406.75))$. It is the closest vector to the considered ideal fuzzy vector $B^* = ((325.5), (358.8), (406.8), (368.5))$. The distance is $D(B', B^*) = 60$. The fuzzy model-based results for Ti-Ni-Zr shows that the optimal alloy composition is: Ti is 'about 46.2%', Ni is 'about 49.8%', Hf is 'about 5%'. The obtained characteristics: M_f is about 351.31, M_s is about 384.92, A_f is about 434.85, and A_s is about 406.75. The mapping induced by the used rules is shown in Fig. 4.3.

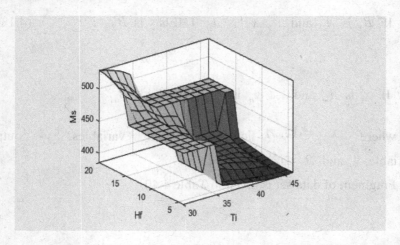

Fig. 4.3. Example of surface viewer interface Ti-Ni-Hf alloy.

4.4. Fuzzy material synthesis by expert system for pressure vessel

To solve Material synthesis problem for Pressure Vessel is used two methods: possibility measure based inference method (by ESPLAN shell, Aliev inference) and Mamdani inference method (by Matlab environment, Fuzzy ToolBox).

4.4.1. Statement of the problem

Defining of the performance index for Pressure Vessel in material synthesis is a very important problem. The basic problem is to evaluate of the performance index by using weighted performance indices.

For determining the performance index, we use data of alloys. There are many types of alloys.

The weighted performance index denoted **out1** is a compound index built from four components each of which is extracted from data set. The four components are: **in1**- scaled pren, **in2**-scaled yield strength, **in3**-scaled weldability, **in4**- scaled impact strength.

Using the above mentioned parameters, the performance index model can be expressed as:

IF x_1 is A_{1L} and ..... x_n is A_{1n} THEN y is B_1

IF B_1 is A_{21} and ..... x_n is A_{2n} THEN y is B_2 (4.13)

....'

IF x_1 is A_{m1} and ..... x_n is A_{mn} THEN y is B_m

where $x_j = 1...n$ -linguistical input variables, y- output variable, A_{ij} and B_i -fuzzy sets,n=4,m=7.

Fragment of data set is given in Table 4.40.

Table 4.40. Fragment of data set (extracted from Big Data).

Scaled PREN	Scaled yield strength	Scaled weldability	Scaled impact strength	Performance index
26.60	3.60	18.40	5.00	53.50
29.70	4.40	23.00	8.60	65.60
19.80	3.60	23.00	5.00	51.30
22.30	3.20	23.00	8.60	57.10
26.00	3.60	18.40	6.80	54.70
22.30	5.40	13.80	11.30	52.70
...	...	...	...	...
47.00	4.60	18.40	13.50	83.50
29.70	4.40	18.40	15.80	68.30
20.40	12.00	18.40	5.00	55.80
21.00	9.80	23.00	4.50	58.30
23.50	4.60	23.00	13.50	64.60
11.80	2.50	18.40	9.00	41.60
15.50	2.50	18.40	8.80	45.10
22.90	5.80	13.80	7.10	49.50
26.60	6.20	4.60	3.20	40.50
...	...	...	...	...
18.60	2.90	18.40	8.80	48.60
32.20	6.20	18.40	6.00	62.70
42.70	4.30	23.00	15.20	85.10
21.00	2.50	18.40	8.80	50.70
21.60	9.50	18.40	4.50	54.00

4.4.2. *Modelling by FCM*

To create this model we use clustering approach, mainly fuzzy C-means. Dataset contains 35 records which extracted BigData. For modelling we use 2/3 of the given data and testing 1/3. Input: x1- Scaled PREN ; x2- Scaled yield , x3- Scaled weldability, x4- Scaled impact strength, Output: Performance index. For simulation FCM based clustering initial data are:

Cluster numbers=7;

Max iteration =1000;

exponent =2;

Min. Improvement=0,000001.

Obtained centers of the clusters is given in Table 4.41.

Table 4.41. Centers of the clusters.

18.5215	3.0384	14.7548	10.7647	46.9898
27.6395	4.4574	21.3502	12.6412	66.0559
26.0329	4.9933	4.8428	3.2598	39.0312
20.8528	9.7068	21.3952	5.0337	56.9826
25.0287	3.5955	19.0063	6.3912	53.9372
46.9418	4.5996	18.4040	13.4963	83.4416
24.1544	6.2895	14.0802	9.7481	54.2839

Representation of the extracted fuzzy rules from BigData by using Fuzzy c-means method fragment is given below and in Fig. 4.4.

1)IF Scaled PREN= about 18 and Scaled yield =about 3 and Scaled weldability =about 14.5 and scaled impact strength = about 10.8 THEN Performance index =about 46.5

2) IF Scaled PREN= about 27 and Scaled yield =about 4.4 and Scaled weldability =about 21 and scaled impact strength = about 12 THEN Performance index =about 65

3) IF Scaled PREN= about 26 and Scaled yield =about 5 and Scaled weldability =about 4.8 and scaled impact strength = about 3 THEN Performance index =about 38.5

4) IF Scaled PREN= about 21 and Scaled yield =about 9 and Scaled weldability =about 21.2 and scaled impact strength = about 5 THEN Performance index =about 55

5) IF Scaled PREN= about 25 and Scaled yield =about 3.6 and Scaled weldability =about 19 and scaled impact strength = about 6 THEN Performance index =about 53.5

6) IF Scaled PREN= about 47 and Scaled yield =about 4.5 and Scaled weldability =about 18 and scaled impact strength = about 13 THEN Performance index =about 83

7) IF Scaled PREN= about 24 and Scaled yield =about 6 and Scaled weldability =about 14 and scaled impact strength = about 10 THEN Performance index =about 54

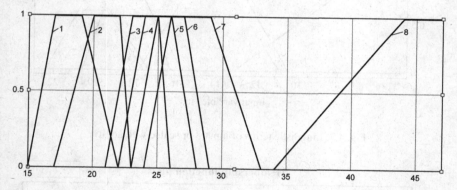

1. if (in1 is about18) and (in2 is about3) and (in3 is about14.5) and (in4 is about10.8) then (out1 is about 46.5) (1)
2. if (in1 is about27) and(in2 is about 4.4) and (in3 is about 21) and (in4 is about 12) then (out1 is about 65) (1)
3. if (in1 is about26) and(in2 is about 5) and(in3 is about 4) and (in4 is about 3) then (out1 is about 38.5) (1)
4. if (in1 is about21) and(in2 is about 9) and(in3 is about 21.2) and (in4 is about 5) then (out1 is about 55) (1)
5. if (in1 is about25) and(in2 is about 3.6) and(in3 is about 19) and (in4 is about 6) then (out1 is about 53.5) (1)
6. if (in1 is about47) and(in2 is about 4.5) and(in3 is about 18) and (in4 is about 13) then (out1 is about 83) (1)
7. if (in1 is about24) and(in2 is about 6) and(in3 is about 14) and (in4 is about 10) then (out1 is about 54) (1)

Fig. 4.4. Extracted fuzzy rules (by using fuzzy C-means method).

Graphical representation of the linguistical terms of inputs and outputs of the rules as trapezoidal fuzzy numbers are given in Figs. 4.5-4.9.

Fig. 4.5. Linguistic terms of input 1 (1 – about 18, 2 – about 21, 3 – about 24, 4 – about 25, 5 – about 26, 6 – about 27, 7 – about 47).

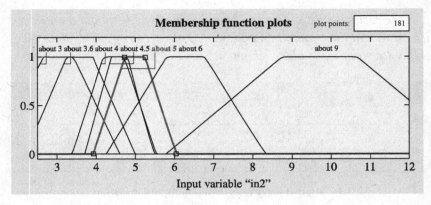

Fig. 4.6. Linguistic terms of input 2 or scaled yield strength.

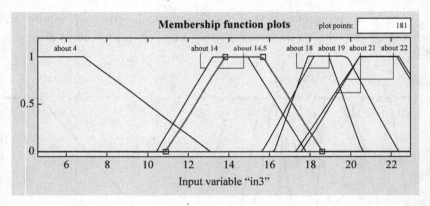

Fig. 4.7. Linguistic terms of input 3 or scaled weldability.

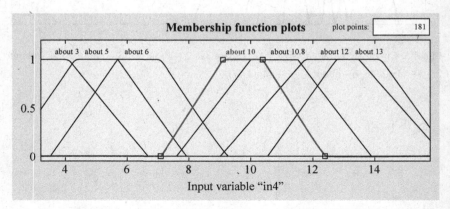

Fig. 4.8. Linguistic terms of input 4 or scaled impact strength.

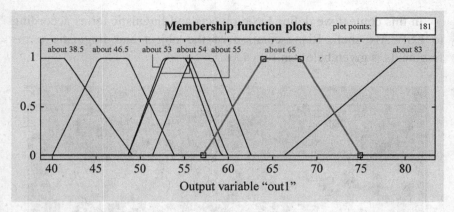

Fig. 4.9. Linguistic terms of outputs or performance index.

Solution by Expert system ESPLAN.

Determine a material with a given level of performance index by using the created fuzzy model given below:

1) IF In1 about 18 and In2 =about 3 and In3 =about 14.5 and In4 = about 10.8 THEN Out1 =about 46.5

2) IF In1 = about 27 and In2=about 4.4 and In3=about 21 and In4= about 12 THEN Out1 =about 65

3) IF In1= about 26 and In2=about 5 and In3=about 4.8 and In4= about 3 THEN Out1 =about 38.5

4) IF In1 = about 21 and In2=about 9 and In3=about 21.2 and In4= about 5 THEN Out1 =about 55

5) IF In1= about 25 and In2=about 3.6 and In3=about 19 and In4= about 6 THEN Out1 =about 53.5

6) IF In1 = about 47 and In2=about 4.5 and In3=about 18 and In4= about 13 THEN Out1 =about 83

7) IF In1= about 24 and In2=about 6 and In3=about 14 and In4= about 10 THEN Out1 =about 54

In this context we define basic objects and linguistic terms according to ESPLAN shell. Representation of the object and linguistic terms fragments is given below in Fig. 4.10.

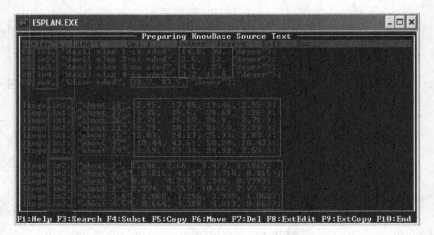

Fig. 4.10. Basic objects of fuzzy material synthesis model.

Also, representation of the object and linguistic terms in working area is given above. Fragment of the preparation of the knowledge base process by using ESPLAN shell is illustrated in Figs. 4.11 and 4.12.

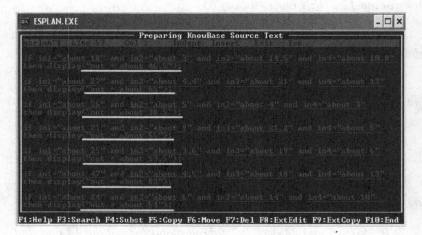

Fig. 4.11. Fragment of the preparation of the knowledge base process.

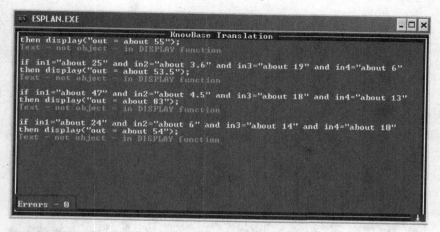

Fig. 4.12. Fragment of the preparation of the knowledge base process (translation part).

The above mentioned model is implemented by using the fuzzy expert system ESPLAN and different tests are performed. Different current information in tests are used.

TEST 1.

IF Scaled PREN= about 18 and Scaled yield =about 3 and
Scaled weldability =about 21 and scaled impact strength = about 12
THEN Performance index =?
The following entering data as initial data is given Expert System (Fig. 4.13) and obtained result is represented in Fig. 4.14.

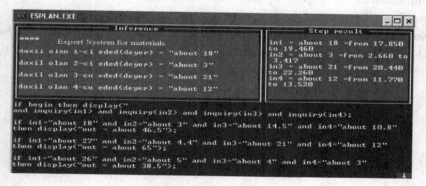

Fig. 4.13. Entering Data as initial data.

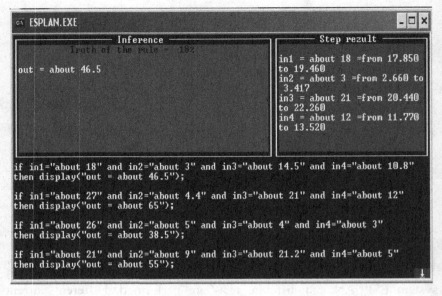

Fig. 4.14. Fragment of computer simulation (Obtained result).

FOR TEST1.

ANSWER:

EXPERT system shell ESPLAN's decision is "Performance index is about 46.5 "**(alloy Monel-400)**.

In this paragraph for the evaluation of alloys performance index fuzzy If-Then rules are used. The fuzzy rules were derived from alloys big data by using FCM method and fuzzy inference within these rules is implemented in expert system shell ESPLAN. The obtained results confirm efficiency of the proposed approach.

Solution by using Mamdani Inference method. General form of the above mentioned rules are as form (4.13).

We can describe fuzzy inference process as follow:

1. Firing level for each rule is defined as follows:

$$\alpha_i = \min_{j=1}^{n}[\max_{x_j}(A_j^{'}(x_j) \wedge A_{ij}(x_j))$$

where $A_j^{'}(x_j)$ are current input values.

2. Outputs for each rule are calculated:

$$B_i'(y) = \min(\alpha_i, B_i(y))$$

3.*Calculate aggregative output:*

$$B'(y) = \max(B_1'(y), B_2'(y), ..., B_m'(y))$$

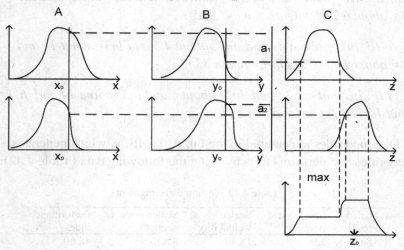

Fig. 4.15. Mamdani inference process.

In our example number of inputs variables is equal to 4 and for each variable linguistic value number is equal to 7.

For example, Scaled PREN variable is evaluated by linguistic evaluations like *about 18*, *about 27*, *about 26*, *about 21*, *about 25*, *about 47*, *about 24*.

Observing the relationship between input and output cluster we may formulate the following linguistic descriptions: productions rules, for example:

1)IF In1 about 18 and In2 =about 3 and In3 =about 14.5 and In4 = about 10.8 THEN Out1 =about 46.5

2) IF In1 = about 27 and In2=about 4.4 and In3=about 21 and In4= about 12 THEN Out1 =about 65

3) IF In1= about 26 and In2=about 5 and In3=about 4.8 and In4= about 3 THEN Out1 =about 38.5

4) IF In1 = about 21 and In2=about 9 and In3=about 21.2 and In4= about 5 THEN Out1 =about 55

5) IF In1= about 25 and In2=about 3.6 and In3=about 19 and In4= about 6 THEN Out1 =about 53.5

6) IF In1 = about 47 and In2=about 4.5 and In3=about 18 and In4= about 13 THEN Out1 =about 83

7) IF In1= about 24 and In2=about 6 and In3=about 14 and In4= about 10 THEN Out1 =about 54

Obtained rules are entered in the Fuzzy ToolBox, which generates fuzzy rules and performs tests by using the following data (Table 4.42):

Table 4.42. Testing data(fragment).

Scaled PREN	Scaled yield strength	Scaled weldability	Scaled impact strength	Performance index
18.60	2.90	18.40	8.80	48.60
21	2.5	18.4	8.8	50.7

Note that when we obtained rules from data is not included to data follows, which is performed tests.

Test 1.

Results. If initial data equals:

IF In1= 18,60 and In2= 2,90and In3= 18,40 and In4= 8,80THEN Out1 =48,60 (alloy 317L)

IF In1= 18,60 and In2= 2,90and In3= 18,40 and In4= 8,80THEN Out1 =50,3(Alloy 317LM)

Then result of computer simulation is given Fig. 4.16.

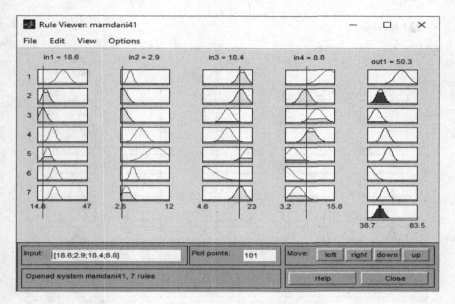

Fig. 4.16. Fragment of computer simulation (test 1).

Consider the following performed test:

If In1=26 and In2=3,6 and In3=18,4 and In4=68,8 Then Out1=54,8

Then result of computer simulation is given Fig. 4.17.

For example, if inputs are 26.3, 3.6, 18.4, 6.8, the performance index equals 54.8.

Comparison expert and testing data (computer simulation result) is given below (Table 4.43):

Table 4.43. Comparison expert and testing data.

Scaled PREN	Scaled yield strength	Scaled weldability	Scaled impact strength	Performance index (Expert data)	Performance index (testing data)
26.00	3.60	18.40	6.80	54.70	54.8(Alloy 1925hMo)

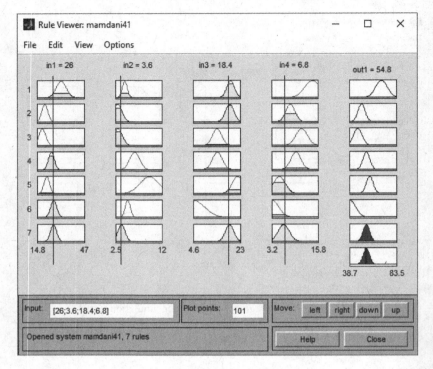

Fig. 4.17. Result of computer simulation.

Deviation between testing and expert data is 0.18% or 0.0018.

4.5. A Fuzzy approach to estimation of phase diagram under uncertain thermodynamic data

Phase-equilibrium problems are important and interesting real-world optimization problems that provide a fundamental basis of material synthesis. An equilibrium state in two and many dimensional phases may induce the best characteristics of materials. From the one side, these problems are of a low dimensionality, but from the other side, a small basin of attraction is surrounded by a large area of global optimum. The latter generates a solution which is not physically possible. The existing approaches to obtain a practically implementable solution include theoretical and computational approaches such as the CALPHAD, approaches based on field theory, statistical mechanics, electrochemical techniques and others [28,133,158,163,164]. Let us mention that development of an adequate thermodynamic model is complicated due to uncertainty in thermodynamic data. More concretely, in phase diagram calculations, it is needed to take into account that boundaries between solidus and liquidus are uncertain. Several approaches can be used for solving this problem. The simplest way is to use some particular data for phase diagram calculations. However, particular data may not sufficiently good to represent the general phenomena adequately. Alternatively, one can use an average of all the available data sets. However, in this case an assumption of the same quality of all the data sets is necessary. At the same time, averaging leads to loss of information that exists in particular data sets. The use of statistical approaches is not suitable when relevant information is incomplete and vague.

Thus, the main disadvantage of majority of the approaches is a low capability of dealing with real-world uncertainty of thermodynamic information intrinsic to these complex problems. At the same time, in the existing studies one-dimensional optimization problems are often considered. In order to deal with mutlidimensionality and real-world uncertainty, we consider an approach for solving two dimensional phase-equilibrium problems by using fuzzy logic and DE optimization.

The quantitative analysis of phase-equilibrium allows to construct a model of relationship between temperature, T, pressure, p, and mole fraction, x. This model describes equilibrium state of several homogeneous phases. The first necessary condition for a problem of equilibrium distribution of k components between two phases is the equality of the chemical potential:

$$\forall i \in \{1,...,k\} : \mu_i^1 = \mu_i^2 \qquad (4.14)$$

In notation μ_i', upper index denotes phases and lower one denotes substances. The dependence of m on T, p, and x is described by a thermodynamic model. Thus, (4.14) can be described as:

$$\forall i \in \{1,...,k\} : x_i^1 \varphi_i^1 = x_i^2 \varphi_i^2 \qquad (4.15)$$

As a rule, concentrations x_i^1 and x_i^2 are found for fixed values of temperature and pressure respectively. The main problem is that such approach may generate trivial solutions $x_i^1 = x_i^2$ that do not have physical meaning (only a critical demixing point has meaning). In order to resolve this problem, it is needed to guess initial conditions for minimization that would not be too far away from the correct solutions.

In the considered problem, objective function (4.16) is used [165] as a measure of the departure from equilibrium state between any two phases of one component:

$$f_1(x^1, x^2) = \sum_{i=1}^{3} \left| x_i^1 \varphi_i^1 - x_i^2 \varphi_i^2 \right| \tag{4.16}$$

Several useful formulations of the second objective exist. A general formulation based on the Euclidean norm of a vector of concentration differences is [165]

$$f_2(x^1, x^2) = \sqrt{2} - \left\| x^1 - x^2 \right\|_2 = \sqrt{2} - \sqrt{\sum_{i=1}^{3} \left(x_i^1 - x_i^2 \right)^2} \tag{4.17}$$

This can be easily extended for more components.

Consider phase diagram for the $UO_2 - BeO_2$ system under uncertainty. The system is characterized by a complete solubility in the solid phase. The following formulas describe the mole fractions of liquidus (x^{Liq}) and solidus (x^{Sol}) for each fixed temperature[180]:

$$x_{UO_2 + Liq}^{Liq}(T) = 1 - \exp\left(\left(\frac{-\Delta H_{UO_2}^M}{RT} \right) \ln\left(\frac{T_{UO_2}^M}{T} \right) \right) \tag{4.18}$$

and

$$x_{Liq + BeO}^{Liq}(T) = \exp\left(\left(\frac{-\Delta H_{BeO}^M}{RT} \right) \ln\left(\frac{T_{BeO}^M}{T} \right) \right) \tag{4.19}$$

$R = 8.314 \, J / mol \, K$ is the gas constant.

In [180] for the first time uncertainty in phase diagram is taken into account in an interval-valued form. The authors consider computation of phase diagram by using one objective function. We will consider this problem on the basis of two objective functions under fuzzy information. The information on values of $\Delta H^M_{UO_2}$, $T^M_{UO_2}$, ΔH^M_{BeO}, and T^M_{BeO} is characterized by fuzzy uncertainty. The corresponding fuzzy evaluations in form of triangular fuzzy numbers (TFNs) are shown in Table 4.44. Fuzziness of these values induces fuzzy uncertainty of information on values of the temperature and melting enthalpy x^{Sol}. In view of this, we will build an adequate model by using fuzzy logic and differential evolution (DE) optimization method.

Table 4.44. Fuzzy values of phase variables.

Variable	Units	Fuzzy value
$\Delta H^M_{UO_2}$	kJ/mol	(40,80,165)
ΔH^M_{BeO}	kJ/mol	(42,85,165)
$T^M_{UO_2}$	K	(3000,3100,3200)
T^M_{BeO}	K	(2700,2800,2900)

The fuzzy graphs describing the considered phase diagram under uncertainty is given in Fig. 4.18.

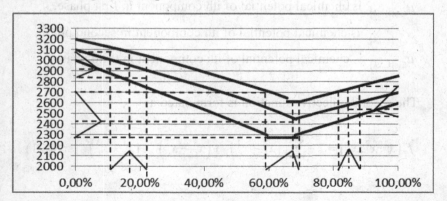

Fig. 4.18. The computed $UO_2 - BeO_2$ fuzzy phase diagram (the core values and bounds).

As one can see, a fuzzy eutectic point exists with the TFN-based coordinates:

$$T=(2300,2500,2700), \quad x_{BeO}=(60\%,68\%,70\%).$$

The fuzziness of this point is the result of intersection of two fuzzy liquid lines describing real-world uncertainty intrinsic to thermodynamic data. In other words, this is a result of the fuzziness of the phase boundaries.

Let's consider calculations of phase diagram for a considered 2 component-3 phase system.

First, let us formulate objective functions. The first objective function is formulated on the basis of phase equilibrium equation as follows:

$$f_1\left(x^1,x^2,x^3\right)=\sum_{i=1}^{2}\left[\left(x_i^1\mu_i^1-x_i^2\mu_i^2\right)^2+\left(x_i^1\mu_i^1-x_i^3\mu_i^3\right)^2\right], \quad (4.20)$$

where the notations are as follows:

$x_{i,i\in\{1,\dots,k\}}^1$ is remaining mole fractions in first phase,

$x_{i,i\in\{1,\dots,k\}}^2$ is remaining mole fractions in second phase,

$x_{i,i\in\{1,\dots,k\}}^3$ is remaining mole fractions in third phase,

$\mu_{i,i\in\{1,\dots,k\}}^1$ is chemical potential of ith component in first phase,

$\mu_{i,i\in\{1,\dots,k\}}^2$ is chemical potential of ith component in second phase,

$\mu_{i,i\in\{1,\dots,k\}}^3$ is chemical potential of ith component in third phase.

The second objective function is formulated as

$$f_2\left(x^1,x^2,x^3\right)=2-\sum_{i=1}^{2}\left[\left(x_i^1-x_i^2\right)^2+\left(x_i^2-x_i^3\right)^2+\left(x_i^1-x_i^3\right)^2\right] \quad (4.21)$$

Next, we need to calculate values of $\mu_i^1, \mu_i^2, \mu_i^3$.

As thermodynamic parameters are uncertain, values of $\mu_i^1, \mu_i^2, \mu_i^3$ become fuzzy. Given these fuzzy values we solve the problems of minimization of objective functions (4.20)-(4.21) by using DE optimization.

Further, we take $P = 1$ bar, change T and concentrations in the three phases and find values of heteroazeotrope temperature T.

Finally, we construct phase diagram (decision variables are T and x by minimizing (4.20)-(4.21).

For the defuzzified case, the considered above phase diagram construction problem is used in [165] for binary water/MMA system (Fig. 4.19).

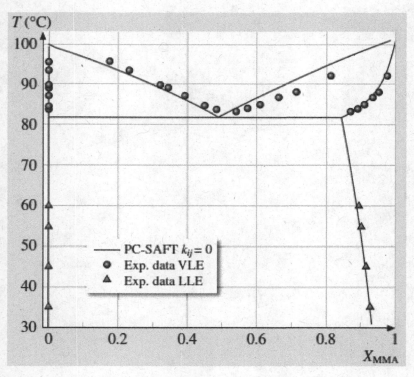

Fig. 4.19. Phase diagram for binary water/MMA system [165].

As one can see, calculation results coincide with experimental data.

Chapter 5

Case Study

5.1. Case study for material selection. Application of Fuzzy Analytic Hierarchy Process to alloy selection problem

Fuzzy Analytic Hierarchy Process (AHP) is the fuzzy extension of the well-known AHP developed by Saaty [170] to solve multiattribute decision problems. AHP utilizes 3-level hierarchy with the objective in the 1st, the criteria in the 2nd and alternatives in the 3rd levels. Importance weights of criteria and criteria values of alternatives are determined by using pairwise comparisons [128]. Fuzzy AHP is used to account for vagueness of linguistic evaluations used in pairwise comparison. In [192] the authors applied fuzzy AHP for the first time by using triangular fuzzy numbers. Further development of fuzzy AHP was considered [46,56]. In this section, we consider the use of fuzzy AHP proposed in [46]. The method is outlined below.

Step 1. A DM conducts pair-wise comparison of criteria (to obtain importance weights) and alternatives (to obtain criteria values) by using linguistic terms (see Table 5.1) to determine fuzzy comparison values.

Table 5.1. The linguistic scale of Saaty.

Saaty scale	Definition	TFN
1	Equally important (Eq. Imp.)	(1,1,1)
3	Weakly important (W. Imp.)	(2,3,4)
5	Fairly important (F. Imp.)	(4,5,6)
7	Strongly important (S. Imp.)	(6,7,8)
9	Absolutely important (A. Imp.)	(9,9,9)
2		(1,2,3)
4	The intermittent values between	(3,4,5)
6	adjacent scales	(5,6,7)
8		(7,8,9)

For example, if a DM says that criterion 1 is "fairly important" than criterion 2, then the corresponding TFN (4,5,6) is used in the pairwise comparison matrix. Accordingly, comparison of criterion 2 to criterion 1 is described by the reciprocal TFN: (1/6,1/5,1/4). Formally, the pairwise comparison matrix is described below:

$$
A = \begin{pmatrix} a_{11} & a_{12},..., & a_{1n} \\ a_{21} & .... & a_{23} \\ a_{n1} & a_{n2},..., & a_{nn} \end{pmatrix}
\tag{5.1}
$$

where a_{ij} is a fuzzy comparison value from the scale (Table 5.1) that describes preference degree (fuzzy comparison value) C_i over C_j.

Step 2. The geometric mean r_i is computed for each criterion C_i to aggregate the fuzzy comparison values:

$$
r_i = \left(\prod_{j=1}^{n} d_{ij} \right)^{1/n}, \quad i = 1,2,...,n
\tag{5.2}
$$

Step 3. The fuzzy importance weights of criteria are computed by linear scaling of r_i and approximated by TFNs:

$$
w_i = r_i \otimes (r_1 \oplus r_2 \oplus ... \oplus r_n)^{-1} = (lw_i, mw_i, uw_i)
\tag{5.3}
$$

Step 4. The TFNs obtained at Step 3 are defuzzified by using the following formula [46]:

$$
M_i = \frac{lw_i + mw_i + uw_i}{3}
\tag{5.4}
$$

Step 5. Values of M_i obtained at Step 4 are normalized to obtain criteria weights:

$$N_i = \frac{M_i}{\sum_{i=1}^{n} M_i}$$ (5.5)

By using the analogous procedure for pairwise comparison of alternatives on the basis of each criterion, the values of criteria C_i for alternatives f_j are computed: x_{ji}. Thus, we arrive at the following decision matrix (Table 5.2):

Table 5.2. Decision matrix.

	C_1 , w_1	C_2 , w_2	$\cdots$	C_n , w_n
f_1	x_{11}	x_{12}	$\cdots$	
f_2	x_{21}	x_{22}	$\cdots$	x_{2n}
.			$\cdots$	
.				
.				
f_m	x_{m1}	x_{m2}	$\cdots$	x_{mn}

The utility of alternative f_i is computed as a weighted average:

$$U(f_j) = \sum_{j=1}^{n} w_j x_{ji}$$ (5.6)

The best alternative is the alternative with the highest utility.

Example. Consider selection of the best alloy for mooring connection[199]. Three alloys as alternatives are considered: alloy 304 (f_1), alloy 316 (f_2), and alloy 254 SMO (f_3). As criteria, the following characteristics are used: C_1 (Hardness), C_2 (PREN), C_3 (yield strength), C_4 (weldability), C_5 (impact strength). The problem hierarchy is shown in Fig. 5.1.

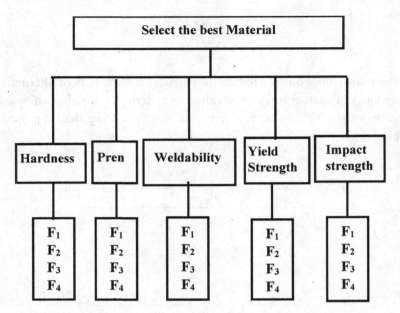

Fig. 5.1 The hierarchy of MCDM problem for alloy selection.

Let us solve the considered problem by using the AHP method.

At Step 1, a DM conducted pairwise comparison of the choice criteria by using the linguistic scale in Table 5.1. The corresponding TFNs are shown in Table 5.3.

Table 5.3. Pairwise comparison of the choice criteria.

C	C_1	C_2	C_3	C_4	C_5
C_1	(1,1,1)	(1/6, 1/5, 1/4)	(1/6, 1/5, 1/4)	(1,1,1)	(1/4, 1/3, 1/2)
C_2	(4,5,6)	(1,1,1)	(1,1,1)	(4,5,6)	(2,3,4)
C_3	(4,5,6)	(1,1,1)	(1,1,1)	(4,5,6)	(2,3,4)
C_4	(1,1,1)	(1/6, 1/5, 1/4)	(1/6, 1/5, 1/4)	(1,1,1)	(1/4, 1/3, 1/2)
C_5	(2,3,4)	(1/4, 1/3, 1/2)	(1/4, 1/3, 1/4)	(2,3,4)	(1,1,1)

At Step 2, for each criterion C_i fuzzy comparison values in Table 5.2 are aggregated by using the geometric mean r_i (Table 5.4).

Table 5.4. The fuzzy values of geometric mean r_i for the criteria.

CRITERIA	r_i		
C1	0.3701	0.4217	0.5000
C2	2.0000	2.3714	2.7019
C3	2.0000	2.3714	2.7019
C4	0.3701	0.4217	0.5000
C5	0.7579	1.0000	1.3195

At Step 3, the TFN-based approximations of fuzzy importance weights of criteria w_i computed by linear scaling of r_i are shown in Table 5.5.

Table 5.5. TFN-based approximations of fuzzy importance weights.

CRITERIA	w_i		
C1	0.0479	0.0640	0.0910
C2	0.2590	0.3600	0.4915
C3	0.2590	0.3600	0.4915
C4	0.0479	0.0640	0.0910
C5	0.0981	0.1518	0.2400

The defuzzified values of w_i and the normalized values are obtained at Step 4 and Step 5 (Table 5.6):

Table 5.6. The defuzzified and normalized values of w_i.

CRITERIA	Mi	Ni
C1	0.0676	0.0651
C2	0.3702	0.3563
C3	0.3702	0.3563
C4	0.0676	0.0651
C5	0.1633	0.1572

Next, the pairwise alternatives comparison on the basis of criteria are conducted (Tables 5.7-5.11) and normalized criteria values are computed (Tables 5.12-5.16). The resulting decision matrix is given in Table 5.17.

Table 5.7. Comparison of alternatives on the basis of C_1.

C_1	A_1	A_2	A_3
A_1	(1,1,1)	(1/3, 1/2 , 1/1)	(1/3, 1/2 , 1/1)
A_2	(1,2,3)	(1,1,1)	(1,1,1)
A_3	(1,2,3)	(1,1,1)	(1,1,1)

Table 5.8. Comparison of alternatives on the basis of C_2.

C_2	A_1	A_2	A_3
A_1	(1,1,1)	(1/3,1/2,1/1)	(1/4, 1/3, 1/2)
A_2	(1,2,3)	(1,1,1)	(1/3, 1/2 , 1/1)
A_3	(2,3,4)	(1,2,3)	(1,1,1)

Table 5.9. Comparison of alternatives on the basis of C_3.

C_3	A_1	A_2	A_3
A_1	(1,1,1)	(1,1,1)	(1/3, 1/2 , 1/1)
A_2	(1,2,3)	(1,1,1)	(1/3, 1/2 , 1/1)
A_3	(1,2,3)	(1,2,3)	(1,1,1)

Table 5.10. Comparison of alternatives on the basis of C_4.

C_4	A_1	A_2	A_3
A_1	(1,1,1)	(1,1,1)	(1,1,1)
A_2	(1,1,1)	(1,1,1)	(1,1,1)
A_3	(1,1,1)	(1,1,1)	(1,1,1)

Table 5.11. Comparison of alternatives on the basis of C_5.

C_5	A_1	A_2	A_3
A_1	(1,1,1)	(1,1,1)	(1,2,3)
A_2	(1,1,1)	(1,1,1)	(1,2,3)
A_3	(1/3, 1/2, 1/1)	(1/3, 1/2, 1/1)	(1,1,1)

Table 5.12. Normalized values of C_1.

Alternative	x_{ji}
A1	0.2268
A2	0.3866
A3	0.3866

Table 5.13. Normalized values of C_2.

Alternative	x_{j2}
A1	0.173
A2	0.3079
A3	0.519

Table 5.14. Normalized values of C_3.

Alternative	x_{j2}
A1	0.2546
A2	0.2546
A3	0.4907

Table 5.15. Normalized values of C_4.

Alternative	x_{j2}
A1	0.3333
A2	0.3333
A3	0.3333

Table 5.16. Normalized values of C_5.

Alternative	x_{j2}
A1	0.3866
A2	0.3866
A3	0.2268

Table 5.17. Decision matrix for alloy selection problem.

	C_1, $w_1 = 0.0651$	C_2, $w_2 = 0.3563$	C_3, $w_3 = 0.3563$	C_4, $w_4 = 0.0651$	C_5, $w_5 = 0.1572$
f_1	0.2268	0.173	0.2546	0.3333	0.3866
f_2	0.3866	0.3079	0.2546	0.3333	0.3866
f_3	0.3866	0.519	0.4907	0.3333	0.2268

The obtained utilities of the alternatives are computed by using (5.6): $U(f_1) = 0.25$, $U(f_2) = 0.31$, $U(f_3) = 0.442$. Thus, the best alternative is f_3, 254 SMO Alloy.

5.2. Computational synthesis of TiNi alloys by using fuzzy rules and big data concepts

Consider a problem of computer synthesis of Ti-Ni alloy with predefined characteristics [30]. A fragment of the big data on relationship between alloy composition, test temperature and three characteristics is shown in Table 5.18:

Table 5.18. A fragment of the big data on Ti-Ni alloy composition.

Composition		Test temperature	Characteristics		
y_1 (Ti,%)	y_2 (Ni,%)	T, C	z_1 (conventional ultimate strength, MPa)	z_2 (conventional yield strength, MPa)	z_3 (unit elongation, %)
49,8	50,2	−196	1260	410	40
49,8	50,2	20	970	150	55
49	51	20	940	550	62
49	51	200	1050	560	28

Assume that the problem of computational synthesis is to find the alloy composition with the characteristics values as close as possible to the following target fuzzy values:

$$z_1 = (1900, 2000, 2100), z_2 = (618, 650, 683), z_3 = (76, 80, 84)$$

These values form ideal fuzzy vector of characteristics $B^* = (B_1^*, B_2^*, B_3^*) = ((1900, 2000, 2100), (618, 650, 683), (76, 80, 84))$.

By using FCM-based clustering we obtained the following fuzzy If-Then rules:

IF y_1 is Medium and y_2 is Medium and y_3 is low
THEN z_1 is High and z_2 is Medium and z_3 is Low medium

IF y_1 is Very high and y_2 is Very low and y_3 is Very high
THEN z_1 is Very low and z_2 is Medium high and z_3 is Medium

IF y_1 is Medium high and y_2 is Low Medium and y_3 is Medium
THEN z_1 is Low and z_2 is Low and z_3 is Very High

IF y_1 is Low and y_2 is Very high and y_3 is High
THEN z_1 is Medium and z_2 is High and z_3 is High

IF y_1 is High and y_2 is Low and y_3 is Very low
THEN z_1 is Very high and z_2 is Medium high and z_3 is Low

The codebooks for the used linguistic terms are shown in Tables 5.19-5.24.

Table 5.19. Linguistic terms for y_1.

Scale	Level of criteria	Linguistic value
1.	Low	(48.75, 48.94, 49.06, 49.26)
2.	Medium	(48.87, 49.28, 49.54, 49.95)
3.	Medium High	(48.97, 49.36, 49.6, 49.99)
4.	High	(49.16, 49.46, 49.65, 49.96)
5.	Very High	(49.27, 49.58, 49.78, 50.08)

Table 5.20. Linguistic terms for y_2.

Scale	Level of criteria	Linguistic value
1.	Very Low	(49.92, 50.22, 50.42, 50.73)
2.	Low	(50.04, 50.35, 50.54, 50.84)
3.	Low Medium	(50.01, 50.4, 50.64, 51.03)
4.	Medium	(50.05, 50.46, 50.72, 51.13)
5.	Very High	(50.74, 50.94, 51.06, 51.25)

Table 5.21. Linguistic terms for T.

Scale	Level of criteria	Linguistic value
1.	Very Low	(−307.3, −222.3, −168, −83.02)
2.	Low	(−254, −176.7, −127.3, −50.06)
3.	Medium	(−104.9, −25.11, 25.87, 105.7)
4.	High	(−38.58, 42.52, 94.35, 175.4)
5.	Very High	(23.84, 166.8, 202.6, 345.5)

Table 5.22. Linguistic terms for z_1.

Scale	Level of criteria	Linguistic value
1.	Very Low	(817.2, 868, 947.5, 998.6)
2.	Low	(854.3, 935.1, 986.7, 1067)
3.	Medium	(884, 948.7, 990.1, 1055)
4.	High	(1094, 1179, 1234, 1320)
5.	Very High	(1128, 1223, 1284, 1380)

Table 5.23. Linguistic terms for z_2.

Scale	Level of criteria	Linguistic value
1.	Low	(6.528, 119.2, 191.2, 303.9)
2.	Low Medium	(265.2, 316.7, 370.6, 422.1)
3.	Medium	(295.7, 371, 419, 494.3)
4.	Medium High	(312.9, 375.9, 416.1, 479.1)
5.	High	(421.7, 520.4, 583.4, 682.1)

Table 5.24. Linguistic terms for z_3.

Scale	Level of criteria	Linguistic value
1.	Low	(16.8, 30.8, 39.7, 53.7)
2.	Low Medium	(32.13, 41.08, 46.81, 55.76)
3.	Medium	(37.69, 44.04, 48.1, 54.45)
4.	High	(41.98, 50.22, 55.48, 63.72)
5.	Very High	(38.05, 51.24, 59.67, 72.86)

These fuzzy rules express data-driven knowledge based model of dependence between composition of alloy and the characteristics. On the basis of this model we need to find such fuzzy input vector $A' = (A'_1, ..., A'_n)$ that the distance between corresponding fuzzy output vector $B' = (B'_1, ..., B'_m)$ and ideal fuzzy vector $B^* = (B^*_1, B^*_2, B^*_3)$ is minimized. We have found that the fuzzy output vector

$$B' = (B'_1, B'_2, B'_3) = ((1176, 1272, 1333, 1430), (309, 371, 420, 481),$$
$$(23, 35, 43, 55))$$

induced by the fuzzy input vector

$$A' = (A'_1, A'_2, A'_3) = ((49.6, 49.65, 49.75, 49.8), (50.2, 50.25, 50.35, 50.4),$$
$$(-200, -197, -192, -194))$$

is the closest one to the considered ideal fuzzy vector $B^* = (B^*_1, B^*_2, B^*_3)$, the distance is $D(B', B^*) = 827.3$.

The best values of characteristics obtained by using experiments were $B' = (B'_1, B'_2, B'_3) = ((1197, 1260, 1323), (390, 410, 430), (38, 40, 42))$.

The obtained distance of this fuzzy vector to the considered ideal fuzzy vector is $D(B', B^*) = 850$.

Thus, the fuzzy model-based computation provides better results than those of natural experiments. The fuzzy model-based results show that the desired alloy composition is Ti is about 49.7%, Ni is about 50.3%, Temp is about 195°C and the obtained characteristics are about 1260, about 410, about 40.

5.3. Validity of the suggested approach. Evaluation of alloy performance by using Z-rules

Let us consider a numerical example on dependence between several alloy characteristics and alloy overall performance. The related information is naturally imprecise and partially reliable. Thus, for modeling of the considered dependence, we will use If-Then rules where antecedents and consequents are described by Z-numbers. Assume that the Z-number valued If-Then rules given below are used:

Rule 1: *If Characteristic 1 is (Average, Usually) and Characteristic 2 is (High, Usually) and Characteristic 3 is (Low, Usually) Then Overall performance is (Very good, Usually)*

Rule 2: *If Characteristic 1 is (Average, Usually) and Characteristic 2 is (Average, Usually) and Characteristic 3 is (Average, Usually) Then Overall performance is (Good, Usually)*

The codebooks of linguistic terms for characteristics values and related reliabilities are shown in Figs. 5.2-5.4.

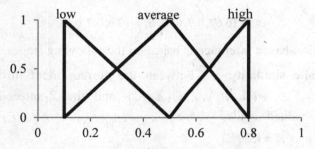

Fig. 5.2. Linguistic terms for antecedents values.

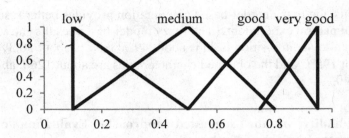

Fig. 5.3. Linguistic terms for consequents values.

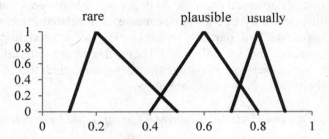

Fig. 5.4. Linguistic terms for reliability.

Let us consider interpolation-based inference on the basis of the considered rules (Chapter 3, Section 3.4.4). Assume that the current values for Characteristic 1, Characteristic 2 and Characteristic 3 are described by Z-numbers $Z_1 = (A_1, B_1)$, $Z_2 = (A_2, B_2)$, $Z_3 = (A_3, B_3)$:

$$A_1 = (0.3, 0.4, 0.5), B_1 = (0.6, 0.7, 0.8);$$

$$A_2 \doteq (0.2, .3, 0.4), B_2 = (0.6, 0.7, 0.8);$$

$$A_3 = (0.62, 0.7, 0.8), B_3 = (0.6, 0.7, 0.8).$$

Interpolation-based inference is based on the following stages.

1) Compute similarity ρ_j between the current input information $Z_1 = (A_1, B_1)$, $Z_2 = (A_2, B_2)$, $Z_3 = (A_3, B_3)$ and the Z-antecedents of Z-number valued rules base $Z_{j1} = (A_{j1}, B_{j1})$, $Z_{j2} = (A_{j2}, B_{j2})$, $Z_{j3} = (A_{j3}, B_{j3})$, $i = 1, 2$.

The values of similarity for the first two rules obtained by using (3.21) are $\rho_1 = 0.42$ and $\rho_2 = 0.69$.

2) Compute the output Z_Y for Z-number valued rules by using (3.20):

$$Z_Y = w_1 Z_{Y,1} + w_2 Z_{Y,2}.$$

The coefficients of interpolation are obtained as $w_1 = 0.38$, $w_2 = 0.62$. For computation of Z_Y, the framework for arithmetic operations over Z-numbers is used (Chapter 1). The computed $A_{12} = A_1 + A_2$ as approximated by a TFN is

$$A_{12} = (0.6, 0.7, 0.92).$$

The approximated B_{12} is found as:

$$B_{12} = (0.5, 0.52, 0.53).$$

By using linguistic approximation to the terms shown in Figs. 5.2 and 5.3 we have: Overall performance is (*"good"*, *"plausible"*).

A. An analysis of the solution

1) Comparative validation

In order to analyze validity of the applied approach we will conduct comparison with fuzzy If-Then rules based approach. In view of this, we transformed Z-number describing antecedents and consequents of the used rules and the current input values into fuzzy numbers according to the method proposed by Kang *et al.* in [124]. Then, by using the interpolative inference with the fuzzy information, we obtained the following output of the fuzzy rules:

$$A = 0.1/0.54 + 0.25/0.62 + 0.5/0.64 + 1/0.75 + 0.5/0.8 + 0/0.85$$

In accordance with the codebook (Fig. 5.2), the overall performance is *"good"*, which coincides with the A part of the Z-number obtained by using Z-number valued rules. However, the use of the fuzzy inference provides evaluation *"good"* under complete reliability. However, if we use Z-number valued If-Then, we obtain (*"good"*, *"plausible"*) evaluation.

Let us now compare two alloys overall performance. The first alloy is of the same characteristics as one considered previously. The characteristics of the second alloy are as follows (described by TFNs):

$$A_1 = (0.4, 0.5, 0.65) , \quad B_1 = (0.7, 0.8, 0.9) ;$$
$$A_2 = (0.6, 0.7, 0.8), \quad B_2 = (0.7, 0.8, 0.9) ;$$
$$A_3 = (0.1, 0.3, 0.5), \quad B_3 = (0.7, 0.8, 0.9) .$$

The result obtained for the 2nd alloy is as follows:

$$A = (0.64, 0.86, 1) \quad B = (0.5, 0.515, 0.53) .$$

By using linguistic approximation on the basis of the terms in Figs. 5.3 and 5.4, Overall performance is evaluated as (*"Very good"*, *"plausible"*). In turn, fuzzy inference based result is

$$A = (0.57, 0.77, 0.85)$$

This can be evaluated as "good" Overall performance (the same as that for the first alloy). Thus, evaluations provided by using of Z-number valued If-Then rules for the alloys differ: ("Very good", "plausible") and ("Good", "plausible"). In turn, fuzzy inference provides qualitatively the same evaluations that may not be realistic. This is due to a loss of information that occurs in transforming Z-numbers to fuzzy numbers. At the same time, reliability information is missed.

2) Sensitivity analysis

Let us analyze sensitivity of the used Z-number valued If-Then rules to the Characteristic 3 antecedent (A and B parts) rule# 2. At first, let us decrease the A part only — from "*average*" level to the fuzzy number (linguistically described as "*low*"):

$$A = (0.005, 0.025, 0.04)$$

The reasoning on the basis of Z-number valued If-Then rules produces the following Z-value of the overall performance:

$$A = (0.63, 0.86, 0.91) , B = (0.5, 0.515, 0.53) .$$

This can be linguistically described as *(very good, plausible)*. Thus, the A part of the Z-number valued overall performance increases from *"good"* to *"very good"*.

Let us now increase A part from *"average"* to the fuzzy number (linguistically described as *"high"*):

$$A = (0.11, 0.54, 0.86).$$

The obtained overall performance evaluation is described by *(good, plausible)*. Thus, the model based on Z-number valued If-Then rules is characterized by higher sensitivity to decrease of the A part of Characteristic 3 than to decrease.

Let us now analyze sensitivity to the B part of Characteristic 3. We found that the model is characterized by higher sensitivity to increase of the B part: for Characteristic 3 value equal to *(average, usually)* the overall performance is *(good, plausible)*, whereas for the case of *(average, low)* it is *(very good, plausible)*.

3) Applicability analysis

Accuracy and interpretability are main criteria of applicability of reasoning under imperfect information[111]. These criteria are naturally conflicting. Higher accuracy can be achieved by increasing a number of rules. Higher number of rules allows to account for a large number of critical cases within a considered pattern. Unfortunately, increase of rules number leads to worse interpretability of a rule base by a human being. This is especially important for MIMO systems. In general, the interpretability is a composite criteria that is described in terms of such subcriteria as complexity, completeness, compactness and transparency (readability) [50]. Let us shortly discuss the transparency criterion. In essence, interpolation-based reasoning approaches are developed for a rule base with a small number of rules. Note that two main approaches for rule construction exist: expert driven and data driven. Indeed, experts may provide 5-10 rules for a relationship considered in this section (or in Section 5.2) as main situations. Data-driven approaches such as FCM method based clustering extract rules from evidence in available data. As a result, a small number of clusters (rules) are determined. Moreover, several methods exist to find an optimal number of clusters. In view of this, the fuzzy If-Then rules and the Z-number valued If-Then rules considered in this section and the chapters of this book are satisfactory in view of the transparency criterion.

Appendix A

Fuzzy Big Database on Candidate Materials (Alloys)

As it is noted in [34], Big Data is the term for a "collection of data sets so large and complex that it becomes difficult to process using on-hand database management tools or traditional data processing applications".

The major differences between traditional data and big data are related to structures of data. Today Data Science sounds similar to new concept of Big Data. But these are different means. Big data consists of voluminous amounts of unstructured, semi-structured or structured data, used to extract meaningful insights from large data sets. Data Science combines statistical, mathematical, programming and problem-solving techniques, application of mentioned techniques for better strategic decision-making.

Usually, big data is defined in terms of the 5 Vs: Volume, Velocity, Variety, Veracity and Value [35]:

Volume: Datasets size ranges from terabytes to zettabyte.

Velocity: Large amounts of data are created at a high speed and analyzed in a short time.

Variety: Structured and unstructured data of different types come from different data sources.

Veracity: Accurateness and trustworthiness of data may not be full.

Value: An extent to which the data are useful for the goal stated in advance.

Often, structured databases have become big enough and qualify as big data, whereas big data is mostly unstructured. Operation or query over Data in Relational Database Management System RDBMS is realized by SQL, but in Big Data both SQL and NoSQL may be used.

Let us consider development of Big data database for materials. The database consists of the following fields (see Table A.1):
- Alloys
- Brand
- Id
- Data sheet
- Material properties
- Characteristic phase transformation temperatures of Ni-Ti ternary alloys
- Characteristic phase transformation temperatures of Ni-Ti alloys
- Transformation temperatures of quaternary alloys
- Mechanical properties of Ti-Ni ternary alloys at room temperature
- Transformation temperatures of heat treated TiNi ternary alloys
- Materials properties database for selection of high-temperature alloys

Table A.1. The fields of big database for candidate materials.

ID
Characteristic phase transformation temperatures of Ni-Ti ternary alloys
Characteristic phase transformation temperatures of Ni-Ti alloys
Transformation temperatures of quaternary alloys
Mechanical properties of Ti-Ni ternary alloys at room temperature
Transformation temperatures of heat treated TiNi ternary alloys
Materials properties database for selection of high-temperature alloys
Titanium alloys properties
International material collection
Open quantum materials database
Materials project
Materials and substance properties

The initial form of Database is given in Fig. A.1.

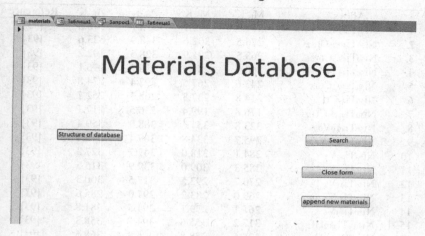

Fig. A.1. Initial form of Big data database.

The Fragment of structure of database is given in Fig. A.2.

Alloy	ID	Data Shee	Material properties
Ti-Ni-X	Characteristic phase transformation temperatures of Ni-Ti ternary alloys	Office Word	
Ti-Ni	Characteristic phase transformation temperatures of Ni-Ti alloys	Office Word	
	Transformation temperatures of quaternary alloys	Office Word	
	Mechanical properties of Ti-Ni ternary alloys at room temperature	Office Word	
	Transformation temperatures of heat treated TiNi ternary alloys	Office Word	
	Materials Properties Database for Selection of High-Temperature Alloys	)F Document	
	Titanium alloys properties		https://app.knovel.com/web/data-search.v?i
	International material collection		https://app.knovel.com/web/browse-a-subji
	Open Quantum Materials Database		http://oqmd.org/materials/
	Materials project		https://www.materialsproject.org/
	materials and substance properties		https://app.knovel.com/web/data-search.v

Fig. A.2. The Fragment of structure of database.

Let us consider queries to the created database.

Query 1. When we select **ID= Characteristic phase transformation temperatures of Ni-Ti ternary alloys,** we obtain the following fragment of information (Table A.2).

Table A.2. Result for Query 1.

	Alloys	M_f, K	M_s, K	A_s, K	A_f, K	Reference
1.	$Ni_{50}Ti_{49.9}Cr_{0.1}$	311.9	342.1	375.7	348.8	[93]
2.	$Ni_{50}Ti_{49.75}Cr_{0.25}$	276.5	302.6	348.9	323.6	[93]
3.	$Ni_{50}Ti_{49.5}Cr_{0.5}$	263.5	291.9	328.5	302.2	[93]
4.	$Ni_{50}Ti_{49.35}Cr_{0.65}$	260.1	284.4	316.3	296.1	[93]
5.	$Ni_{50}Ti_{49.2}Cr_{0.8}$	243.6	267.5	297.4	274.8	[93]
6.	$Ni_{50}Ti_{49}Cr_1$	214.8	237.3	268.3	252.1	[93]
7.	$Ni_{50}Ti_{48.75}Cr_{1.25}$	176.8	199.4	236.5	217.1	[93]
8.	$Ni_{50}Ti_{49.9}V_{0.1}$	323.8	354.7	388.9	359.4	[93]
9.	$Ni_{50}Ti_{49.75}V_{0.25}$	295.7	334.8	369.4	342.4	[93]
10.	$Ni_{50}Ti_{49}V_1$	284.1	318.0	347.7	327.3	[93]
11.	$Ni_{50}Ti_{48}V_2$	285.3	309.0	339.9	315.5	[93]
12.	$Ni_{50}Ti_{47}V_3$	270.7	292.5	317.5	300.3	[93]
13.	$Ni_{50}Ti_{45}V_5$	269.0	283.2	297.0	285.6	[93]
14.	$Ni_{50}Ti_{44}V_6$	261.1	279.1	294.5	281.8	[93]
15.	$Ni_{49.8}Ti_{48.2}Hf_2$	317.2	355.6	394.7	358.3	[93]
16.	$Ni_{49.8}Ti_{46.2}Hf_4$	325.5	358.8	406.8	368.5	[93]
17.	$Ni_{49.8}Ti_{44.2}Hf_6$	329.0	363.9	421.4	381.3	[93]
18.	$Ni_{49.8}Ti_{42.2}Hf_8$	355.9	384.1	448.3	418.1	[93]
19.	$Ni_{49.8}Ti_{40.2}Hf_{10}$	377.7	401.1	464.8	438.4	[93]
20.	$Ni_{49.8}Ti_{39.2}Hf_{11}$	389.8	414.9	475.9	449.0	[93]
21.	$Ni_{49.42}Ti_{35.95}Hf_{14.63}$	380	460	435	510	[91]
22.	$Ni_{49.8}Ti_{35.2}Hf_{15}$	451.0	480.0	530.9	512.0	[93]
23.	$Ni_{49.8}Ti_{30.2}Hf_{20}$	546.4	573.1	610.6	595.8	[93]
24.	$Ni_{45}Ti_{50}Pd_5$	307.7	328.5	355.2	335.2	[93]
25.	$Ni_{43}Ti_{50}Pd_7$	302.3	323.3	347.1	331.3	[93]
26.	$Ni_{41}Ti_{50}Pd_9$	322.3	329.4	341.3	331.2	[93]
27.	$Ni_{39}Ti_{50}Pd_{11}$	318.2	335.7	347.6	334.7	[93]
28.	$Ni_{37}Ti_{50}Pd_{13}$	332.1	348.5	365.3	352.8	[93]
29.	$Ni_{35}Ti_{50}Pd_{15}$	351.3	364.9	377.5	367.2	[93]
30.	$Ni_{33}Ti_{50}Pd_{17}$	365.9	383.2	397.3	385.6	[93]

Query 2. ID=Characteristic phase transformation temperatures of Ni-Ti alloys. Fragment of Result is given below (Table A.3):

Table A.3. Fragment of result on Query 2.

№	Alloy Composition		Transition temperatures				Ref.
	X_1	X_2	Y_1	Y_2	Y_3	Y_4	
	Ti, в at.%	Ni,in at. %	M_f, K	M_s, K	A_s,K	A_f,K	
1.	53.4	46.6	285	330	354	390	[77]
2.	52.4	47.6	301	310	352	407	[77]
3.	51.9	48.1	433	373	396	413	[77]
4.	51.4	48.6	347	374	451	426	[77]
5.	51.0	49.0	289	339	329	366	[77]
6.	50.6	49.4	278	330	336	379	[77]
7.	50.5	49.5	292	320	326	353	[77]
8.	50.4	49.6	286	306	348	387	[77]
9.	50.01	49.99	311.7	338.7	352.1	380.2	[77]
10.	49.81	50.19	296.1	325.8	337.1	365.8	[93]
11.	49.8	50.2	303	222	306	305	[77]
12.	49.61	50.39	275.9	302.1	319.4	339.3	[93]
13.	49.6	50.4	220	243	261	273	[77]
14.	49.5	50.5	242	278	301	317	[77]
15.	49.41	50.59	263.4	290.2	302.0	324.6	[93]
16.	49.20	50.80	245.3	272.1	284.2	308.3	[93]
17.	49.14	50.86	237.9	266.0	277.9	301.3	[93]
18.	49.00	51.00	222.4	246.1	245.5	268.0	[93]
19.	48.90	51.10	207.5	226.9	240.9	254.0	[93]

Query 3. ID= Transformation temperatures of quaternary alloys.

Fragment of Result is given below (Table A.4):

Table A.4. Fragment of result on Query 3.

	Composition	Condition	Transformation temperatures			
		Stress,(MPa)	M_f, K	M_s, K	A_s, K	A_f, K
1.	$Ti_{35.5}Ni_{49.5}Hf_{15}Nb_0$	100	431	462	502	537
2.	$Ti_{35.5}Ni_{49.5}Hf_{15}Nb_0$	200	430	465	507	544
3.	$Ti_{35.5}Ni_{49.5}Hf_{15}Nb_0$	300	436	482	516	564
4.	$Ti_{35.5}Ni_{49.5}Hf_{15}Nb_0$	400	446	499	527	597
5.	$Ti_{35.5}Ni_{49.5}Hf_{15}Nb_0$	500	452	508	536	625
6.	$Ti_{30.5}Ni_{49.5}Hf_{15}Nb_5$	100	411	441	483	518
7.	$Ti_{30.5}Ni_{49.5}Hf_{15}Nb_5$	200	394	437	474	513
8.	$Ti_{30.5}Ni_{49.5}Hf_{15}Nb_5$	300	398	442	478	549
9.	$Ti_{30.5}Ni_{49.5}Hf_{15}Nb_5$	400	411	461	492	587
10.	$Ti_{30.5}Ni_{49.5}Hf_{15}Nb_5$	500	414	484	507	621
11.	$Ti_{25.5}Ni_{49.5}Hf_{15}Nb_{10}$	100	367	406	452	489
12.	$Ti_{25.5}Ni_{49.5}Hf_{15}Nb_{10}$	200	359	403	441	484

(*Continued*)

Table A.4 (*Continued*)

Composition	Condition	Transformation temperatures			
	Stress,(MPa)	M_f, K ·	M_s, K	A_s, K	A_f, K
13. $Ti_{25.5}Ni_{49.5}Hf_{15}Nb_{10}$	300	362	411	445	512
14. $Ti_{25.5}Ni_{49.5}Hf_{15}Nb_{10}$	400	360	435	458	552
15. $Ti_{25.5}Ni_{49.5}Hf_{15}Nb_{10}$	500	391	453	479	571
16. $Ti_{20.5}Ni_{49.5}Hf_{15}Nb_{15}$	100	331	345	433	454
17. $Ti_{20.5}Ni_{49.5}Hf_{15}Nb_{15}$	200	325	356	426	451
18. $Ti_{20.5}Ni_{49.5}Hf_{15}Nb_{15}$	300	327	363	424	461
19. $Ti_{20.5}Ni_{49.5}Hf_{15}Nb_{15}$	400	328	390	417	490
20. $Ti_{20.5}Ni_{49.5}Hf_{15}Nb_{15}$	500	333	422	419	534
21. $Ti_{50}Ni_{25}Pd_{25}Cu_0$	100	432	446	461	470
22. $Ti_{50}Ni_{25}Pd_{25}Cu_0$	300	439	474	482	513
23. $Ti_{50}Ni_{25}Pd_{25}Cu_0$	500	460	503	508	554
24. $Ti_{50}Ni_{25}Pd_{25}Cu_0$	650	471	518	517	577
25. $Ti_{50}Ni_{20}Pd_{25}Cu_5$	100	428	460	465	484

Query 4. ID= Mechanical properties of Ti-Ni ternary alloys at room temperature.

Fragment of Result is given below (Table A.5):

Table A.5. Fragment of result on Query 4.

№	Alloy composition	Condition		Transformation temperatures				Ref.
		Heat treatment, °C	Time ,h	M_f, °C	M_s, °C	A_s,° C	A_f, °C	
1.	$Ti_{47.7}Ni_{52}Re_{0.3}$	1000	24	93	132	139	161	[80]
2.	$Ti_{47.7}Ni_{52}Re_{0.3}$	300	3	64	86	95	117	[80]
3.	$Ti_{47.7}Ni_{52}Re_{0.3}$	400	3	68	92	102	129	[80]
4.	$Ti_{47.7}Ni_{52}Re_{0.3}$	500	3	81	112	119	142	[80]
5.	$Ti_{47.7}Ni_{52}Re_{0.3}$	600	3	94	123	131	149	[80]
6.	$Ti_{50.4}Ni_{44.6}Cu_5$	400	1	93	132	139	161	[84]
7.	$Ti_{50.4}Ni_{44.6}Cu_5$	450	1	64	86	95	117	[84]
8.	$Ti_{50.4}Ni_{44.6}Cu_5$	500	1	68	92	102	129	[84]
9.	$Ti_{50.4}Ni_{44.6}Cu_5$	550	1	81	112	119	142	[84]
10.	$Ti_{50.4}Ni_{44.6}Cu_5$	600	1	94	123	131	149	[84]
11.	$Ti_{44}Ni_{47}Nb_9$	750	15	-63	-29.4	0.9	29.8	[179]
12.	$Ti_{44}Ni_{47}Nb_9$	800	15	-58.6	-24.3	7.4	35.4	[179]
13.	$Ti_{44}Ni_{47}Nb_9$	850	15	-58.8	-24.4	10.8	40.2	[179]
14.	$Ti_{44}Ni_{47}Nb_9$	900	15	51.3	-21.2	10.7	39.3	[179]
15.	$Ti_{44}Ni_{47}Nb_9$	950	15	45.8	-20.9	14.2	40.3	[179]

Query 5. ID= **Materials Properties Database for Selection of High-Temperature Alloys**

Fragment of result based on extraction data from Internet sources is given below (Fig. A.3):

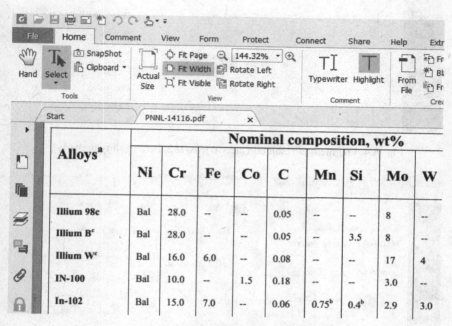

Alloys[a]	Nominal composition, wt%								
	Ni	Cr	Fe	Co	C	Mn	Si	Mo	W
Illium 98c	Bal	28.0	--	--	0.05	--	--	8	--
Illium B[c]	Bal	28.0	--	--	0.05	--	3.5	8	--
Illium W[c]	Bal	16.0	6.0	--	0.08	--	--	17	4
IN-100	Bal	10.0	--	1.5	0.18	--	--	3.0	--
In-102	Bal	15.0	7.0	--	0.06	0.75[b]	0.4[b]	2.9	3.0

Fig. A.3. Fragment of result on Query 5.

Query 6. ID= **Titanium alloys properties**

Fragment of result based on extraction data from Internet sources is given below (Figs. A.3, A.4, and A.5):

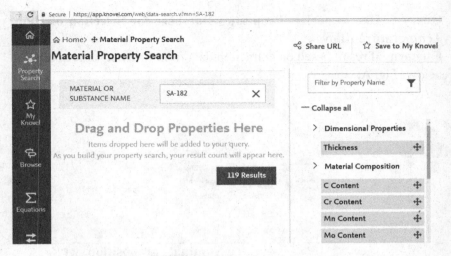

Fig. A.4. Fragment of result on Query 6 (SA-182, Permeability property).

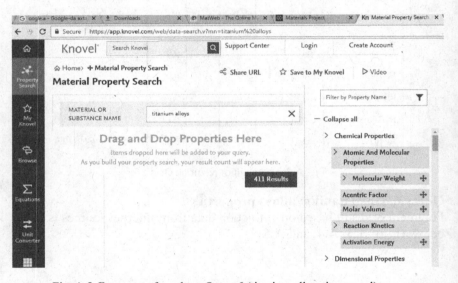

Fig. A.5. Fragment of result on Query 6 (titanium alloys in general).

Query 7. ID= International material collection

Fragment of result based on extraction data from Internet sources is given below:

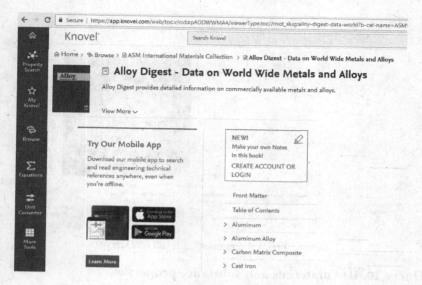

Fig. A.6. Fragment of result on Query 7.

Query 8. ID= Quantum Materials Database.

Fragment of result based on extraction data from Internet sources is given below:

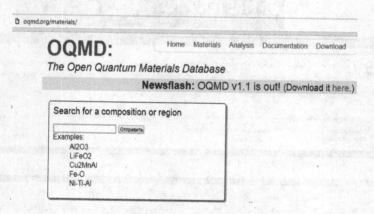

Fig. A.7. Fragment of result on Query 8.

Query 9. ID= Materials project

Fragment of result based on extraction data from Internet sources is given below:

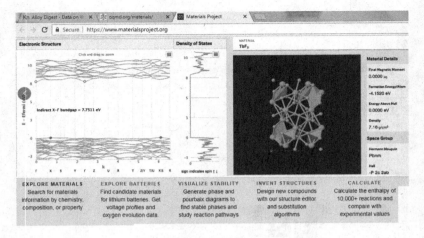

Fig. A.8. Fragment of result on Query 9.

Query 10. ID= materials and substance properties.
Fragment of Result is given below:

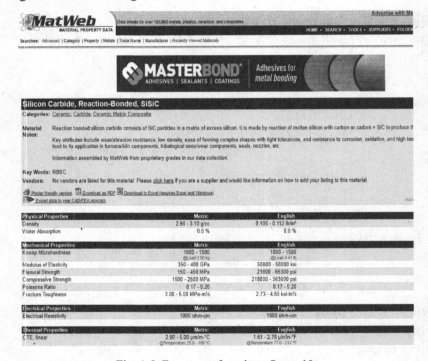

Fig. A.9. Fragment of result on Query 10.

Appendix B

Fuzzy Big Database on Material Synthesis

Let us consider queries to the created database to support material synthesis.

Query 1. When we select ID= Mechanic characteristics of Ti-Ni alloys, we obtain the following fragment of information (Table B.1).

Table B.1. A fragment of the big data on Ti-Ni alloy composition.

Composition		Test temperature	Characteristics		
y_1 (Ti, %)	y_2 (Ni,%)	T , C	z_1 (conventional ultimate strength, MPa)	z_2 (conventional yield strength, MPa)	z_3 (unit elongation, %)
49.8	50.2	−196	1260	410	40
49.8	50.2	20	970	150	55
49	51	20	940	550	62
49	51	200	1050	560	28

Query 2. When we select **ID= Characteristic phase transformation temperatures of Ni-Ti ternary alloys,** we obtain the following fragment of information (Table B.2).

Table B.2. Result for Query 2.

	Alloys	M_f, K	M_s, K	A_s, K	A_f, K	References
1.	$Ni_{29}Ti_{50}Pd_{21}$	406.4	424.5	440.3	426.6	[1]
2.	$Ni_{20}Ti_{50}Pd_{30}$	515.3	533.8	546.8	534.9	[1]

(*Continued*)

Table B.2.   (*Continued*)

	Alloys	M_f, K	M_s, K	A_s, K	A_f, K	Reference
3.	$Ni_{34.5}Ti_{50.5}Pd_{15}$	338	346	348	356	[93]
4.	$Ni_{49.5}Ti_{49.5}Zr_1$	322.3	353.2	388.9	358.3	[93]
5.	$Ni_{49.5}Ti_{47.5}Zr_3$	313.2	345.9	395.8	355.6	[93]
6.	$Ni_{49.5}Ti_{45.5}Zr_5$	304.2	338.7	401.6	352.4	[93]
7.	$Ni_{49.5}Ti_{40.5}Zr_{10}$	344.6	372.4	428.2	401.8	[93]
8.	$Ni_{49.5}Ti_{35.5}Zr_{15}$	435.2	464.0	505.9	483.4	[93]
9.	$Ni_{48.78}Ti_{33.01}Zr_{18.21}$	410	490	470	550	[88]
10.	$Ni_{49.5}Ti_{30.5}Zr_{20}$	535.7	560.4	606.4	584.7	[93]
11.	$Ni_{28.5}Ti_{50.5}Pt_{21}$	548.3	597.6	626.2	585.5	[93]
12.	$Ni_{43}Ti_{52}Cu_5$	307.1	327.7	355.4	337.0	[93]
13.	$Ni_{43.5}Ti_{51.5}Cu_5$	313.6	333.4	358.8	342.4	[93]
14.	$Ni_{44}Ti_{51}Cu_5$	311.3	333.0	360.4	341.1	[93]
15.	$Ni_{44.25}Ti_{50.75}Cu_5$	312.6	333.5	356.5	337.4	[93]
16.	$Ni_{44.5}Ti_{50.5}Cu_5$	309.2	332.8	358.1	337.4	[93]
17.	$Ni_{44.6}Ti_{50.4}Cu_5$	316.3	338.4	360.7	341.1	[93]
18.	$Ni_{44.75}Ti_{50.25}Cu_5$	324.3	341.8	362.9	346.2	[93]
19.	$Ni_{45}Ti_{50}Cu_5$	316.7	344.7	367.7	339.6	[93]
20.	$Ni_{45.2}Ti_{49.8}Cu_5$	301.7	326.6	350.7	328.3	[93]
21.	$Ni_{45.3}Ti_{49.7}Cu_5$	299.3	318.4	339.6	320.7	[93]
22.	$Ni_{45.5}Ti_{49.5}Cu_5$	284.4	303.8	329.8	313.0	[93]
23.	$Ni_{45.7}Ti_{49.3}Cu_5$	270.6	288.8	311.5	294.6	[93]
24.	$Ni_{45.9}Ti_{49.1}Cu_5$	257.3	271.5	288.6	278.3	[93]
25.	$Ni_{46.0}Ti_{49.0}Cu_5$	241.5	261.9	285.3	266.1	[93]
26.	$Ni_{46.1}Ti_{48.9}Cu_5$	234.1	250.9	272.3	259.7	[93]
27.	$Ni_{46.2}Ti_{48.8}Cu_5$	224.4	240.3	259.2	244.0	[93]
28.	$Ni_{47.5}Ti_{50}Cu_{2.5}$	317.9	344.6	380.2	354.2	[93]
29.	$Ni_{42.5}Ti_{50}Cu_{7.5}$	319.7	337.0	356.9	342.7	[93]

Query 3. ID=Characteristic phase transformation temperatures of Ni-Ti alloys. Fragment of Result is given below (Table B.3):

Table B.3. Fragment of result on Query 3.

№	Alloy Composition		Transition temperatures				Ref.
	X_1	X_2	Y_1	Y_2	Y_3	Y_4	
	Ti, в at.%	Ni, in at. %	M_f, K	M_s, K	A_s, K	A_f, K	
1.	53.4	46.6	285	330	354	390	[77]
2.	52.4	47.6	301	310	352	407	[77]
3.	51.9	48.1	433	373	396	413	[77]
4.	51.4	48.6	347	374	451	426	[77]
5.	51.0	49.0	289	339	329	366	[77]
6.	50.6	49.4	278	330	336	379	[77]

(*Continued*)

Table B.3. (*Continued*)

№	Alloy Composition		Transition temperatures				Ref.
	X_1	X_2	Y_1	Y_2	Y_3	Y_4	
	Ti, в at.%	Ni,in at. %	M_f, K	M_s, K	A_s,K	A_f,K	
7.	50.5	49.5	292	320	326	353	[77]
8.	50.4	49.6	286	306	348	387	[77]
9.	50.01	49.99	311.7	338.7	352.1	380.2	[77]
10.	49.81	50.19	296.1	325.8	337.1	365.8	[93]
11.	49.8	50.2	303	222	306	305	[77]
12.	49.6	50.4	220	243	261	273	[77]
13.	49.5	50.5	242	278	301	317	[77]
14.	49.41	50.59	263.4	290.2	302.0	324.6	[93]
15.	49.20	50.80	245.3	272.1	284.2	308.3	[93]

Query 4. ID= Transformation temperatures of quaternary alloys.

Fragment of Result is given below (Table B.4):

Table B.4. Fragment of result on Query 4.

	Composition	Stress, (MPa)	Transformation temperatures			
			M_f, K	M_s, K	A_s, K	A_f, K
1.	$Ti_{35.5}Ni_{49.5}Hf_{15}Nb_0$	100	431	462	502	537
2.	$Ti_{35.5}Ni_{49.5}Hf_{15}Nb_0$	200	430	465	507	544
3.	$Ti_{35.5}Ni_{49.5}Hf_{15}Nb_0$	300	436	482	516	564
4.	$Ti_{35.5}Ni_{49.5}Hf_{15}Nb_0$	400	446	499	527	597
5.	$Ti_{35.5}Ni_{49.5}Hf_{15}Nb_0$	500	452	508	536	625
6.	$Ti_{30.5}Ni_{49.5}Hf_{15}Nb_5$	100	411	441	483	518
7.	$Ti_{30.5}Ni_{49.5}Hf_{15}Nb_5$	200	394	437	474	513
8.	$Ti_{30.5}Ni_{49.5}Hf_{15}Nb_5$	300	398	442	478	549
9.	$Ti_{30.5}Ni_{49.5}Hf_{15}Nb_5$	400	411	461	492	587
10.	$Ti_{30.5}Ni_{49.5}Hf_{15}Nb_5$	500	414	484	507	621
11.	$Ti_{25.5}Ni_{49.5}Hf_{15}Nb_{10}$	100	367	406	452	489
12.	$Ti_{25.5}Ni_{49.5}Hf_{15}Nb_{10}$	200	359	403	441	484
13.	$Ti_{25.5}Ni_{49.5}Hf_{15}Nb_{10}$	300	362	411	445	512
14.	$Ti_{25.5}Ni_{49.5}Hf_{15}Nb_{10}$	400	360	435	458	552
15.	$Ti_{25.5}Ni_{49.5}Hf_{15}Nb_{10}$	500	391	453	479	571
16.	$Ti_{20.5}Ni_{49.5}Hf_{15}Nb_{15}$	100	331	345	433	454
17.	$Ti_{20.5}Ni_{49.5}Hf_{15}Nb_{15}$	200	325	356	426	451
18.	$Ti_{20.5}Ni_{49.5}Hf_{15}Nb_{15}$	300	327	363	424	461
19.	$Ti_{20.5}Ni_{49.5}Hf_{15}Nb_{15}$	400	328	390	417	490
20.	$Ti_{20.5}Ni_{49.5}Hf_{15}Nb_{15}$	500	333	422	419	534
21.	$Ti_{50}Ni_{25}Pd_{25}Cu_0$	100	432	446	461	470
22.	$Ti_{50}Ni_{25}Pd_{25}Cu_0$	300	439	474	482	513
23.	$Ti_{50}Ni_{25}Pd_{25}Cu_0$	500	460	503	508	554
24.	$Ti_{50}Ni_{25}Pd_{25}Cu_0$	650	471	518	517	577
25.	$Ti_{50}Ni_{20}Pd_{25}Cu_5$	100	428	460	465	484
26.	$Ti_{50}Ni_{20}Pd_{25}Cu_5$	300	443	487	488	520

(*Continued*)

Table B.4. (*Continued*)

	Composition	Stress, (MPa)	Transformation temperatures			
			M_f, K	M_s, K	A_s, K	A_f, K
27.	$Ti_{50}Ni_{20}Pd_{25}Cu_5$	500	459	512	506	558
28.	$Ti_{50}Ni_{20}Pd_{25}Cu_5$	650	469	526	520	583
29.	$Ti_{50}Ni_{20}Pd_{25}Cu_5$	700	476	534	523	595

Query 5. ID= Mechanical properties of Ti-Ni ternary alloys at room temperature. Fragment of Result is given below (Table B.5):

Table B.5. Fragment of result on Query 5.

	Composition	Stress, MPa		Transformation temperatures				Ref.
		Heat treat.,°C	Time, h	M_f, °C	M_s, °C	A_s, °C	A_f, °C	
1.	$Ti_{47.7}Ni_{52}Re_{0.3}$	1000	24	93	132	139	161	[80]
2.	$Ti_{47.7}Ni_{52}Re_{0.3}$	300	3	64	86	95	117	[80]
3.	$Ti_{47.7}Ni_{52}Re_{0.3}$	400	3	68	92	102	129	[80]
4.	$Ti_{47.7}Ni_{52}Re_{0.3}$	500	3	81	112	119	142	[80]
5.	$Ti_{47.7}Ni_{52}Re_{0.3}$	600	3	94	123	131	149	[80]
6.	$Ti_{50.4}Ni_{44.6}Cu_5$	400	1	93	132	139	161	[84]
7.	$Ti_{50.4}Ni_{44.6}Cu_5$	450	1	64	86	95	117	[84]
8.	$Ti_{50.4}Ni_{44.6}Cu_5$	500	1	68	92	102	129	[84]
9.	$Ti_{50.4}Ni_{44.6}Cu_5$	550	1	81	112	119	142	[84]
10.	$Ti_{50.4}Ni_{44.6}Cu_5$	600	1	94	123	131	149	[84]
11.	$Ti_{44}Ni_{47}Nb_9$	750	15	−63	−29.4	0.9	29.8	[179]
12.	$Ti_{44}Ni_{47}Nb_9$	800	15	−58.6	−24.3	7.4	35.4	[179]
13.	$Ti_{44}Ni_{47}Nb_9$	850	15	−58.8	−24.4	10.8	40.2	[179]
14.	$Ti_{44}Ni_{47}Nb_9$	900	15	51.3	−21.2	10.7	39.3	[179]
15.	$Ti_{44}Ni_{47}Nb_9$	950	15	45.8	−20.9	14.2	40.3	[179]

Query 6. ID= Austenitic Transformation temperatures of Ti-Ni ternary alloys. Fragment of Result is given below (Table B.6):

Table B.6. Fragment of result on Query 6.

Composition			Transformation temperatures			
x_1 (Ni, %)	x_2 (Ti, %)	x_3 (Hf, %)	y_1(martensitic finish temperature, K)	y_2(martensitic start temperature, K)	y_3(austenitic start temperature, K)	y_4(austenitic finish temperature, K)
49.8	46.2	4	325,5	358.8	406,8	368,5
49.8	44.2	6	329,0	363,9	421,4	381.3
49,8	35,2	15	451,0	480,0	530,9	512,0
49,8	30.2	20	546,4	573,1	610,6	595,8
.	.	.	.	.	.	.
.	.	.	.	.	.	.
.	.	.	.	.	.	.

Query 7. ID=weighted performance indices for pressure vessel.
Fragment of Result is given below (Table B.7):

Table B.7. Fragment of result on Query 7.

Scaled PREN	Scaled yield strength	Scaled weldability	Scaled impact strength	Performance index
26,60	3,60	18,40	5,00	53,50
29,70	4,40	23,00	8,60	65,60
19,80	3,60	23,00	5,00	51,30
22,30	3,20	23,00	8,60	57,10
26,00	3,60	18,40	6,80	54,70
22,30	5,40	13,80	11,30	52,70
...	...	...	...	...
47,00	4,60	18,40	13,50	83,50
29,70	4,40	18,40	15,80	68,30
20,40	12,00	18,40	5,00	55,80
21,00	9,80	23,00	4,50	58,30
23,50	4,60	23,00	13,50	64,60
11,80	2,50	18,40	9,00	41,60

(*Continued*)

Table B.7. (*Continued*)

Scaled PREN	Scaled yield strength	Scaled weldability	Scaled impact strength	Performance index
15,50	2,50	18,40	8,80	45,10
22,90	5,80	13,80	7,10	49,50
26,60	6,20	4,60	3,20	40,50
...	...	...	...	...
18,60	2,90	18,40	8,80	48,60
32,20	6,20	18,40	6,00	62,70
42,70	4,30	23,00	15,20	85,10
21,00	2,50	18,40	8,80	50,70
21,60	9,50	18,40	4,50	54,00

Query 8. ID=material properties of candidate austenitic stainless steel. Fragment of Result is given below (Table B.8):

Table B.8. Fragment of result on Query 8.

Designation				Properties			
Industry	UNS	Fy (MPa)	Ft (MPa)	Young's Modulus	Density (g/cm3)	CTE (μm/m•°C)	ThrmCond (W/m•K)
304	S30400	205	515	193	8.00	17.2	16.2
316	S31600	205	515	193	8.00	15.9	16.2
316L	S31603	170	450	193	8.00	16.0	16.2
317L	S31703	240	585	200	8.00	16.5	14.4
317LM	S31725	205	515	200	8.00	17.5	16.2
254 SMO	S31254	300	650	200	8.00	16.0	13.0
AL-6XN	N08367	365	690	200	8.06	15.3	11.8
Alloy 825	N08825	300	690	206	8.13	13.9	11.1
904L	N08904	270	605	196	7.95	15.3	11.5
1925hMo	N08926	300	650	193	8.10	16.1	12.0

Query 9. ID=material properties of candidate duplex   stainless steel.
Fragment of Result is given below (Table B.9):.

Table B.9. Fragment of result on Query 9.

Designation		Properties					
UNS	Industry	Fy (MPa)	Ft (MPa)	Young's Modulus	Density (g/cm3)	CTE (μm/m•°C)	ThrmCond (W/m•K)
S31803	2205	450	620	200	7.82	16.5	14.6
S32304	2304 Ferralium	400	600	200	7.80	13.0	18.0
S32550	255 Zeron	550	760	210	7.81	11.9	14.2
S32760	100 7-Mo	550	750	190	7.84	12.8	12.9
S32950	PLUS	480	690	200	7.74	11.5	15.3

Query 10. ID=material properties of candidate Ferritic   stainless steel. Fragment of Result is given below (Table B.10):

Table B.10. Fragment of result on Query 10.

Designation		Properties					
UNS	Industry	Fy (MPa)	Ft (MPa)	Young's Modulus	Density (g/cm3)	CTE (μm/m•°C)	ThrmCond (W/m•K)
S43000	430	205	415	200	7.80	10.4	26.1
S44627	E-Brite	275	450	200	7.66	9.9	16.7
S44635	Monit	515	620	200	7.80	~10	~16
S44660	Sea-Cure	450	585	214	7.70	9.5	16.4
S44735	29-4C	415	550	200	7.67	9.2	15.2
S44800	29-4-2	415	550	200	7.70	9.2	15.1

Query 11. ID=material properties of candidate Aluminum Alloys.
Fragment of Result is given below (Table B.11):

Table B.11. Fragment of result on Query 11.

Designation		Properties				
		Fy	Ft	Young's	Density	CTE
UNS	Industry	(MPa)	(MPa)	Modulus	(g/cm3)	(μm/m·°C)
A92014	2014 O	97	186	72	2.80	22.5
A93003	Alcad 3003 H14	110	150	70	2.73	23.2
A93004	3004 H32	170	215	70	2.72	23.2
A94043	4043 H16	180	205	70	2.68	22.0
A95052	5052 H34	214	262	69	2.68	23.2
A95083	5083 O	145	290	70	2.66	24.2
A95086	5086 H34	255	325	71	2.66	13.2
A96061	6061 T6	276	310	69	2.70	23.6
A96063	6063 T4	90	172	68	2.69	23.4
A97072	7072	97	131	68	2.72	23.6
A97075	7075 O	103	228	71	2.80	23.4

Query 12. ID=material properties of candidate Nickel Alloys.

Fragment of Result is given below (Table B.12):

Table B.12. Fragment of result on Query 12.

Designation		Properties					
		Fy	Ft	Young's	Density	CTE (μm/m·°C)	ThrmCond
UNS	Industry	(MPa)	(MPa)	Modulus	(g/cm3)	°C)	(W/m·K)
N04400	Monel 400	240	550	180	8.80	13.9	21.8
N04405	Monel R-405	240	550	180	8.80	13.7	21.8
N05500	Monel K-500	790	1100	180	8.44	13.7	17.5
N06022	C-22	370	715	205	8.69	12.4	10.1
N06030	G-30	310	690	199	8.22	12.8	10.2
N06059	Alloy 59	380	770	210	8.60	12.2	10.4
N06200	C-2000	110	750	206	8.50	12.4	10.8
N06625	Alloy 625	517	930	207	8.44	12.8	9.8
N07718	Alloy 718	1000	1240	211	8.19	13.0	11.4
N06686	Alloy 686	700	940	207	8.73	12.0	~10

(Continued)

Table B.12. (*Continued*)

Designation		Properties					
		Fy	Ft	Young's	Density	CTE (μm/m•ºC)	ThrmCond
UNS	Industry	(MPa)	(MPa)	Modulus	(g/cm3)	ºC)	(W/m•K)
N010276	C-276	355	790	205	8.89	11.2	9.8
R20033	Alloy 33	380	720	195	7.90	15.3	13.4

Query 13. ID=material properties of candidate Copper Alloys.

Fragment of Result is given below (Table B.13):

Table B.13. Fragment of result on Query 13.

Designation		Mechanical Properties						
		Fy	Ft	Elong	Density	CTE (μm/m•ºC)	ThrmCon	Impact
UNS	Industry	(MPa)	(MPa)	%	(g/cm3)	ºC)	(W/m•K)	Strng
C61400	Al Bronze	310	535	40	7.89	16.2	56.5	81
C63000	NiAl Bronze 90-10	407	776	59	7.58	16.2	37.7	18
C70600	CuproNi 70-30	338	415	20	8.94	17.1	40.0	60
C71500	CuproNi	140	380	45	8.94	16.2	29.0	107
C72200	CuproNi w/ Cr	125	315	46	8.94	15.8	34.5	80
C83600	85-5-5-5	117	255	30	8.83	18.0	72.0	14
C86500	Mn Bronze	195	490	30	8.30	20.3	87.0	42
C95500	Al Bronze 9D	275	620	6	7.53	16.2	42.0	14
C95700	MnAl Bronze	275	620	20	7.53	17.6	12.1	40
C95800	Alpha NiAl Bronze	240	585	15	7.64	16.2	36.0	22
C96200	90 Cu-10 Ni	172	310	20	8.94	16.2	45.0	135
C96400	70-30 CuNi	255	470	28	8.94	16.0	29.0	105

Query 14. ID=composition of candidate Nickel Alloys.

Fragment of Result is given below (Table B.14):

Table B14. Fragment of result on query 14.

| Designation | | Composition | | | | | | | |
UNS	Industry	Al%	C%	Co%	Cr%	Cu%	Fe%	Mn%	Mo%
N04400	Monel 400	-	0.30 max	-	-	28.0 - 34.0	2.5 max	2.0 max	-
N04405	Monel 405	-	0.30 max	-	-	28.0 - 34.0	2.5 max	2.0 max	-
N05500	Monel K-500	2.3 - 3.2	0.18 max	-	-	27.0 - 33.0	2.0 max	1.5 max	-
N06022	C-22	-	0.02 max	2.5 max	20.0 - 23.0	-	2.0 - 6.0	0.50 max	12.5 - 14.5
N06030	G-30	-	0.03 max	5.0 max	28.0 - 31.5	-	13.0 - 17.0	1.5 max	4.0 - 6.0
N06059	Alloy 59	0.1 - 0.4	-	-	22.0 - 24.0	-	1.5 max	0.50 max	16.5 max
N06200	C-2000	-	0.01 max	2.0 max	22.0 - 24.0	1.3 - 1.9	3.0 max	0.50 max	15.0 - 17.0
N06625	Alloy 625	0.4	0.10 max	1.0 max	20.0 - 23.0	-	5.0 max	0.50 max	8.0 - 100
N07718	Alloy 718	0.2 - 0.8	0.08 max	1.0 max	17.0 - 21.0	0.30 max	balance	0.35 max	2.8
N09925	Alloy 925	0.1 - 0.5	0.03 max	-	19.5 - 22.5	1.5 - 3.0	22.0 min	1.0 max	2.5 - 3.5
N06686	Alloy 686	-	0.01 max	-	19.0 - 23.0	-	1.0 max	0.75 max	15.0 - 17.0
N08926	1925hMo	-	0.02 max	-	20.0 - 21.0	0.8 - 1.0	0.40 max	1.0 max	6.0 - 6.8
N10276	C-276	-	0.01 max	2.5 max	14.5 - 16.5	-	4.0 - 7.0	1.0 max	15.0 - 17.0
R20033	Alloy 33	-	0.02 max	-	31.0 - 35.0	0.3 - 1.2	balance	2.0 max	0.50 - 2.0

Query 15. ID=composition of candidate Copper Alloys. Fragment of Result is given below (Table B.15):

Table B15. Fragment of result on query 15

UNS	Designation	Composition						
		Al%	C%	Cr%	Cu%	Fe%	Mn%	
C61400	Al Bronze	6.0 - 8.0	-	-	balance	1.5 - 3.5	1.0 max	
C63000	NiAl Bronze	9.0 - 11.0	-	-	balance	2.0 - 4.0	1.5 max	
UNS	Industry	Al%	C%	Cr%	Cu%	Fe%	Mn%	
C70600	90-10 CuproNi	-	-	-	balance	1.0 - 1.8	1.0 max	
C71500	70-30 CuproNi	-	-	-	balance	0.40 - 1.0	1.0 max	
C72200	CuproNi w/ Cr	-	0.03 max	0.30 - 0.7	balance	0.5 - 1.0	1.0 max	
C83600	85-5-5-5	0.01 max	-	-	balance	0.30 max	-	
C86500	Mn Bronze	0.5 - 1.5	-	-	balance	0.40 - 2.0	0.10 - 1.5	
C95500	Al Bronze 9D	10.0 -11.5	-	-	balance	3.0 - 5.0	3.5 max	
C95700	MnAl Bronze	7.0 - 8.5	-	-	balance	2.0 - 4.0	11.0 - 14.0	
C95800	Alpha NiAl Bmz	8.5 - 9.5	-	-	balance	3.5 - 4.5	0.8 - 1.5	
C96200	90 Cu-10 Ni	-	0.10 max	-	balance	1.0 - 1.8	1.5 max	
C96400	70-30 CuNi	-	0.20 max	-	balance	0.25 - 1.5	1.5 max	

Documentation of ZNCalc Software for Computation with Z-numbers

In recent years Z-number concept naturally arise in the areas of control decision making, forecasting, modeling of complex systems and others. Unfortunately to date there are no effective software for Z-arithmetic is in existence. Here is presented software for Z-arithmetic ZNCalc. Exploration of this software shows that the suggested software satisfies all requirements of software quality standards ISO 9126.

C.1. Algorithm description

Software was developed on the VBA MS Excel language. This is allowed to realize the all inclusive principle (all in one file). System is presented as MS excel workbook with macros. Using MS Excel and VBA has some advantages — *usable* user interface and visualization environment, embedded tools which allow to reduce development time. Help also included in workbook. As data structures worksheet ranges were used. It is convenient method for data communication between modules. Software uses 3 worksheets: Worksheet 1 is used for input data and output results. Worksheet 2 is used for implementation of basic calculations. Worksheet 3 is used for fuzzy arithmetic. User can see trace of all calculation (intermediate results) and use them for additional analysis. MS Excel workbook include also test data for verification program. User can save results of calculations in archive spreadsheet. Software consist of 3 parts which are loaded from main user form (Fig. C.1). Type of arithmetic operation is chosen by ComboBox.

Button for cleaning worksheets 1 and 2 are located on the userform. Cleaning worksheet 3 is realized before computations with fuzzy arithmetic.

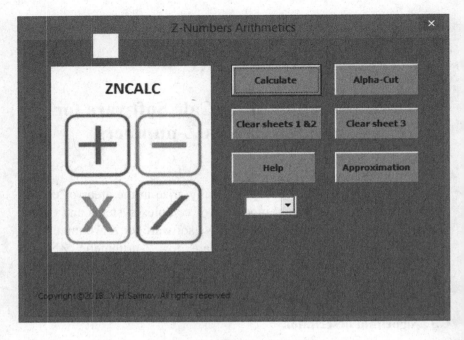

Fig. C.1. Main userform.

Software consists of main module and several functional modules.

-**MAİN** is a core module of program realized for control of computation processes, calculate convolution of probability distributions and membership functions of resulting z-number.

-**TRAP1()** generates discrete values on base of parametric representation.

-**SOLVER1()** prepares the data to apply Solver Add-In that solves goal programming problem to determine probability distributions.

-**OPSUMİNDEX()** implementation of arithmetic calculations, determination of indexes of duplications.

Data can be presented in parametric format or non parametric by discrete values. Switch between mode (parametric/Non parametric) is organized by ComboBox (Fig. C.2). Also Button RUN is used to load UserForm. A user indicates dimensions of first sides of Z-numbers as Na1 and Na2 , for second side Nb1 and Nb2. In case of parametric presentation data are entered in corresponding cells as it is shown on the

Fig. C.2. For triangular numbers b=c. Parametric presentation is converted to discrete values by special module TRAP1().

Fig. C.2. Panel for run program and switch data input mode.

Z1	a	b	c	d	Na1	a	b	c	d	Nb1
A	107,00	112,50	115,50	129,00	11	0,47	0,58	0,58	0,78	5

Z2	a	b	c	d	Na2	a	b	c	d	Nb2
A	7,00	7,50	8,50	9,00	11	0,80	0,85	0,86	0,91	8

Fig. C.3. Parametric data input.

In case of non parametric data presentation data are entered in corresponding cells as it is shown on the Fig. C.4.

№	A1	Mu1	A2	Mu2	Mu1	№	B1	Mu1	B2	Mu2
1	0,07	0	0,32	0		1	0,558031	0	0,595924	0
2	0,0912	0,25	0,3456	0,25		2	0,589341	0,25	0,616166	0,25
3	0,1124	0,5	0,3712	0,5		3	0,620652	0,5	0,636408	0,5
4	0,1336	0,75	0,3968	0,75		4	0,651962	0,75	0,656651	0,75
5	0,1548	1	0,4224	1		5	0,683272	1	0,676893	1
6	0,17999999	1	0,45	1		6	0,710687	1	0,700001	1
7	0,20999999	0,8	0,474	0,8		7	0,732876	0,8	0,720001	0,8
8	0,23999999	0,6	0,498	0,6		8	0,755065	0,6	0,740001	0,6
9	0,26999999	0,4	0,522	0,4		9	0,777254	0,4	0,760001	0,4
10	0,29999999	0,2	0,546	0,2		10	0,799443	0,2	0,780001	0,2
11	0,32999998	0	0,57	0		11	0,821632	0	0,800001	0

Fig.C.4. Nonparametric data entering.

Consider the description of the implementation of main module of program. (Fig. C.5)

Unit 1. Set entering mode (Parametric/Non Parametric) (Fig. C.2).

Unit 2. Input parameters of given Z-numbers (Fig. C.3).

Unit 3. Call module TRAP1() which provides generation of discrete values and their presentation on the Worksheet.

Unit 4. Direct entering data in the ranges of Worksheet 1 (Fig. C.4).

Unit 5. Copy all necessary data from Worksheet 1 to Worksheet 2.

Unit 6. Initialization of arrays dimensions.

Unit 7. Control of loop for calculations of probability distributions of Z_1.

Unit 8. Preparing data for module Solver1(), which calls Solver Add-Ins.

Unit 9. Calls Solver1(), gets results and forms the P_1 matrix of probability distribution for Z_1.

$$\min\left(\sum_{i=1}^{n}(p_i\mu_i - b_k)\right)^2 \qquad \sum_{i=1}^{n}\frac{x_i\mu_i}{\sum_{i=1}^{n}\mu_i} = \sum_{i=1}^{n}x_i p_i \qquad p_i \geq 0, \sum_{i=1}^{n}p_i = 1$$

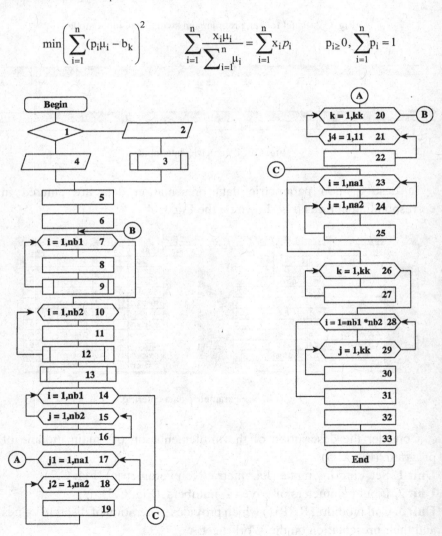

Fig. C.5. Flowchart of main module.

Unit 10. Control of loop for calculations of probability distributions of Z_2.

Unit 11. Preparing data for module Solver1(), which is used as Solver Add-Ins.

Unit 12. Call Solver1(), get results and form the P2 matrix of probability distribution for Z_2.

Unit 13. Call Opsumindex(). Calculation of support A_{12}, duplications indexes and amount of non duplicated results.

Unit 14,15. Control loop of calculation of distribution function P_{12}.

Unit 16. Computation of membership functions of Z_{12}.

Unit 17, 18. Control loop for join probability distribution function P_{12}

Unit 19. Calculation of join probability distribution function P_{12}.

$$p_{12}(x) = \sum p_1(x_1)p_2(x_2)$$

Unit 20, 21. Control loop for calculation convolution.

Unit 22. Calculation of convolutions.

$$p_{12}(x) = \sum_{x=x_1{}^*x_2} p_1(x_1)p_2(x_2)$$

Unit 23, 24. Control loop for calculation of membership function of A_{12} (first part of Z_{12}).

Unit 25. Calculation of membership function of A_{12}.

Unit 26. Control loop for removing duplications of results.

Unit 27. Final calculation of membership function of A_{12}.

Unit 28, 29. Control loop for calculation support of B_{12}.

Unit 30. Calculation of B_{12}.

Unit 31. Sorting B_{12}, and membership function of B_{12}.

Unit 32. Sorting A_{12}, and membership function of A_{12}.

Unit 33. Copy results to worksheet 1.

Results of program are presented on values format (Fig. C.6) and graphical format (Fig. C.7).

N	A12	Mu12	Mu12-alpha				B12	Mu12
			Results					
1	0,39	0	0				0	0
2	0,4112	0	0				0	0
3	0,4156	0	0				0	0
4	0,4324	0	0				0	0
5	0,4368	0,25	0,25				0	0
6	0,4412	0	0,25				0	0
7	0,4536	0	0,25				0	0
8	0,458	0,25	0,25				0	0
9	0,4624	0,25	0,25				0	0
10	0,4668	0	0,25				0	0

Fig. C.6. Output of results.

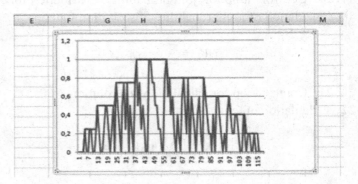

Fig. C.7. Membership function for result A12.

C.2. User guideline

When file is opened press on button Parameters of macros security warning and choose option Enable this content.

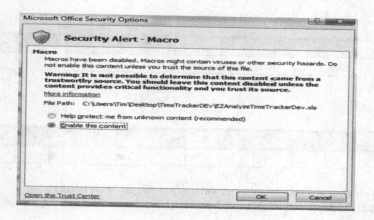

1. Automatically is opened UserForm, close it for first start.

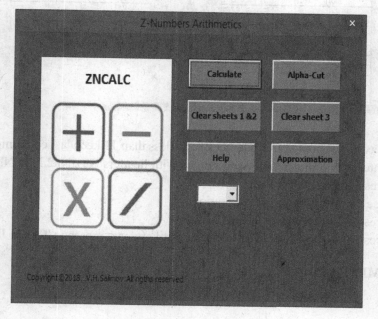

2. Choose Worksheet 1 and switch ComboBox (Fig. C.2) value to **Nonparametric** if you want to enter directly discrete values or to **Parametric** when we want to use parametric input In this case enter values into cell with headers a b c d (Fig. C.3)

Z1	A					B				
	a	b	c	d	Na1	a	b	c	d	Nb1
	107,00	112,50	115,50	129,00	11	0,47	0,58	0,58	0,78	5

Z2	A					B				
	a	b	c	d	Na2	a	b	c	d	Nb2
	7,00	7,50	8,50	9,00	11	0,80	0,85	0,86	0,91	8

3. If you choose first variant enter values into ranges with headers
A1,Mu1,A2,Mu2 and B1,Mu1, B2 ,Mu2 .

№	A1	Mu1	A2	Mu2
1	100	0,02	7	0,02
2	101,25	0,265	7,125	0,265
3	102,5	0,51	7,25	0,51
4	103,75	0,755	7,375	0,755
5	105	1	7,5	1
6	110	1	8,5	1
7	112	0,8	8,6	0,804
8	114	0,6	8,7	0,608
9	116	0,401	8,8	0,412
10	118	0,201	8,9	0,216
11	120	0,001	9	0,02

№	B1	Mu1	B2	Mu2
1	0,5	0,091	0,8	0,167
2	0,6	1	0,84	1
3	0,7	1	0,85	1
4	0,8	0,091	0,9	0,167
5				
6				
7				
8				
9				
10				
11				

4. Max dimension =11, if number of data less than 11 keep last cells empty.

5. Enter actual dimensions into ranges with headers Na1,Na2,Nb1,Nb2.

6. Press on the button Run.

7. Use ComboBox and set operation.

8. Press on button Clear sheets 1&2.

9. Press on button Calculate and wait until appears message **TASK IS**.

COMPLETED

10. Ok and press on button Clear Sheet 3.

11. Press on button Alpha-Cut and wait until appears Message **TASK IS COMPLETED**.

12. You can use Approximation if membership functions like trapeziodal function.

13. Ok and press on button Approximation.

14. Switch on sheet 1 and analyze results in ranges A12,Mu12, Mu12-Alpha,B12,MU12.

			RESULTS		
N	A12	Mu12	Mu12-alpha	B12	Mu12
1	107	0,02		0,464923	0,091
2	107,125	0,02		0,478525	0,091
3	107,25	0,02		0,481534	0,091
4	107,375	0,02		0,49699	0,091
5	107,5	0,02		0,54708	0,167
6	108,25	0,02		0,563623	1
7	108,375	0,265		0,56727	1
8	108,5	0,265		0,585701	0,167
9	108,6	0,02		0,627726	0,167
10	108,625	0,265		0,647358	1
11	108,7	0,02		0,651655	1
12	108,75	0,265		0,673058	0,167
13	108,8	0,02		0,70033	0,091
14	108,9	0,02		0,724824	0,091
15	109	0,02		0,730223	0,091
16	109,5	0,02		0,75693	0,091

15. In cells A,B,C,D are presented parameters for trapezoidal approximation.

A	B	C	D
107	112,5	118,5	129

A	B	C	D
0,464923	0,563623	0,651655	0,75693

16. Also join Graph of Mu12, Mu12alpha is presented.

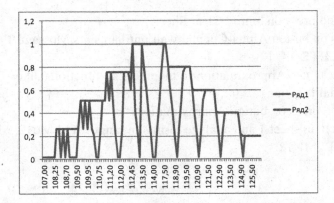

17. Copy Sheet1 in archive (recommended).

18. Use test examples to verify this program.

19. Good Luck!!!

During the running of the program some error situations may happen. Program generate corresponding alerts. User should correct input data and run program again (press Run button). List of error alerts are presented below

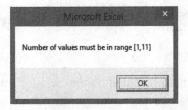

It is happened when you enter the number of points (Na1,Na2,Nb1,Nb2) out of range [1,11].

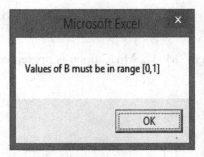

It means that support of B is probability.

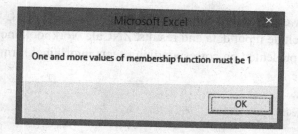

It means the membership function must have as minimum one value 1.

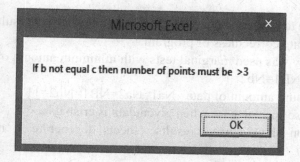

This is happened when we use trapezoidal fuzzy numbers (Parametric mode).

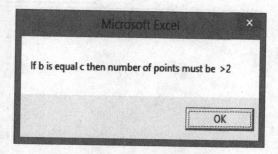

This is happened when we use triangular fuzzy numbers (Parametric mode).

Software verification

According to SDLC (software development life cycle) ZNCalc was tested.

For testing were prepared some **test cases** by experts (Figs. C.8 and C.9). Case test include input data and results. ZNCalc workbook include 2 case tests which presented on corresponding sheets in original format.

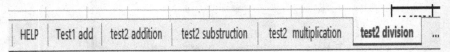

Fig. C.8. List of test case worksheets.

Using these test-cases show that ZNCalc give the correct results.

It demonstrate correctness of program.

Additionally was used marginal tests with minimum amount of data
Na1=Na2=NB1=Nb2=1

And maximum amount of data   Na1=Na2=NB1=Nb2=11

Also was use special case when given data is crisp data

Test session show correct results. (sheets degenerate 1, marginal 1, marginal 2)

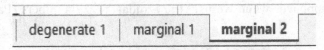

Fig. C.9. List of special test case worksheets.

Z1=(A1,B1)

x1	memb_A1	b1	memb_B1
10	0	0,2	0
11	0,2	0,35	1
12	0,4	0,5	0
13	0,6		
14	0,8		
15	1		
16	0,8		
17	0,6		
18	0,4		
19	0,2		
20	0		

Z2=(A2,B2)

x2	memb_A2	b2	memb_B2
100	0	0,5	0
102	0,2	0,6	1
104	0,4	0,7	0
106	0,6		
108	0,8		
110	1		
112	0,8		
114	0,6		
116	0,4		
118	0,2		
120	0		

results

x12	memb_A12
110	0
111	0
112	0
113	0,2
114	0,2
115	0,2
116	0,4
117	0,4
118	0,4
119	0,6
120	0,6
121	0,6
122	0,8
123	0,8
124	0,8
125	1
126	0,8
127	0,8
128	0,8
129	0,6
130	0,6
131	0,6
132	0,4
133	0,4
134	0,4
135	0,2
136	0,2
137	0,2
138	0
139	0
140	0

B12:

b12	memb_B12
0,538918	0
0,554576	0
0,568046	0
0,587226	0
0,606843	1
0,624977	0
0,62963	0
0,655111	0
0,678353	0

Results of ZNCalc for this test case

№	A1	Mu1	A2	Mu2
1	10,00	0,00	100,00	0,00
2	11,00	0,20	102,00	0,20
3	12,00	0,40	104,00	0,40
4	13,00	0,60	106,00	0,60
5	14,00	0,80	108,00	0,80
6	15,00	1,00	110,00	1,00
7	16,00	0,80	112,00	0,80
8	17,00	0,60	114,00	0,60
9	18,00	0,40	116,00	0,40
10	19,00	0,20	118,00	0,20
11	20,00	0,00	120,00	0,00

№	B1	Mu1	B2	Mu2
1	0,20	0,00	0,50	0,00
2	0,35	1,00	0,60	1,00
3	0,50	0,00	0,70	0,00
4				
5				
6				
7				
8				
9				
10				
11				

Results

N	A12	Mu12	Mu12-alpha		B12	Mu12
1	110,000	0,000	0,000		0,539	0,000
2	111,000	0,000	0,000		0,587	0,000
3	112,000	0,000	0,000		0,630	0,000
4	113,000	0,200	0,200		0,555	0,000
5	114,000	0,200	0,200		0,607	1,000
6	115,000	0,200	0,200		0,655	0,000
7	116,000	0,400	0,400		0,568	0,000
8	117,000	0,400	0,400		0,625	0,000
9	118,000	0,400	0,400		0,678	0,000
10	119,000	0,600	0,600			
11	120,000	0,600	0,600			
12	121,000	0,600	0,600			
13	122,000	0,800	0,800			
14	123,000	0,800	0,800			
15	124,000	0,800	0,800			
16	125,000	1,000	1,000			
17	126,000	0,800	0,800			
18	127,000	0,800	0,800			
19	128,000	0,800	0,800			
20	129,000	0,600	0,600			
21	130,000	0,600	0,600			
22	131,000	0,600	0,600			
23	132,000	0,400	0,400			
24	133,000	0,400	0,400			
25	134,000	0,400	0,400			
26	135,000	0,200	0,200			
27	136,000	0,200	0,200			
28	137,000	0,200	0,200			
29	138,000	0,000	0,000			
30	139,000	0,000	0,000			
31	140,000	0,000	0,000			

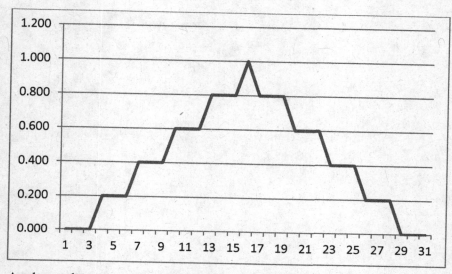

Analogously *test-case* 2 and other *test-cases* can be verified.

Bibliography

1. Abreu, M. P. (2007). On the development of computational tools for the design of beam assemblies for Boron neutron capture therapy, *J Comput Aided Mater Des*, 14, pp. 235-251.
2. Ağirgün, B. (2012). Supplier Selection Based on Fuzzy Rough-AHP and VIKOR, *Nevşehir Üniversitesi Fen Bilimleri Enstitü Dergisi*, 2, pp. 1-11.
3. Agrawal, A, Deshpande, P. D., Cecen, A., Basavarsu, G. P., Choudhary, A. N. and Kalidindi, S. R. (2014). Exploration of data science techniques to predict fatigue strength of steel from composition and processing parameters, *Integr Mater Manuf Innovation*, 3, pp. 1-19.
4. Agrawal, A. and Choudhary, A. (2016). Perspective: Materials informatics and big data: Realization of the 'fourth paradigm' in science in materials science, *APL Mater*, 4(5), 053208.
5. Ahn, K. K. and Nguyen, B. K. (2008). Modeling and control of shape memory alloy actuators using Preisach model, genetic algorithm and fuzzy logic, *Mechatronics*, (18), pp. 141-152.
6. AI-Powered Materials Data Platform. https://citrination.com.
7. Aleksendric, D. and Carlone, P. (2015). *Soft Computing in the Design and Manufacturing of Composite Materials*, (Woodhead Publishing).
8. Aliev R. A., Huseynov O. H. and Serdaroglu R. (2016). Ranking of Z-Numbers and Its Application in Decision Making, *Int J Inf Tech Decis*, 15(6), pp. 1503-1519.
9. Aliev, R. A. (2017). *Uncertain Computation-Based Decision Theory*, (World Scientific, Singapore).
10. Aliev, R. A., Alizadeh, A. V., Huseynov, O. H. and Jabbarova KI. (2015). Z-number based Linear Programming, *Int J Intell Syst*, 30(5), pp.563-589.
11. Aliev, R. A., Guirimov, B. G., Huseynov O.H. (2018). Z-number based clustering for knowledge discovery with reliability measure of results. *Proc. International Conference on Information Society and Smart Cities, ISC 2018*, Fitzwilliam College, University of Cambridge, Cambridge city, United Kingdom, 27-28 June, 2018.
12. Aliev, R. A. and Aliyev, R. R. (2001) *Soft Computing and Its Applications*. (World Scientific, New Jersey, London, Singapore, Hong Kong).
13. Aliev, R. A. and Guirimov, B. G. (2012). *Type-2 Fuzzy neural networks and their applications*, (Springer.)
14. Aliev, R. A. and Huseynov O.H. (2014). *Decision theory with imperfect information*. (New Jersey, London, Singapore: World Scientific).

245

15.   Aliev, R. A., Aliev, F. T. and Babaev, M. D. (1991) *Fuzzy Process Control and Knowledge Engineering.* (Verlag TUV Rheinland, Koln).

16.   Aliev, R. A., Alizadeh A. V., Huseynov O. H. (2015). The arithmetic of discrete Z-numbers, *Inform. Sciences*, 290(1), pp.134-155.

17.   Aliev, R. A., and Kreinovich, V. (2017). Z-Numbers and Type-2 Fuzzy Sets: A Representation Result, *Intell Autom Soft Co*, 2017, published online, https://doi.org/10.1080/10798587.2017.1330310.

18.   Aliev, R. A., Pedrycz, W., Guirimov, B. G., Aliev, R. R., Ilhan, U,, Babagil, M. and Mammadli, S. (2011). Type-2 fuzzy neural networks with fuzzy clustering and differential evolution optimization, *Inf Sci*, 181, pp.1591-1608.

19.   Aliev, R. A., Pedrycz, W., Huseynov, O. H. and Eyupoglu, S. Z. (2017). Approximate Reasoning on a Basis of Z-number valued If-Then Rules, *IEEE Trans Fuzzy Syst*, 25(6), pp.1589-1600.

20.   Aliev, R.A., Huseynov, O.H., Aliyev, R.R. and Alizadeh, A.V. (2015). *The Arithmetic of Z-numbers. Theory and Applications* (World Scientific Singapore).

21.   Allen, F. H. (2002). The Cambridge structural database: A quarter of a million crystal structures and rising, *Acta Crystallogr B*, 58, 380-388.

22.   Andersson, J-O, Helander, T, Höglund, L., Shi, P. and Sundman, B. (2002). Thermo-Calc & DICTRA, computational tools for materials science, *Elsevier, Calphad*, 26(2), pp. 273-312.

23.   ARGUS Metal Prices. www.metalprices.com.

24.   Ashby, M. (2000). Multi-objective optimization in material design and selection, *Acta Materilia*; 48, pp.359-369.

25.   Ashby, M. (2010). *Materials Selection in Mechanical Design.* (Butterworth-Heinemann).

26.   ASM International Materials Collection (1952-2015). https://app.knovel.com/web/browse-a-subject-area.v/catid:225/cat_slug:asm-international-materials-collection.

27.   Athawale, V. M. and Chakraborty, S. (2012). Material selection using multi-criteria decision-making methods: A comparative study, *Proc. Institution of Mechanical Engineers, Part L, Journal of Materials: Design and Applications*, 226(4), pp. 267-286.

28.   Averill, B. A. and Eldredge, P. (2012). *Principles of General Chemistry*, (McGraw-Hill Education).

29.   Babanli, M. B., Mamedov, Q. and Aslanov, J. (2016). Increasing reliability of the improved machines and equipment determination of productivity criteria. Bulletin of Environment, *Pharmacology and Life Sciences.Bull. Envv. Pharmacol. Life Sci.*, 5(12), pp. 95-98.

30.   Babanli, M.B. (2017). Synthesis of new materials by using fuzzy and big data concepts, *Procedia Comput Sci*, 120, pp. 104-111.

31.   Babanli, M.B., Huseynov, V.M. (2016). Z-number-based alloy selection problem, *Procedia Comput Sci*, 102, pp.183 – 189.

32.   Babanli, M.B., Kolomytsev V., Musienko R., Sezonenko A., Ochin P., Dezellus A., Plaindoux P., Portier R. and Vermaut P. (2001). Thermodynamic Properties and thermal stability of the multicomponent TiNi Based alloy Ribbons, *Metal Physics and Advanced Technologies*, 23, pp. 111-124.

33.   Babanli, M.B., Kolomytsev V., Musienko R., Sezonenko A., Ochin P., Dezellus A., Plaindoux P., Portier R. and Vermaut P. (2001). Multicomponent TiNi based shape memory alloys general considerations and selection rules for an initial precursor amorphous state, *Journal Phys.IV France*, 11(8), pp.457-462.

34. Babanli, M.B., Kolomytsev V., Pasko A., Shpak A, Sych T., Ochin P., Vermaut P., Portier R.,Cesari, E.and Rafaja, D. (2008). Shape Memory Behavior in Some $(Ti,Zr,Hf)_{50}(Ni,Cu)_{50}$ Alloys Elaborated by Glass Devitrification, *Advances in Science and Technology,* 59, pp. 113-118.

35. Babanli, M.B., Kolomytsev V., Sezonenko A., Ochin P., Portier R., Vermaut P. and Pasko A. (2002). Mechanical and functional properties of quarternary (Ti,Hf) (Ni,Cu) based shape memory melt-spun ribbons, *Proc. 10th International conference Martensitic transformations,* ICOMAT 02, pp. 889-892.

36. Babanli, M.B., Kolomytsev V., Sezonenko A., Pasko A., Ochin P., Portier R.and Vermaut P. (2003). Glass forming ability and thermodynamic properties of Ti (Zr,Hf) (Ni Cu) shape memory alloys, *Journal Phys.IV France,*.112, pp.1055-1058.

37. Babanli, M.B., Pasko A., Kolomytsev V., Sezonenko A., Ochin P., Portier R. and Vermaut P. (2003). Mechanical and functional properties of quarternary (Ti,Hf) (Ni,Cu) based shape memory melt-spun ribbons, *Journal Phys.IV France,*.112, pp. 889-892.

38. Baldwin, J. F. and Pilsworth, B. W. (1979). A model of fuzzy reasoning through multivalued logic and set theory, *Int. J. Man-Machines Studies,* 11, pp. 351-380.

39. Bede, B. (2013). *Mathematics of Fuzzy Sets and Fuzzy Logic.* (Springer-Verlag Berlin Heidelberg).

40. Belsky, A., Hellenbrandt, M., Karen, V. L. and Luksch, P. (2002). Acta Crystallogr B, 58, pp.364-369.

41. Berman, H. M., Westbrook, J., Feng, Z., Gilliland, G., Bhat, T., Weissig, H., Shindyalov, I. N. and Bourne, P. E. (2000). The Protein Data Bank. *Nucleic Acid Res,* 28, pp.235-242.

42. Bezdek, J. C. (1981). *Pattern Recognition with Fuzzy Objective Function Algorithms,* Plenum Press, New York.

43. Big data. Wikipedia. https://en.wikipedia.org/wiki/Big_data.

44. Billingham, J. and Laws, P. A. (1994). Fatigue Crack Propagation in High Strength Steels for Use Offshore, *Mater Eng,* 3, pp. 129-139.

45. Borgelt, C. Fuzzy and Probabilistic Clustering, http://www.cost-ic0702.org/summercourse/files/clustering.pdf.

46. Buckley, J. J. (1985). Fuzzy hierarchical analysis, *Fuzzy Sets Syst,* 17(1), pp. 233-247.

47. Cai, A.-H., Chen, H., An, W.-K., Li, X.-S., and Zhou, Y. (2008). Optimization of composition and technology for phosphate graphite mold, *Mater Design,* 29: pp.1835-1839.

48. Casasnovas, J. and Riera, J. V. (2006). On the addition of discrete fuzzy numbers. *WSEAS Transactions on Mathematics,* 5(5), pp.549–554.

49. Casasnovas, J. and Riera, J. V. (2007). Discrete fuzzy numbers defined on a subset of natural numbers, *Adv. Soft Comp.,* 42, pp. 573-582.

50. Casillas, J., Cordón, O, Herrera Triguero, F. and Magdalena, L. (2003). Interpretability Improvements to Find the Balance Interpretability-Accuracy in Fuzzy Modeling: An Overview, eds. J. Casillas, O. Cordón, T. Herrera Triguero, L. Magdalena, *Interpretability Issues in Fuzzy Modeling,* Berlin, Heidelberg: Springer, pp. 3-22.

51. Cavallini, C., Giorgetti, A., Citti, P. and Nicolaie, F. (2013). Integral aided method for material selection based on quality function deployment and comprehensive VIKOR algorithm, *Mater Design,* 47, 27-34.

52.   Cebon, D. and Ashby, M. (2003). Data systems for optimal material selection, *Adv Mater Processes*, 161(6), pp. 51-54.
53.   Ceder, G., Hautier, G., Jain, A. and Ong, S. P. (2011). Recharging lithium battery research with first-principles methods, *MRS Bull*, 36, pp.185–191.
54.   Chaira, T. (2011). A novel intuitionistic fuzzy c means clustering algorithm and its application to medical images, *Appl Soft Comput*, 11, pp.1711-1717.
55.   Chang, Ch.-T., Lai, J. Z. C. and Jeng M.-D. (2011). A Fuzzy K-means Clustering Algorithm Using Cluster Center Displacement, *J Inf Sci Eng*, 27, pp.995-1009.
56.   Chang, D. Y. (1996). Applications of the extent analysis method on fuzzy AHP, *Eur J of Oper Res*, 95(3), pp.649–655.
57.   Chatterjee, P. and Chakraborty, Sh. (2012). Material selection using preferential ranking methods. *Mater Design* , 35, pp. 384–393.
58.   Chatterjee, P., Athawale V. M. and Chakraborty, Sh. (2011). Materials selection using complex proportional assessment and evaluation of mixed data methods, *Mater Design*, 32(2), pp. 851-860.
59.   Chatterjee, P., Chakraborty S. (2016). Comparative analysis of VIKOR method and its variants, *Decis Sci Letters,* 5(4), pp. 469-486.
60.   Chen, D. D. (2017). Dislocation substructures evolution and an adaptive-network-based fuzzy inference system model for constitutive behavior of a Ni-based superalloy during hot deformation, *J Alloys Compd*, 708, pp.938-946.
61.   Chen, D., Li, M. and Wu, S. (2003). Modeling of microstructure and constitutive relation during super plastic deformation by fuzzy-neural network, *J Mater Process Technol*, 142, pp.197-202.
62.   Chen, S-M. (1997). A new method for tool steel materials selection under fuzzy environment, *Fuzzy Sets Sys*, 92, pp. 265-274.
63.   Cheng, J., Feng, Y., Tan, J. and Wei, W. (2008). Optimization of injection mold based on fuzzy moldability evaluation, *J Mater Process Technol*, 21, pp. 222-228.
64.   Chowdhury, S., Poet, R. and Mackenzie, L. (2013). Multicriteria Optimization to Select Images as Passwords in Recognition Based Graphical Authentication Systems, *Conf. HAS*, pp.13-22.
65.   Christodoulou, J. A. (2013). Integrated computational materials engineering and materials genome initiative: Accelerating materials innovation, *Adv Mater Processes*, 171(3), pp. 28–31.
66.   Col, M., Ertunc, H. M. and Yilmaz, M. (2007). An artificial neural network model for toughness properties in microalloyed steel in consideration of industrial production conditions, *Mater Des*, 28, pp. 488-495.
67.   Conduit, B. D., Jones, N. G., Stone, H. J. and Conduit G. J. (2017). Probabilistic design of a molybdenum-base alloy using a neural network. *Elsevier, Scripta Mater*, 146, pp. 82-86.
68.   Conduit, B. D., Jones, N. G., Stone, H. J. and Conduit, G.J. (2017). Design of a nickel-base superalloy using a neural network, *Mater Design*, 131, pp.358-365.
69.   Date, Christopher J. (2012). *Introduction to Database Systems*. (Pearson).
70.   Datta, S. and Chattopadhyay, P P. (2007). Soft computing techniques in advancement of structural metals, *Int Mater Rev*, 58(8), pp. 475-504.
71.   Dean J., and Ghemawat, S. (2004). MapReduce: Simplified Data Processing on Large Clusters, *Proc. the 6th Symposium on Operating System Design and Implementation, OSDI'04*, Berkeley, CA, USA, vol. 6, pp.137-150.

72. Dehghannasiri, R., Xue, D., Balachandran, P. V. Mohammadmahdi, R. Y., Dalton, L. A., Lookman, T. and Dougherty, E. R. (2017). Optimal experimental design for materials discovery, *Comput Mater Sci*,. 129, pp. 311–322.

73. Dental Amalgam: A Scientific Review and Recommended Public Health Service Strategy for Research, Education and Regulation Final Report of the Subcommittee - on Risk Management of the Committee to Coordinate Environmental Health and Related Programs Public Health Service. Department of Health and Human Services Public Health Service(1993) https://health.gov/environment/amalgam1/selection.htm.

74. Diebold F. (2012) On the Origin(s) and Development of the Term "Big Data". *Pier working paper archive, Penn Institute for Economic Research, Department of Economics, University of Pennsylvania,* http://www.ssc.upenn.edu/~fdiebold/papers/paper112/Diebold_ Big_Data.pdf.

75. Dieter, G. E. (1986). *Mechanical Metallurgy* (Mc Graw-Hill Book Company).

76. Downs, R. T. and Hall-Wallace, M. (2003). *Am. Miner.*, 88,pp.247-250.

77. Duerig, T.W., Pelton, A.R. (1981). The mechanical properties of NiTi-based shape memory alloys, *Acta Metallurgica*, 29(2), pp. 393-398.

78. Edwards K. l. (2005). Selecting Materials for Optimum Use in Engineering Components, *Mater Design*, 26, pp.469–474.

79. Edwards, K. and Ashby, M. (1994). Optimal selection of composite materials in mechanical engineering design, *Proc. 4th Int Conf of Comput Aided Design in Composite Material Technology*, pp. 85-92.

80. El-Bagoury, N, Hessien, M. M. and Zaki Z. I. (2014). Influence of Aging on Microstructure, Martensitic Transformation and Mechanical Properties of NiTiRe Shape Memory Alloy. *Met. Mater. Int.*, 20(6), pp. 997-1002.

81. Elishakoff, I. and Ferracuti, B. (2006a). Fuzzy sets based interpretation of the safety factor, *Fuzzy Sets Syst,* 157, pp.2495-2512.

82. Elton, D. C., Boukouvalas, Z., Butrico, M. S., Fuge, M. D. and Chung P. W. (2018). Applying machine learning techniques to predict the properties of energetic materials, *Sci Rep.*, 8(1), 9059.

83. Ermolaeva, N. A., Kaveline, K. G. and Spoormaker, J. L. (2002). Materials selection combine with optimal structure design: concept and some result, *Mater Des,* 23, pp. 459-470.

84. Fabregat-Sanjuan, A., Ferrando, A. F., De la Flor S. (2015). Influence of heat treatment on internal friction spectrum in NiTiCu shape memory alloy. *Materials Today: Proceedings* 2(S3), pp. S755-S758.

85. Factors Influencing Materials Selection. http://mechanical-materials technology.blogspot.com/2011/08/factors-influencing-materials-selection.html.

86. Fang, S. F., Wang, M. P., Qi, W. and Zheng, F. (2008). Hybrid genetic algorithms and support vector regression in forecasting atmospheric corrosion of metallic materials, *Comput Mater Sci*, 44(2), pp.647-655.

87. Farag, M. and El-Magd, E. (1992) An Integrated Approach to Product Design, Materials Selection and Cost Estimation, *Mater Design*, 13(6), pp. 323-327.

88. Farina, M. and Amato, P. (2004). A fuzzy definition of "optimality" for many-criteria optimization problems, *IEEE Trans Syst Man Cybernt A,* 34(3), pp. 315-326.

89. Fayazbakhsh, K., Abedian, A., Manshadi, B. D. and Khabbaz, R. S. (2009). Introducing a novel method for materials selection in mechanical design using Z-transformation in statistics for normalization of material properties, *Mater Design,* 30, pp. 4396–4404.

90. Fellet, M. (2017). Big Data Analytics Deliver Materials Science Insights, http://www.lindau-nobel.org/blog-big-data-analytics-deliver-materials-science-insights/.

91. Firstov, G.S., Humbeecka, J. Van, Koval Y.N. (2004). High-temperature shape memory alloys: some recent developments. *Materials Science and Engineering A,* 378 1(2), pp. 2–10.

92. Frang, M. (2002). *Quantitative methods of material selection.* Handbook of material selection. (John Wiley and Sons).

93. Frenzel, J., Wieczorek, A., Opahle, I., Maa, B., Drautz, R. and Eggeler, G. (2015). On the effect of alloy composition on martensite start temperatures and latent heats in Ni–Ti-based shape memory alloys, *Acta Mater,* pp.213–231.

94. Gaultois, M. W., Oliynyk, A. O., Mar, A., Sparks T. D., Mulholland, G. J. and Meredig, B. (2016). Perspective: Web-based machine learning models for real-time screening of thermoelectric materials properties, *APL Materials,* 4, 053213.

95. Ghemawat S., Gobioff H. and Leung S.T. (2003). The Google File System, Proc. the 9th *ACM Symposium on Operating Systems Principles,* New York, USA, pp. 29–43.

96. Girubha, R. J. and Vinodh, S. (2012). Application of fuzzy VIKOR and environmental impact analysis for material selection of an automotive component, *Mater Design,* 37, pp. 478–486.

97. Gosain, A. and Dahiya, S. (2016). Performance Analysis of Various Fuzzy Clustering Algorithms: A Review, *Elsevier, Procedia Comput Sci,* 79, pp.100-111.

98. Goupee, A. J. and Vel, S. S. (2007). Multi-objective optimization of functionally graded materials with temperature-dependent material properties, *J Mater Process Technol* ,28, pp.1861-1879.

99. Gražulis, S., Chateigner, D., Downs, R. T. , Yokochi, A. F. T. , Quirós, M., Lutterotti, L., Manakova, E., Butkus, J., Moeck, P.and Le Bail A. (2009). *J Appl Crystallogr,* 42, pp.726-729.

100. Gul, M., Celik, E., Gumus, A.T., Guneri, A.F. (2018). A fuzzy logic based PROMETHEE method for material selection problems. *Beni-Suef University Journal of Basic and Applied Sciences* 7(1), pp. 68-79.

101. Hadoop MapReduce, http://www.hadoop.apache.org/docs/stable/mapred_tutorial.html 17.

102. Hadoop Distributed File System, http://www.hadoop.apache.org/docs.

103. Halevi, G. (2012) The Evolution of Big Data as a Research and Scientific Topic, *Research Trends,* 30, pp.3-6.

104. Hancheng, Q, Bocai, X, Shangzheng, L. and Fagen, W. (2002). Fuzzy neural network modeling of material properties, *J Mater Process Technol,* 122, pp. 196-200.

105. Hand, D., Mannila, H. and Smyth, P. (2001). *Principles of Data Mining.* The MIT Press *Massachusetts.*

106. Hashimoto, K., Kimura, M. and Mizuhara, Y. (1998). Alloy design of gamma titanium aluminides based on phase diagrams, *Intermetallics,* 6(7-8), pp.667-672.

107. Hey, T., Tansley, S. and Tolle, K. (2009). *The Fourth Paradigm: Data-Intensive Scientific Discovery*, Microsoft Corporation, p. 287.

108. Hill, J., Mulholland, G., Persson, K., Seshadri, R., Wolverton, Ch. and Meredig, B. (2016). Materials science with large-scale data and informatics, *Unlocking new opportunities Materials Research Society*, MRS Bulletin, 41, pp. 399-409.

109. Huang, L. and Massa, L. (2013). Applications of energetic materials by a theoretical method (discover energetic materials by a theoretical method), *Int. J. Ener. Mat. Chem. Prop*, 12(3), pp.197–262.

110. Ignizio, J. P. (1991). *Introduction to Expert Systems: The Development and Implementation of RuleBased Expert Systems.* (McGraw-Hill, New York, NY).

111. Ishibuchi, H. and Nojima, Y. (2007). Analysis of interpretability-accuracy tradeoff of fuzzy systems by multiobjective fuzzy genetics-based machine learning, *Int. J. Approx. Reason*, 44(1), pp. 4-31.

112. Jabbarova, A.I. (2016). Solution for the Investment Decision Making Problem through Interval Probabilities, *Procedia Comput Sci*, 102, pp.465-468.

113. Jahan, A., Bahraminasab, M. and Edwards, K. L. (2012). A target-based normalization technique for materials selection, *Mater Design*, 35, pp. 647-654.

114. Jahan, A., Edwards, K. and Bahraminasab, M. (2016). *Multi-criteria Decision Analysis for Supporting the Selection of Engineering Materials in Product Design.* (Butterworth-Heinemann).

115. Jahan, A., Ismail, M. Y., Sapuan, S. M. and Mustapha F. (2010). Material screening and choosing methods – A review, *Mater Design*, 31, pp. 696–705.

116. Jahan, A., Ismail, Md Y., Shuib. S., Norfazidah, D. and Edwards, K. L. (2011). An aggregation technique for optimal decision-making in materials selection. *Mater Design,* 32(10), pp.4918-4924.

117. Jain, A. K., Murty, M. N. and Patrick J. F. (1999). Data clustering: a review, ACM computing surveys (CSUR), *Association for Computer Machinery*, 31(3),pp. 264- 323.

118. Jain, A., Persson, K. A. and Ceder, G. The materials genome initiative: Data sharing and the impact of collaborative ab initio databases. *APL Materials*, 4(5), 053102.

119. Jang, J.-S.R. (1993). ANFIS: adaptive-network-based fuzzy inference system, *IEEE Trans Syst Man Cybern*, 23 (3), pp.665-685.

120. Jee, D-H., Kang K-J. (2000). A method for optimal material selection aided with decision making theory, *Mater Design*, 21(3), pp.199-206.

121. Jeffreys, S (1988). Finite element analysis doing away with prototypes, *Ind Comput*, pp. 34-36.

122. Jenkins, J. F. and Mishra, B. (1999). Deep Water Corrosion Fundamentals, *Int Workshop on Corrosion Control for Marine Structures and Pipeline*, Galveston, Texas, 1999, pp. 35-58.

123. Jina, X., Benjamin W. Waha, Chenga X., Wanga Y. (2015). Significance and Challenges of Big Data Research, *Big Data Research*, 2(2), pp. 59–64.

124. Kang, B., Wei, D., Li, Y. and Deng, Y. (2012). Decision making using Z-numbers under uncertain environment, *J Comput Inform Syst*, 8(7), pp. 2807-2814.

125. Kaur, P., Soni, A. K. and Gosain, A. (2011). Robust Intuitionistic Fuzzy C-means clustering for linearly and nonlinearly separable data, *Int Conf on Image Information Processing (ICIIP)*, pp. 1-6.

126. Kaur, P., Soni, A. K. and Gosain, A. (2013). Robust kernelized approach to clustering by incorporating new distance measure, *Eng Appl Artif Intel*, 26(2), pp. 833-847.

127. Kesavaraj, G. and Sukumaran, S. (2013). A study on classification techniques in data mining, *4th Int Conf on Computing, Communications and Networking Technologies (ICCCNT)*, pp. 1-7.

128. Kilincci, O., and Onal, S. A. (2011). Fuzzy AHP approach for supplier selection in a washing machine company, *Expert Syst Appl*, 38(8), pp. 9656-9664.

129. Kiong S. C. *et al.* (2013). Decision Making with the Analytical Hierarchy Process (AHP) for Material Selection in Screw Manufacturing for Minimizing Environmental Impacts, *Applied Mechanics and Materials*, 315, pp. 57-62.

130. Kóczy, L. T., and Hirota, K. (1991). Rule Interpolation by α-Level Sets in Fuzzy Approximate Reasoning, *J. BUSEFAL*, 46, pp.115-123.

131. Koker, R., Altinkok, N. and Demir, A. (2007). Neural network based prediction of mechanical properties of particulate reinforced metal matrix composites using various training algorithms, *Mater, Des*, 28, pp. 616-627.

132. Kosmač, A. (2017). Factors affecting material selection for high temperature applications — review. https://steelmehdipour.net/wp-content/uploads/2017/02/Factors-affecting-material-selection-for-high-temperature-applications.pdf.

133. Laidler, K. J. and Meiser, J. H. (1982). *Physical Chemistry*. Benjamin/Cummings Pub. Co.

134. Laney, D. (2001) 3D Data Management: Controlling Data Volume, Velocity and Variety. Technical report, META Group, Inc (Gartner, Inc.), http://blogs.gartner.com/.

135. Larson, E. (2015). *Thermoplastic Material Selection, A Practical Guide*. (William Andrew, New York).

136. Lee, Y.-H. and Kopp, R. (2001a). Application of fuzzy control for a hydraulic forging machine, *Fuzzy Sets Syst*, 99, pp.99-108.

137. Lesiak, B.; Zemek, J.; Jiricek, P. and Jozwik, A. (2007). Investigation of CoPd alloys by XPS and EPES using the pattern recognition method, *J Alloys Compd*, 428(1-2), pp. 190-196.

138. Lei X., Chunxiao J., Jian W., Jian Y., Yong R. (2014). Information Security in Big Data: Privacy and Data Mining, *IEEE Access*, 2, pp. 1149–1176.

139. Liu, P. and Zhang, L. (2015). The Extended VIKOR Method for Multiple Criteria Decision Making Problem Based on Neutrosophic Hesitant Fuzzy Set, *General Math*, pp.1-13.

140. Lookman, T., Balachandran, P. V., Xue, D., Pilania, G., Shearman, T., Theiler, J., Gubernatis, J. E., Hogden, J., Barros, K., BenNaim E. and Alexander, F. J. (2016). *A Perspective on Materials Informatics:State-of-the-Art and Challenges*, Information Science for Materials Discovery and Design, *Springer Series in Materials Science*, 225, ch.1, p. 11.

141. Maier M. (2013). Towards a Big Data Reference Architecture, http://www.win.tue.nl/~gfletche/Maier_MSc_thesis.pdf. Eindhoven University of Technology, *Department of Mathematics and Computer Science*.

142. Material Property Search. https://app.knovel.com/web/data-search.v.

143. Material Property Search. Titanium Alloys. https://app.knovel.com/web/data-search.v?mn=titanium%20alloys.

144. Materials Database National Institute of Materials Science http://smds.nims.go.jp/fatigue/index_en.html accessed on Jan 12, 2016.

145. Menges, A. (2015). *Material Synthesis: Fusing the Physical and the Computational*, (Wiley).

146. Milani, A. S., Shanian, A., Madoliat, R. and Nemes, J. A. (2005). The effect of normalization norms in multiple attribute decision making methods: a case study in gear material selection. *Struct Multidisc Optim*, 29, pp.312–318.

147. Moise, I. Evangelos Pournaras, Dirk Helbing (2015). Introduction to Data Mining and Machine Learning Techniques. https://www.ethz.ch/content/dam/ethz/special-interest/gess/computational-social-science-dam/documents/education/Spring2015/datascience/introduction-data-mining.pdf.

148. Montgomery, D. C. (1997). *Design and analysis of experiments*, (5th Ed.), (Wiley).

149. Moore, R.E. (1966) Interval analysis. (Prentice Hall, Englewood Cliffs, New Jersey).

150. Mueller, T., Kusne, A. G. and Ramprasad, R. (2016). Machine Learning In Materials Science: Recent Progress And Emerging Applications. In A. L. Parrill and K. B. Lipkowitz, editors, *Reviews in Computational Chemistry*, 29, John Wiley & Sons.

151. Nandi, A. K. and Pratihar, D. K. (2004a). Automatic design of fuzzy logic controller using a genetic algorithm-to predict power requirement and surface finish in grinding, *J Mater Process Technol*, 148, pp. 288-300.

152. Odejobi, O. A. and Umoru, L. E. (2009). Applications of soft computing techniques in materials engineering: A review, *Afr J Math Comput Sci Res*, 2(7), 104-131.

153. Olson, G. B. and Kuehmann, C. J. (2014). Materials genomics: From CALPHAD to flight, *Scr Mater*, 70, pp. 25–30.

154. Opricovic, S. (2011). Fuzzy VIKOR with an application to water resources planning, *Expert Syst Appl*. 38, pp. 12983–12990.

155. OQMD: The Open Quantum Materials Database. http://oqmd.org.

156. Otsuka, K., Ren, X. (1999). Recent developments in the research of shape memory alloys, *Intermetallics*, 7(5), pp.511-528.

157. Pal, N. R., Pal, K., Keller J. and Bezdek, J. C. (2005). A Possibilistic Fuzzy c- Means Clustering Algorithm, *IEEE Trans Fuzzy Syst*, 13(4), pp.517-530.

158. Papon, P.;Leblond, J. and Meijer, P. H. E. (2002). *The Physics of Phase Transition : Concepts and Applications*, Berlin: Springer.

159. Patel, B. N., Prajapati, S. G. and Lakhtaria, K. I. (2012). Efficient Classification of Data Using Decision Tree, *Bonfring International Journal of Data Mining*, 2(1), pp. 6-12.

160. Pedrycz W. and Gomide F. (2007) *Fuzzy Systems Engineering. Toward Human-Centric Computing*. (John Wiley & Sons, Hoboken, New Jersey).

161. Pedrycz, W. (2001). Fuzzy equalization in the construction of fuzzy sets, *Elsevier, Fuzzy Sets Syst*, 119(2), pp. 329–335.

162. Pedrycz, W., Peters, J. F. (1998). *Computational Intelligence in Software Engineering. Advances in Fuzzy Systems, Applications and Theory*, (World Scientific, Singapoure).

163. Petrucci, R. H.; Harwood, W. S.; Herring, F. G. (2002). *General Chemistry. Principles and Modern Applications*(8th ed.). Prentice Hall, p. 477.

164. Predel, B.; Hoch, M. and Pool, M (2004). *Phase Diagrams and Heterogeneous Equilibria: A Practical Introduction*. (Springer, Berlin).

165. Preuss, M., Wessing, S., Rudolph, G. and Sadowski, G. (2015) Solving Phase Equilibrium Problems by Means of Avoidance-Based Multiobjectivization, eds. Kacprzyk J., Pedrycz W. Springer Handbook of Computational Intelligence, Springer, Berlin, Heidelberg.

166. Rai, D., Jha, G. K., Chatterjee, P. and Chakraborty, Sh. (2013). Material Selection in Manufacturing Environment Using Compromise Ranking and Regret Theory-based Compromise Ranking Methods: A Comparative Study, *Univers J Mater Sci*, 1(2), pp. 69-77.

167. Rao, C. N. R. and Biswas, K. (2015). *Essentials of Inorganic Materials Synthesis* (Wiley).

168. Rao, H. S., Mukherjee, A. (1996). Artificial neural networks for predicting the macromechanical behaviour of ceramic-matrix composites, *Comput Mater Sci*, 5, pp. 307-322.

169. Reuben, R. L. (1994). *Materials in Marine Technology*, Springer-Verlag, London.

170. Saaty, T. L., (1980). *The Analytic Hierarchy Process*, McGraw-Hill, New York, USA.

171. Sakundarini, N., Taha, Z., Abdul-Rashid, S. H. and Ghazilla, R. A. R. (2014). Incorporation of high recyclability material selection in computer aided design, *Mater Design*, 56, pp. 740-749.

172. Sampath, R. and Zabaras, N. (1999). An object-oriented implementation of a front tracking FEM for directional solidification processes. *Int J Numer Methods Eng*, 44, pp. 1227-1265.

173. Saravanakumar. K. (2017). Parallel Database — Intraquery Parallelism — Advanced Database Management System. http://www.exploredatabase.com/2014/03/parallel-database-intraquery-parallelism.html.

174. Sen, P. and Yang, J-B (1995). Multiple-criteria decision-making in design selection and synthesis, *J Eng Des*, 6(3), pp.207-224.

175. Seshadri, R. and Sparks, T. D. (2016). Perspective: Interactive material property databases through aggregation of literature data. *APL Material*, 4(5), 053206.

176. Sha, A. A., Dr. Reddy, T.V.Sh., Manafuddin, Sh. and Dr. Kumar,T. S. (2014), A review of soft computing techniques in materials engineering, *Int J of Advanced Research in Engineering and Technology (IJARET)*, 5(10), pp. 134-150.

177. Shifler, D. A. (2005). Understanding Material Interactions in Marine Environments to Promote Extended Structural Life, *Corros Sci*, 47, pp. 2335-2352.

178. Shimin, V. V., Shah, V. A. and Lokhande, M. M. (2016). Material selection for semiconductor switching devices in electric vehicles using Analytic Hierarchy Process (AHP) method. *IEEE 1st Int Conf on Power Electronics, Intelligent Control and Energy Systems (ICPEICES)*.

179. Shu, X.Y., Lu, S.Q., Li, G.F., Liu, J.W., Peng, P. (2014). Nb solution influencing on phase transformation temperature of $Ni_{47}Ti_{44}Nb_9$ alloy. *Journal of Alloys and Compounds*, 609, pp. 156–161

180. Stan, M. and Reardon, B. J. (2003). A Bayesian approach to evaluating the uncertainty of thermodynamic data and phase diagrams, *Computer Coupling of Phase Diagrams and Thermochemistry*, 27(3), pp.319-323.

181. Stewart, J. (2012). Flywheels move from steam age technology to Formula 1. http://www.bbc.com/future/story/20120629-reinventing-the-wheel.

182. Sumpter, B. G., Vasudevan, R. K., Potok, T. and Kalinin, S. V. (2015). A bridge for accelerating materials by design, *npj Comput Mater* 1, 15008.
183. Tajdari, M., Ghaffarnajad M. A. and Khoogar, A. R. (2010). Shear strength prediction of Ni–Ti alloys manufactured by powder metallurgy using fuzzy rule-based model, *Mater Design*, 31, pp.1180–1185.
184. Takahashi, K. and Tanaka, Y (2016). Material synthesis and design from first principle calculations and machine learning. *Comp Mater Sci*, 112, pp. 364–367.
185. The five V's of big data. https://www.bbva.com/en/five-vs-big-data/.
186. The Materials Project. Web-based Access to Computer Information on Materials. http://www.materialsproject.org.
187. The Materials Research Laboratory. Energy Materials Data Mining. www.mrl.ucsb.edu:8080/datamine/thermoelectric.jsp.
188. The NOMAD Laboratory. A European Centre of Excellence. https://nomad-coe.eu/.
189. Topcu, I. B., Karakurt, C. and Saridemir, M. (2008). Predicting the strength development of cements produced with different pozzolans by neural network and fuzzy logic, *Mater Design*, 29 (10), pp.1986-1991.
190. Uros, Z., Franc, C and Edi, K. (2009). Adaptive network based inference system for estimation of flank wear in end-milling, *J Mater Process Technol*, 209(3), pp.1504-1511.
191. Vafaeenezhad, H., Seyedein, S. H., Aboutalebi, M. R. and Eivani, A. R. (2017). Application of constitutive description and integrated ANFIS – ICA analysis to predict hot deformation behavior of Sn-5Sb lead-free solder alloy, *J Alloys Compd*, 697, pp. 287-299.
192. Van Laarhoven, P. J. M. and Pedrycz, W. (1983). A fuzzy extension of Saaty's priority Theory, *Fuzzy Sets Syst*, 11(1-3), pp.199-227.
193. Villars, P. (2007). *Pearson's Crystal Data: Crystal Structure Database For Inorganic Compounds* (ASM International).
194. Wang, Ch.-H. and Pang, Ch.-T. (2011). Using VIKOR Method for Evaluating Service Quality of Online Auction under Fuzzy Environment, *Int J Comput Sci Eng Technol*, 1(6), pp. 307-314.
195. Wang, G., Wu, C. and Zhao, C. (2005). Representation and Operations of discrete fuzzy numbers, *Southeast Asian Bulletin of Math.*, 28, pp. 1003-1010.
196. Wang, S. T. , Chung, K. F., Shen, H. B. and Zhu, R. Q. (2004). Note on the relationship between probabilistic and fuzzy clustering, *J Soft Comput*, 8(7), pp. 523–526.
197. Wei Cai, Liu Ailian, Jiehe Sui and Liancheng Zhao. (2006) Effects of Cerium Addition on Martensitic Transformation and Microstructure of $Ti_{49.3}Ni_{50.7}$ *Alloy Materials Transactions*, Vol. 47, No. 3 pp. 716-719.
198. Weinert, M., Schneider, G., Podloucky, R. and Redinger, J. (2009). FLAPW: applications and implementations, *J Phys Condens Matter*, 21(8), 084201.
199. Welling, D. A. (2011). A Fuzzy Logic Material Selection Methodology for Renewable Ocean Energy Applications. *Proquest, Umi Dissertation Publishing*, p. 154.
200. White, A. (2013). Workshop makes recommendations to increase diversity in materials science and engineering, *MRS Bull*, 38, pp.120–122.
201. White, A. A. (2013). Big data are shaping the future of materials science, *MRS bulletin*, 38, pp. 594-595.

202. White, A. A. (2013). Interdisciplinary collaboration, robust funding cited as key to success of materials genome initiative program, *MRS Bull*, 38, pp.894–896.
203. White, A. A. (2013). Universities prepare next-generation workforce to benefit from the materials genome initiative, *MRS Bull*, 38, pp.673–674.
204. Wu, X., Kumar, V. and Quinlan, J. R.et al. (2008). Top 10 algorithms in data mining, *Knowl Inf Syst*, 14(1), pp.1-37.
205. Xue, Y.-X, You, J.-X., Lai, X.-D., and Liu, H.-Ch. (2016). An interval-valued intuitionistic fuzzy MABAC approach for material selection with incomplete weight information, *Appl Soft Comput*, 38, pp. 703–713.
206. Yang, Z. G., Stevenson, J. W., Paxton, D. M., Singh, P. and Weil, K. S. (2002). Materials Properties Database for Selection of High-Temperature Alloys and Concepts of Alloy Design for SOFC Applications , *Pacific Northwest National Laboratory Richland, Washington* 99352, p. 78.
207. Yao, L. and Weng, K-S. (2012). On A Type-2 Fuzzy Clustering Algorithm, *Proc. 4th Int Conf on Pervasive Patterns and Applications, PATTERNS*, pp. 45-50.
208. Yazdani, M. and Graeml, F. R. (2014). VIKOR and its Applications: A State-of-the-Art Survey, *Int J Strat Decis Sci*, 5(2), pp. 56-83.
209. Yazici, I. and Kahraman, C. (2015). VIKOR method using interval type two fuzzy sets, *J Intell Fuzzy Syst*, 29(1), pp. 411-421.
210. Zadeh, L. A. (1965). Fuzzy Sets, *Inform. Control*, 8, pp. 338-353.
211. Zadeh, L. A. (1975). The concept of a linguistic variable and its applications in approximate reasoning, *Inform. Sciences*, 8, pp.43–80, pp. 301–357; 9, pp. 199–251.
212. Zadeh, L. A. (1996). Fuzzy logic — computing with words, *IEEE T. Fuzzy Syst.*, 4(2), pp. 103-111.
213. Zadeh, L. A. (2011). A note on Z-numbers, *Inform. Sciences*, 181, pp. 2923–2932.
214. Zafarani, H. R., Hassani, A. and Bagherpour, E. (2014). Achieving a desirable combination of strength and workability in Al/SiC composites by AHP selection method, *J Alloys Compd*, 589, pp. 295-300.
215. Zha, X. F. (2005). A web-based advisory system for process and material selection in concurrent product design for a manufacturing environment. *Int J Adv Manuf Technol*, 25(3-4), pp. 233-243.
216. Zhang, H. M., Xu, Z. S. and Chen, Q. (2007). On clustering approach to intuitionistic fuzzy sets, *Control and Decision*, 22(8), pp. 882-888.
217. Zienkiewicz, O. C. and Taylor, R. L. (1994). *The Finite Element Method* (McGraw-Hill).

Index

Printed in the United States
By Bookmasters